Deconstructing Youth

Deconstructing Youth

Youth Discourses at the Limits of Sense

Fleur Gabriel
Monash University, Australia

First published 2013 by
PALGRAVE MACMILLAN

Palgrave Macmillan in the UK is an imprint of Macmillan Publishers Limited, registered in England, company number 785998, of Houndmills, Basingstoke, Hampshire RG21 6XS.

Palgrave Macmillan in the US is a division of St Martin's Press LLC, 175 Fifth Avenue, New York, NY 10010.

Palgrave Macmillan is the global academic imprint of the above companies and has companies and representatives throughout the world.

Palgrave® and Macmillan® are registered trademarks in the United States, the United Kingdom, Europe and other countries.

ISBN 978–0–230–36333–5

This book is printed on paper suitable for recycling and made from fully managed and sustained forest sources. Logging, pulping and manufacturing processes are expected to conform to the environmental regulations of the country of origin.

A catalogue record for this book is available from the British Library.

A catalog record for this book is available from the Library of Congress.

Contents

v

Acknowledgements

Thank you Susan Yell, Simon Cooper, Robert Briggs and Paul Atkinson for all your guidance, support and feedback in the development and refinement of this work. I am ever grateful for the help you have provided to me over many years. Thanks also to Felicity Plester, Catherine Mitchell and Chris Penfold at Palgrave Macmillan for your kind and professional service. Finally, thank you Mum, Dad, Barb, Leah, Cara, Melly, Chantal and the rest of my dear family and friends for being a constant source of encouragement and for seeing me through this and all my endeavours with love.

1
Introduction

The Australian Government's 'National Binge Drinking Strategy' (2008–2010) sought to address the 'binge drinking epidemic' among the country's youth (Australian Labor Party, 2008, np). Part of this strategy involved a confronting advertising campaign designed to shock young people about the impact of binge drinking, similar to campaigns targeting smoking, HIV/AIDS and the road toll. The campaign was also designed with a particular focus on personal responsibility. Using the tagline 'Don't turn a night out into a nightmare', the campaign was 'designed to encourage teenagers and young adults to think about the choices they make about drinking, and particularly the possible negative consequences of excessive alcohol consumption' (Department of Health and Ageing, undated, np). However, the advertisements encouraging young people to take personal responsibility in regulating their own drinking behaviour were also designed, in the words of the then Prime Minister Kevin Rudd, to scare 'the living daylights out of young people about the health impact of binge drinking' (cited in Cooper, 2008, np). For example, a group of teenage boys are depicted joking around together by a city roadside until one is hit by a car; violence erupts in a nightclub over a spilled drink; a woman falls through a coffee table while drunk at a house party; another woman is photographed having sex in a park (Curry, 2008, np). Thus the campaign was organised in terms of two conflicting aims or logics: alongside expectations of personal responsibility and self-regulation – what might be considered expressions of adult-level rationality – was the paternalism of a scare campaign designed to elicit unreflective, fear-based compliance.

While this contradiction might simply speak to the inconsistencies of a particular political programme, it is perhaps symptomatic of a more general ambivalence that inheres in broader attitudes towards and even concepts of the identity of youth in the developed Western world. Underlying a conflicting desire to scare young people into acting in a particular way (even if that way is deemed 'responsible') and to encourage them to take personal responsibility for their own drinking choices is an uncertainty about what exactly youth is or means. Young people are treated here as being in need of guidance and instruction *and* as being capable of taking responsibility for themselves. This capability makes them like adults, but this capability is also imagined as something to be acquired, such that the *lack* of a particular social competence marks them as *other* than the fully functional adult subject that they are directed, even destined, to become. By the same token, the apparent inevitability of the transformation of young people into mature, rational adults posits a continuity that belies the marked distinction of youth's 'essential' identity. Accordingly, youth is marked as a distinct life stage and identity category by virtue of its difference from what marks the category adult, but what youth 'is' is also its very becoming something else. What young people do that is taken to be particular to them is also what is leading them towards becoming something other than themselves. At the basic level of definition, then, there are contradictions in operation here: youth is simultaneously the same and different, distinct and emerging, central and marginal.

The very existence of such ambivalence and contradiction raises the possibility, if nothing else, of reading (Western) youth discourses in a way that is attentive to these contradictions and it is this possibility that I seek to explore in the following discussion. More particularly, I aim to reflect on how, where and why such contradictions go unnoticed, and to consider what might be gained from revealing such oversights. Surprisingly, perhaps, one source that might be helpful in beginning such a reading is John Hartley's work on television. In *Tele-ology* (1992), Hartley utilises deconstructive theory to demonstrate the ways in which television texts challenge the purity and certainty of existing analytical categories and subject boundaries employed in textual analysis, revealing instead their conceptual ambiguity. As part of this reading, he describes the textual representation of youth as a particular example of 'categorical ambiguity' (1992, p. 31). Hartley explains that the opposing terms of a binary pair (such as 'reader' and 'text') are ordinarily understood to be mutually exclusive, but that closer inspection reveals that 'there is a margin between the two that is ambiguous', a margin that is 'neither one thing nor the other, and both one and the other' (1992, p. 31). For Hartley, the category of youth occupies one such ambiguous boundary or margin. It is marked by its difference from both child and adult (it is neither of these) but it also displays the attributes and potentialities of both. In this way, according to Hartley, youth serves to mark or make apparent the limit between the terms in the binary pair child/adult by existing as a 'nominated ambiguous boundar[y]' against an ex-nominated (naturalised, unnamed, assumed and implicit) centre – adult (1992, p. 31).

The category 'child' is, of course, also marked by its difference from an ex-nominated centre, and might thus be 'read' for what it says about adulthood, but the categories of 'child' and 'youth' each have different relationships to the category 'adult'. As the binary opposite of adult, childhood is a more stable category than 'youth'. The boundaries of childhood are drawn more clearly in comparison to youth which exists in mediation between 'child' and 'adult' and represents the transition between the two. We might say that childhood marks a socially legitimated zone of 'purposelessness', which is to say that the purpose of childhood is just to *be* a child. This notion of childhood is reflected in the Australian Federal Government's 'Early Years Learning Framework' for early childhood education and care. First endorsed in 2009 by the Council of Australian Government (Department of Education, Employment and Workplace Relations, undated, np), the framework describes children's play as enabling them 'to simply enjoy being' and such play provides 'opportunities for children to learn as they discover, create, improvise and imagine' (Bita, 2009, np). What then distinguishes 'youth' from 'child' is that the play that is used by children to explore, create and interpret the world around them is actually put to use. Such activity eventually becomes subject to the regulatory expectation that it be directed towards the goal, or purpose, of becoming adult. In this way, it may be said that there is a conflation between the categories of 'child' and 'youth.' As such, my focus on youth is not to the exclusion of the activities and concerns of childhood (for example, the preservation of innocence, what constitutes timely development), when the activities of childhood become subject to a specific set of expectations that characterise youth. There are, however, some noteworthy differences between the two terms which call for further elaboration.

As presented here, youth is like a 'third' term, *the exclusion of which* makes the child/adult 'binary' possible. But given that the binary is dependent on this prior exclusion, youth is also more like the 'first' term. Either way, however, it is through the 'forgetting' or 'suppression' of youth as (or at) the ambiguous boundary between the terms 'child' and 'adult' that each can appear as distinct forms of identity or subjectivity that are characterised by the absence of the attributes of the other (for example, a self-gratifying will versus dispassionate reason, or innocence versus worldliness). To use a Derridean term, youth is the 'undecidable' relation between, but also the condition of, the two, and this margin manifests in social contexts in terms of thinking about how a child becomes an adult. What must happen to bring about this transition? What must 'youth' 'do'? What characteristics should young people therefore possess and not possess, and how is this shaped by gender, race, class and age? What happens 'in between' child and adulthood is quite important for it signals the future, the shape of the society to come, and to discuss youth reveals much about the dreams and investments of the wider culture.

There is, however, anxiety associated with this transition from child to adult. The category of youth 'offends against binary logic' (Hartley, 1992, p. 31) because, even as the category has been produced by that logic, the category transgresses the logic by having attributes that belong to both sides and to neither side of the binary (for example, child/adult, innocence/knowledge, irresponsible/responsible, unreason/reason). I argue that youth discourses as they operate in situated contexts unreflexively incorporate this contradictory foundation in the work of making sense of youth. This is important to understand because a common element which emerges from a close reading of youth discourses is a confidence in the ability to distinguish between youth and adult on the basis of their distinct qualities. Despite the fact that youth is an ambiguous category, it is possible to identify totalising assumptions and essentialist reductions underpinning discussion about youth. Discourses on youth sexuality, for example, operate from assumptions of biological and also emotional innocence, hence the anxiety over how and when it is appropriate to transition out or away from this state without causing harm by prematurely ending that 'innocence'. What remains unseen here is the ambiguous margin that makes it possible to articulate such grounding assumptions and the binary positions from which interpretive work proceeds. So to treat youth as an exclusive and distinct identity category, despite its negative definition via the positively defined 'adult' and its other, 'child', is to allow for only a narrow and predictable range of constitutive and interpretive options regarding youth. More particularly, the effect of assuming an essential nature to youth is to have youth discourses fall short of their own explanatory demands.

To elaborate, this means that, as a concept, youth is produced from a child/adult binary, but the effect of this is to produce a subject position that cannot be contained within the available terms provided by the binary system. This excess is threatening to the system's coherence, because it has not originated from any 'outside', but from within. The effect of this conceptual (dis)order, as I demonstrate in the chapters to follow, is that things considered 'normal' and necessary for youth to do (for example, reach physical, cognitive and emotional maturity; assert their independence; become sexually active) are also taken as dangerous, problematic or troublesome, and as grounds for disciplinary action to regulate youth behaviour. Crucially, these behaviours and actions are taken as having come from somewhere 'outside' (like the threat of strangers) and are treated as such. But to respond on the grounds that a dominant (internal) order is being threatened by something external to it is to fail to see that the existing explanatory framework *requires* for its intelligibility the same (antagonistic) subject position in order to be reaffirmed and restored. The effect of this process or structure, as I hope to show, is that the same problematic effects occur and the same arguments against youth are made over and over in a bid to restore order. Youth is posited as something threatening, a point of tension, and as potentially responsible for the collapse of social order, when its antagonistic position and function is also consistent with the dominant conceptual order; indeed, this position is the order's founding condition of possibility.

When youth is defined as a threat in this way, and consequently treated as a social problem that needs to be 'fixed', the seemingly logical response is to call for more empirical research, more analysis and more policy (for example, more advertising campaigns on the dangers of binge drinking, the introduction of drug testing in schools to discourage teen drug use) in order to overcome the problem that young people pose. While research, analysis and policy action are all important and necessary, it may well be that part of the problem also lies with the founding concepts as much as any lack of empirical knowledge. At a conceptual level, the first principles governing the construction of youth – identity as distinct, binary logic as mutually exclusive – offer too little by assuming too much. These principles operate on an assumption or expectation that it is possible to rigorously or sufficiently identify the nature of youth. This assumption covers over the conditions on the basis of which such a position is made possible, such that the conceptual excess or ambiguous margin that is a condition of intelligibility of this assumption must be both ignored and implicitly relied upon. By following through on its own logic, this assumption must enforce certain explanatory limits or else risk its own intelligibility. The problem, then, is not a lack of knowledge as such, but a lack of awareness at a theoretical level of the manner of the constitution of 'youth' and the limits of that constitution's own conceptuality.

In order to keep thinking youth, then, what is needed is a focus on *how* youth is thought, on *how* knowledge about youth is being constructed. In saying this I am assuming that the term ought to not be abandoned despite its problematic status. However, it may rightly be asked whether these issues would need to be dealt with if the term were to be eliminated altogether. Is the better solution to not think 'youth' at all, rather than go to so much effort to deconstruct it? After all, 'youth' is a term that quickly evaporates or is exhausted once it is used, because what it seeks to define and describe is not an essential presence but a movement, a transition. Youth is not child and not adult; it is becoming not child and becoming adult. None of this 'is' youth, so the category cannot be adequately defined. In other words, 'youth' is not where the word is located. But at the same time, there is a gap to be accounted for between child and adult. Empirically, child becomes adult, and this process happens with or without a notion of youth as it is understood in any particular cultural context. Theoretically, any explanation could be offered to explain how this process occurs, what it means and how it should or should not be facilitated, but abandoning the category of youth does not eliminate the empirical gap that exists here. The gap still needs to be accounted for even if only to nominate an age when childhood ends and adulthood begins. Accordingly, this analysis does not aim to do away with youth or with a concept of youth. It does not seek to change things by replacing a flawed logic with something less problematic, and it does not seek to 'break' with binary thinking in order to get to youth in (or as) a pure state of being. The aim, rather, is to reveal the blind spots in the existing logic and the tensions inherent in its constitution, and to pay attention to them in order to offer a more effective way of analysing, debating and negotiating existing ideals and expectations about youth (and how these ideals and expectations are understood and experienced according to differentiations of age, gender, race and class).

Approaching the question of youth deconstructively allows for this. Deconstructive theory has already been productively applied to questions of gender identity and the status of the colonial 'other', and youth shares some similarities with these areas. As will be discussed in Chapter 3, feminist and post-colonial theorists reveal how discourses of race and gender dominate and constrain their objects of study (women and racial others) based on an unacknowledged dependence on the subordinated identity category in order for the dominant subjectivities of men and the West to appear as pure, natural and inevitable. Similarly for youth, the categories of 'child' and 'adult' appear as a natural ground via an unrecognised dependence on 'youth' as the ambiguous margin between the two, and ideas about youth proceed as though produced *from* this binary distinction. Paying attention to these tensions opens up possibilities for working against the subordination of youth, as much as of women and racial others, in a way that does not simply reverse this condition (by instituting a reverse essentialism, for example). This focus offers ways of approaching identity that are responsive to the manner of its conceptualisation – to the contingencies in place that undermine assumptions of absolute self-presence and essential truth. In such an approach, the importance of identity is not lost, but neither can it be taken for granted.

My aim is to open up similar, but thus far unexamined, possibilities for youth. As this method is well-established in these other areas, I seek to adopt a similar methodology in analysing youth discourses as they operate in Western cultural contexts. Specifically, I draw on techniques from deconstruction which have underpinned much of the feminist and postcolonial analyses of subjectivity, identity and the 'other.' Utilising Jacques Derrida's work and applying in particular the notions of undecidability, differance, iterability, supplementarity and the event, I trace the interpretive logic of dominant youth discourses in order to reveal their blind spots or conceptual tensions. I point to the excess of meaning these tensions create, which cannot be adequately explained or contained within available interpretive frameworks. I go on to offer a way of thinking youth that works *with* this antagonism but does not require the perpetuation of self-contradictory conceptual frameworks in order to keep existing orders intact. Paradoxically, it is in opening up the limits of youth discourses (the ex-nominated categories at play in producing dominant discourses of youth) that a less reductive and more responsive approach to understanding youth is enabled. It becomes possible to think youth more 'directly'. That is, again paradoxically, to work *against* assumptions that posit a notion of direct access to oneself – essential difference, authentic identity, of context as 'exhaustively determinable', or where there is a saturation (not an excess) of meaning (Derrida, 1988, p. 18) – and to work *with* the contingencies that make a concept of youth possible (undecidability, supplementarity, trace and so on). With a greater reflexivity and a heightened awareness of discursive limits, there is an opportunity to address existing markers of youth (youth as the future, youth as becoming adult, youth as a distinct identity category and life stage), and the often troublesome behaviour these markers produce, in a way that does not necessarily risk the intelligibility of explanatory systems in making sense of youth. In other words, a deconstructive reflexivity does not demand an interpretation of youth that preserves discursive parameters by inadvertently creating the conditions for their ongoing self-displacement.

This is actually a way of making youth *more* meaningful and valuable, not less, even though it may not seem so at first. This work puts at risk certain essentialist assumptions about youth (youth as an inherent state, as innocence, biology as destiny), but doing so means getting closer to what youth discourses articulate in the first place – the process of becoming adult. It is also possible to explain and respond to issues such as youth violence, sexuality and cognitive maturation without losing sight of the very object of investigation due to an inability to contain the effects of youth discourses within essentialist frameworks. This is to say that the regulatory discourses and policy frameworks that are used to explain and respond to such issues – discourses around safe sex and alcohol consumption and policies on the treatment of young offenders – are shaped by certain ways of thinking about youth, and what deconstruction calls for is greater attention to and awareness of how these ways of thinking work. Seeking to approach youth deconstructively is not, therefore, about trying to present alternative discourses whose effects can be contained or controlled, but about bringing to the discussion of youth a greater responsibility for the *effects* of such talk. This awareness brings the possibility of thinking through the limits of existing ways of thinking, towards actually enacting the possibilities of youth that already exist.

Chapter 2 examines several dominant and influential ways of thinking and speaking about youth and analyses how they come up against their own conceptual limits. This is done by looking at a range of theoretical traditions that have contributed to dominant discourses on youth and how these traditions work to shape (and limit) how young people are thought and spoken about in both popular and academic contexts. The chapter does not attempt to provide an exhaustive analysis of youth theory; rather, it focuses on three theoretical traditions with the understanding that *any* attempt to articulate such an ambivalent category as youth must necessarily impose limits on the category and in turn be limited in its capacity to understand or explain youth.

The chapter opens with a description of two incidents that sparked controversy in the media and I identify the kinds of discursive responses they mobilised. I then consider the theoretical influences underpinning these discourses. I look at how youth is conceptualised by Enlightenment thinkers John Locke and Jean-Jacques Rousseau, by developmental theorists Erik Erikson and Jean Piaget, and then from a critical political economy perspective focusing on the work of Henry Giroux. Finally, I examine youth according to subculture and post-subculture theory. These theoretical strands contribute differently to youth discourse (by underpinning it or interrogating it), but across all of them is an underlying assumption of youth as an identifiable and animating form of subjectivity whether this form of subjectivity is understood as grounded in physiology or social location. I raise the question of what is at stake in this formation – what is lost, what is gained and why it matters.

Chapter 3 introduces deconstructive theory in taking up the question of what it means to approach youth in terms of identity when such definition comes via the prior definition of an adult subject. Deconstruction has been applied in interrogating the identity positions of women and racial others who have been similarly defined and I look to this work for what it can offer a reading of youth. Postcolonial and feminist theorists such as Judith Butler, Homi Bhabha and Gayatri Spivak argue that the assumptions on which a notion of identity is based (self-presence, fundamental difference) cannot adequately account for the subjectivity of marginalised people. They also suggest that dominant subjects are not self-sufficient, but depend on these subordinated positions in their appearance as natural. The work of these theorists provides a model for how to approach the question of identity in ways that are responsive to these issues and how to use such an approach to challenge dominant identity structures.

The next three chapters are case studies which present a series of deconstructive analyses of the discursive tensions and contradictions inherent in youth discourse. The first is on a body of scientific research on the maturation of the teen brain and the development of reason. The second concerns constructions of young female sexuality within the discourse of 'coming of age'. The third is on the Columbine massacre as a defining event in the history of mass school shootings perpetrated by young men. In Chapter 4, on the teen brain, I work to show that there is an underlying reliance on a notion of originary presence in framing and interpreting research on how the teenage brain reaches adult-level cognitive function and maturity. I argue that this actually creates problems when it comes to accounting for the development of reasoning ability in young people. Youth are posited as lacking intuitive reason and as being impulsive and irresponsible, closer to nature and the senses. But this way of thinking is shown to be self-contradictory when held rigorously to the concept and standards of reason which informs the research in question.

The chapter argues that when youth is seen as secondary to the adult subject, and yet prior to it, the very notion of (adult) reason and originary presence is put in question. Working from the Derridean notions of supplementarity and the trace – which is to say understanding the key concepts of 'origin' and the 'subject' as discursive effects – allows one to begin to think the human subject and the meaning of human reason and the categorisation of youth in relation to this in ways that do not produce contradictory effects. But this has consequences for the authority of the long-standing theoretical traditions informing the science. A *secondary* 'originary' presence is the only way to imagine how young people grow into reason, which changes the concept of reason that is at work here. Doing so does not invalidate such research on youth, but it does address the conceptual shortfall that creates a need for more research only to reveal the same conclusions about youth as lacking reason.

Chapter 5 selects three films which construct (female) youth sexuality – *Lolita* (1997), *Towelhead* (2007) and *Thirteen* (2003) – and analyses the discourse of 'coming of age' in light of debate about the sexualisation of youth. Based on a binary opposition of innocence/knowledge, 'coming of age' signals the transition young people undergo from one into the other. The problem, however, is that when this happens, the defining markers of youth – innocence and a lack of self-knowledge – are viewed as having been transgressed. This is taken as threatening to the distinctions of youth and, by implication, the distinctions of adulthood, even as such transgression is necessary to the definition of each. Every attempt to assert the meaning of youth identity actually undermines how it is supposed to function, hence the paradoxical nature of 'coming of age'. An innocence/knowledge split creates the 'problem' of youth sexuality in that it cannot account for the movement from one to the other. To adopt forms of adult behaviour as is expected and required of young people leads to perceptions of youth deviancy and the dangers associated with female sexual precociousness. This is especially troublesome when, as demonstrated by *Lolita* and *Towelhead*, it involves a paedophilic relationship. In response to such concerns, I offer a way of thinking about innocence as performative. Such an interpretive basis allows for a response to the issue of young female sexuality that does not have to risk its own conceptual coherence in order to meet its own explanatory expectations and protective intentions.

Chapter 6 focuses on an event which foregrounds discourses of youth violence – the 1999 Columbine massacre. This event has served as a model for making sense of more recent shooting tragedies, and so serves as my particular focus in investigating the effects of the conceptual shortfall I have described here with regard to the demand to explain this tragic event. The two boys who carried out this school shooting operated in a way that both anticipated and negated many of the explanations that were put forward as to why the massacre happened. Survivors and others have therefore struggled to 'place' the boys within some kind of recognisable explanatory order, and attempts to 'fix' the boys within existing explanatory frameworks have not been able to offer explanation enough for what happened. I consider an alternative construction of youth intention that offers the possibility of answers by, paradoxically, not demanding a final explanation for what happened. By not assuming that meaning can be absolutely or exhaustively determined, there is a way to move forward that does not have to leave out of the explanatory framework what it depends on in order to make sense.

In arguing that part of the 'problem' of youth is the very means by which youth is articulated and understood, the analyses performed here work to offer a way of conceptualising youth that does not reproduce the conditions which first position youth as a social problem. By attending to the implicit assumptions that ground current constructions of youth in Western society, this book sets up an alternative way of approaching the question of youth. The following chapter proceeds, therefore, to examine the conceptual underpinnings of contemporary youth discourses.

2
The State of Contemporary Youth: Conceptual Underpinnings of Dominant Youth Discourses

Various discourses contribute to 'thinking' youth in particular ways and this chapter examines a selection of these discourses and considers the question of what is at stake in such formations. The discussion references a range of contemporary issues about youth, but it opens with an examination of two controversial events and the media attention they generated as examples that mobilise a cluster of discursive responses concerning youth. In identifying a number of these discourses in their popular and academic forms – specific aspects of which will be addressed further in Chapters 4, 5 and 6 – I look to the discursive history that they emerge from. This involves an analysis of different conceptual paradigms and how they inform contemporary youth discourses. Starting with a developmental paradigm, I examine the work of Enlightenment thinkers John Locke and Jean-Jacques Rousseau and then analyse a developmental psychology perspective. Following this, I consider a critical political economy paradigm by focusing on the work of education theorist, Henry Giroux. Finally I look at youth within a (sub)cultural studies paradigm, addressing both classic subculture theory and more recent scholarship on 'post-subculture' theory[1]. I examine how each approach conceptualises youth, exploring what assumptions each approach makes about youth as a category, and how each approach contributes to a set of discourses which inform commonsense understandings of youth. While these approaches differ in their conceptualisation of youth (as based in physiology, or as the product of social structures), they can all be seen to approach 'youth' in terms of its key difference to what constitutes 'adult' or the 'dominant culture'.

The Teenage Kings of Werribee

In October 2006, Australian current affairs programme *Today Tonight* aired footage of a group of teenage boys shown bullying and sexually assaulting a girl on the banks of the Werribee River in Werribee, an outer western suburb of Melbourne in Victoria, Australia. It was also reported that a DVD of the footage called 'Cunt The Movie' (Medew, 2007a, p. 3) made by the boys who featured in it was being sold to school students in the local area for five dollars. The public response to the story was outrage. Up to a dozen boys aged between 16 and 17 were involved in the incident. They are seen laughing and taunting the girl – a 17-year-old reported to have a 'mild developmental delay' ('Father's Plea', 2006, np) – urinating on her, setting fire to her hair, throwing her clothes into the river, and forcing her to perform oral sex.

Calling themselves the 'Teenage Kings of Werribee', the DVD included footage not just of the assault by the river but of the boys 'making chlorine bombs, dropping flares on a homeless man and throwing eggs at taxi drivers' (Miletic, 2006, np). The DVD had been edited together with titles and credits (from which police were able to track down perpetrators), and it even included an R rating. The footage had been shot the previous June and had been uploaded to video-sharing site YouTube where it and two other videos had accumulated more than 9,000 viewings (Ziffer, 2006a, np) before it was picked up by *Today Tonight* and subsequently removed from the website. The deletion of alleged gang member MySpace accounts followed, along with the launch of a police investigation, and calls for any copies of the DVD to be handed into police. Arrests were made in the following months and charges of procuring sexual penetration by intimidation, assault, and making and producing child pornography were laid (Shtargot, 2007, np). Eight of the boys pleaded guilty – an indication of their remorse, according to the judge on the case (Shtargot, 2007, np) – and another three contested the charges. In October 2007, the Children's Court convicted seven of the eight who pleaded guilty and sentenced them to youth supervision orders, requiring them to report weekly to a youth justice worker who would provide counselling and possibly require them to undertake community service as part of their sentence (Medew, 2007a, p. 3). Julia Medew reports that 'all of the boys were ordered to complete the Male Adolescent Program for Positive Sexuality', a programme run by the Royal Children's Hospital that is 'designed to prevent re-offending'. The programme focuses on 'victim awareness, relapse prevention, social skills, sex and sexuality' and is targeted at youth aged 10–21 years, 'a time when research suggests their behaviour is more likely to change as a result of education and therapy than it is for adults undergoing similar treatment' (2007b, p. 3).

Gobs 2012

In April 2012, another YouTube clip was the focus of a brief media sensation, this time centring on the disturbing actions of a group of teenage girls. Five high school students from Adelaide, Australia used a smartphone to record three of the girls offering (but not performing) 'gobs' (oral sex) for 80 cents per minute in a (pretend) bid to raise money for the prevention of sexual assault. The three Year 9 girls are shown sitting on a bench on school grounds in their school uniforms and the footage was uploaded to YouTube and 'went viral', accumulating 10,000 viewings before being removed from the site less than a day later (Tilley, 2012, np). The clip was labelled 'Gobs 2012' in satirical reference to the media campaign known as 'Kony 2012'. This campaign, launched in March 2012, received sensational (if short lived) media attention across the globe in response to another 'viral video', this time a short film released on YouTube and an accompanying social media campaign designed to raise awareness and gain support for the arrest of Central African war criminal, Joseph Kony (see http://www.kony2012.com). The girls responsible for Gobs 2012 were suspended by their school and the matter was referred to the South Australian police as a precautionary measure (South Australian Education Department Statement in Tilley, 2012, np).

Social media researcher Nina Funnell suggests that the girls were doing more in their video than simply offering oral sex. She argues that they were actually trying to be funny by parodying the Kony campaign (cited in Tilley, 2012, np). Offering 'gobs', in the schoolgirls' words, to 'make the world a better place' (cited in Tilley 2012, np) was meant to satirise the earnest discourse of social cause campaigning. The girls also offer 'action packs' in their video, including wrist bands, a familiar marketing tool in similar social action movements like the 'Make Poverty History' campaign (see http://www.makepovertyhistory.org). Funnell suggests that the girls demonstrate an obvious, if ill-conceived and poorly executed, attempt to play with the conventions of genre and to be subversive, which should be taken into consideration in making sense of the video (cited in Tilley, 2012, np). In contrast, news coverage of the story focused on the shocking prospect of 15-year-old girls offering sexual favours online, which appears to confirm fears of the sexualisation of culture, its negative impact on young girls and young people's unsafe use of the internet.

Both these cases challenge assumptions about youth. A situation in which a group of boys film scenes of violence and sexual assault, broadcast and distribute it, and are charged with making child pornography, breaches many norms and expectations about how youth are expected and thought to behave. Similarly, teen girls offering oral sex in an attempt to parody a social action campaign challenges expectations about the sexual knowledge, attitudes and availability of girls. These cases also confirm some norms and expectations as well: teen boys as out of control, violent and dangerous threats to society, and girls as increasingly sexually precocious in a media and sex saturated society, the effect of which is to put their health, safety, reputations and futures at risk. While these are two examples amongst countless others in which the behaviour of young people has been the cause of concern and outrage in the community, these incidents are interesting to consider for what they highlight about the state of contemporary youth in terms of the discursive structures employed to make sense of it. Some of these discourses are considered below.

Youth, sex, violence and the media

One quite striking, and for many extremely alarming, element of both cases is the sexual behaviour and attitudes expressed by the participants. The Werribee Kings case involves the apparent contradiction of having kids producing child pornography. It is commonly accepted that child pornography is inherently exploitative on the basis that 'children' are unable to give their free and informed consent to any sexual act due to the presumption of childhood innocence (meaning that children cannot understand what they are consenting to). But who exactly is doing the exploiting in the case of the Werribee Kings when the makers are also underage? Clearly, it is other children, but the power imbalance comes not from age, but from gender and cognitive ability. While perhaps the boys did not set out to make 'child porn', they produced something 'porn-like' in the sexual attitude they expressed towards the girl (forcing her to perform oral sex, writing the name of the movie on her breasts, throwing her clothes away), and in filming the incident, distributing it online and producing a saleable product from it. Likewise, whatever the Gobs 2012 girls were aiming to achieve with their video, and however successful (or otherwise) their attempt at satire is deemed to be, the predominant interpretation of their video was that they were offering themselves sexually in a commercial and highly public way. This kind of behaviour from young people, both boys and girls, transgresses not just social expectations concerning youth, but the perceived limits of youth behaviour if grounded in an assumption of innocence and a limited self-awareness.

According to education professor and prominent researcher on youth and media David Buckingham, 'children's access to sexual knowledge is often regarded as part of a more general permissiveness, equated with a rise in violence, drug use and criminal activity amongst the young' (2003, p. 4). Buckingham also points out that the rise of new media technology is making it incredibly easy for minors to access explicit material (2003, p. 3), and it would seem that it is also very easy for young people to *make* sexually explicit, even pornographic, material thanks to this technology. The rise of 'sexting', for instance, in which young people use camera phones to take sexually explicit photos of themselves and then send them as a text message to others in their peer group, is leading to serious legal trouble for minors because sending photos of underage kids and teens, even if made by the teens themselves, constitutes child pornography (Sacco et al., 2010, p. 3). There has been widespread media coverage on this phenomenon in recent years, as well as the emergence of an extensive body of literature – from governments, journalists and academics – examining the sexualisation of culture and especially its impact on girls (and women)[2]. The concern articulated across much of this literature is that this rise in sexualised communication, media content and behaviour is causing girls to develop sexual identities too soon and at the expense of their childhoods and their innocence. This implies that it would be possible to take on such an identity in a more timely and appropriate way, an issue which I explore further in Chapter 5 on the discourse of 'coming of age'.

There is a conflict here, however, where, according to Buckingham, 'children's awareness of sexuality can be seen as a healthy, natural phenomenon', but 'it can also be viewed as precocious or unnatural', something that weakens 'the boundaries between childhood and adulthood, which are apparently designed to protect children' (2003, p. 5). For Buckingham, 'the recurrent claim that children are being "sexualised" at the hands of the media obviously implies that they were not sexual in the past, and have now become so' (2003, p. 4). The basis for such concerns, in Buckingham's account, seems to be an assumption of 'a golden age of innocence' now lost due to the media age, and which we should strive to get back to (2003, p. 4).

Another troublesome aspect of the Werribee Kings case is its violence: throwing flares at a homeless person, reports of a sequel to 'Cunt the Movie', 'CTM2', showing the boys breaking into and trashing homes, and defecating and urinating in kettles and cups (Crawford, 2006, np). In the days following the release of the story, there were discussions about the influence of violent media such as the pay-TV programme, *Jackass* – a show deliberately setting out to push acceptable boundaries and social mores through its reckless style of stunt work. *Jackass* star Johnny Knoxville, in Australia at the time the story broke, said when questioned over the incident: 'I'm sorry, but we didn't invent cameras or doing something stupid... Those little bastards are evil, what they did to some girl... how the f--- do you put that on us?' (cited in Ziffer, 2006b, p. 3). According to *Jackass* director Jeff Tremaine the 'spirit' of the show is 'to shock the public, not involve them in dangerous stunts', and the team actually turned to making R-rated films instead of the television show so as to prevent children from watching (Ziffer, 2006b, p. 3). Ultimately, though, Tremaine does not feel responsible for so-called copycat behaviour as he believes 'it would happen with or without us' (cited in Ziffer, 2006b, p. 3).

Public commentators are quick to link such behaviour to new media technology, thus conflating two 'moral panics': youth violence (both physical and sexual) and youth media use. Similarly, Gobs 2012 and the phenomenon of sexting highlight another dual moral panic: youth sex and youth media use. The former Federal Communications Minister of Australia, Helen Coonan, said in response to the Werribee Kings story that 'there could be no more glaring example of how [media] technology is aiding and abetting acts such as these to reach a wider audience at a remarkable pace' (cited in Rennie, 2006, np). These comments can equally be applied to Gobs 2012. The internet and new media technologies have brought new ways of using and interacting with media and media content to a point where there is now a blurring of lines between production and consumption, text and audience, and techno 'savvy' teens are at the forefront of the development of these new relationships.

It is commonly asserted that the problem with this advancement of media technology is that traditional modes and means of regulation are being bypassed, and adults are struggling to keep up with the speed of these changes and to make sense of what they mean. In the aftermath of the Werribee Kings incident, an editorial in Melbourne newspaper *The Age* suggested that 'the dazzling attractions of cyberspace and new technologies can blur the ethical boundaries we navigate in the real world' when, with mobile phone cameras and ease of upload to online sites, people can witness recorded footage of someone being bullied or harassed, for example, and yet maintain a viewing distance and therefore not feel compelled to act against it ('The DVD that shocked the nation', 2006, p. 14). This distance is thanks to the conflation of the real and the virtual enabled by the technology; 'the medium makes it easier for people to bear witness and not testify, to distance themselves from their own conscience' ('The DVD that shocked the nation', 2006, p. 14). One response to this trend has been the development of cyber-safety programmes in schools as an attempt to educate students on the dangers of cyberspace and in ethical and safe online behaviour. A statement from the South Australian Education Department in response to the Gobs 2012 incident confirmed that the high school in question 'has a strict cyber safety policy in place' (cited in Tilley, 2012, np). This is particularly pertinent in relation to this case as a former student of the school was murdered by an online predator in 2007[3], a tragedy in which the absolute worst fear for parents and cyber-safety experts as to what could happen to young people online was realised. (Disconcertingly, the girls in the Gobs 2012 video sit near a memorial to the murdered student [Kinkade, 2012, np].)

This question of the place of new media technology in teens' experience and expression of themselves is explored in detail in Chapter 6. For the moment, however, it is sufficient to note that, in addition to cyber-safety programmes, an obvious response to these new mediated social situations and contexts is to seek to monitor kids' online activity more closely, the underlying assumption being that kids lack the ability to regulate themselves online, or anywhere for that matter. Moreover, teens are not expected to regulate themselves, as it is the responsibility of adults to do so. That the Werribee Kings thought that doing what they did would be 'a laugh' (Medew, 2007c, p. 3) can be taken as evidence of this lack of self-regulation and self-awareness, and this is reflected in then Prime Minister John Howard's comments that the youths' behaviour was probably a result of peer pressure and a lack of parental authority ('DVD school in despair', 2006, np). Funnell speculates that the girls meant their video to be taken as a joke, but their big mistakes were wearing their school uniforms (thus making identification easy and, of course, implicating their school in the scandal), and also choosing to release the clip online because 'you have no control over it or how it gets distributed [once online], or the sorts of interpretations that people will map onto [it]' (cited in Tilley, 2012, np). For child psychologist Michael Carr-Gregg, this incident 'goes to highlight how little these girls knew and understood about the rights and responsibilities of social media' (cited in Kinkade, 2012, np), indicating a lack of comprehension of the consequences of their actions. Funnell notes that it is important in comedy or in any public performance to 'know your audience' (cited in Tilley, 2012, np) and the girls appear to have quite seriously misjudged this. So rather than being read as comic satire on a controversial topic, the incident has predominantly been read quite literally as teen girls offering oral sex for money. What is important to note here is how these perspectives reproduce a very familiar discourse on youth. Kids are assumed to lack sufficient maturity and self-awareness and to be open to undue peer and media influence which therefore calls for parental authority to discipline and guide them (and yet they are also expected to know their audience and understand the rights and responsibilities of social media).

In contrast, instead of linking the behaviour of the Werribee Kings and the Gobs 2012 girls to the adverse effect of media use on vulnerable or impressionable teens or on the sexualisation of culture, it is possible to see evidence of a more developed self-awareness. While the Gobs 2012 girls speak very explicitly about sex, if considered within the context of satire, as Funnell does, then the offer of oral sex is not to be taken seriously at all but can be read as an attempt to subversively play with the kinds of stylistic conventions seen in Kony 2012 and other genres like infomercials (cited in Tilley, 2012, np). Despite the fact that the girls themselves do not directly explain their intentions for the video, leaving reporters and commentators to speculate as to their aims, that the girls tell their viewers that they are offering 'gobs' to help prevent men from raping girls (Williamson, 2012, np), as well using phrases like 'we are trained professionals' (cited in Terry, 2012, np), can nevertheless be understood to demonstrate a comprehension of media conventions more complex and reflexive than would be attributed to them if explained either by reference to youthful ignorance or by the corrupting influence of popular culture on their developing sexualities.

Similarly, comments from Werribee Kings group members themselves show an awareness of the kinds of discourses used by others to make sense of their film. For example, someone claiming to be the film's producer wrote in an online post that 'you probably know me best by my f----- up, illegal movie, which I find funny and do not regret at all' (cited in Crawford, 2006, np). This statement signals an awareness of a normative judgement on the group's behaviour in explicitly rejecting the expectation that he should feel remorse for his actions. Another example includes calling the girl 'the victim' in the DVD (cited in Miletic, 2006, np). This shows the boys' conscious awareness and placement of the girl as the victim (and not, presumably, in the manner intended by the Positive Sexuality programme), which in turn signals their awareness of how their behaviour would be framed. Yet in using the line 'no one messes with us, we only mess with them' on the cover of the DVD (cited in Miletic, 2006, np), they clearly reject this framing.

This awareness suggests that the question of the influence of violent media (or sexual content), for example, is not as simple as arguing that youth passively assume violent or sexualised behaviour. Such awareness can be seen to suggest, in these cases at least, that the young people involved *consciously work with* available discourses. The Werribee Kings subvert discourses of 'perpetrator/victim', or of 'crime/guilt/remorse', and mimic the language of American street culture found in rap and hip hop music and Hollywood movies in using the line 'no one messes with us, we only mess with them'. The girls mimic infomercials and social awareness campaigns. This performativity complicates the assumption that their level of maturity would not enable such awareness (an issue that is discussed further in Chapter 5 and at length in Chapter 6).

What is indicated from this discussion of different ways of making sense of these cases is that the identity of youth is inherently ambivalent. The image of youth projected here is one of fragility, innocence, passivity and vulnerability on the one hand, and of precocity, danger and threat on the other; of teens as knowing, active and powerful. Youth are discursively positioned (by others) either as being negatively or adversely influenced by certain forces (due to their susceptibility to peer pressure, or media influences), or (by themselves) as consciously acting outside the 'norm'. Especially noteworthy is how new media technologies exacerbate this ambivalent status. The internet and mobile phones, online chat services and networking sites (such as Facebook, MySpace, YouTube, Twitter, Tumblr) allow youth to exist and be thought of as an abstract, virtual community in ways not possible before the introduction and uptake of these technologies. Furthermore, such virtual interaction enables (and requires) a level and kind of self-conscious thought and behaviour, or 'performativity', that confounds or confronts existing assumptions about, and expectations of, youth self-awareness (the notion of performativity will be taken up in detail in following chapters). Academic discourses, however, must necessarily contain or limit this conceptual variability in order to be able to analyse youth and approach it as an object of study and research. In the next section, I look at ways in which this is done, and then at how academic discourses on youth flow back into commonsense discourses. This then leads me to consider (at the end of this chapter and in the next) the limits of these discourses and the effects of these limits in framing and making sense of youth behaviour.

Youth in academic discourse

Today, youth has become an object of the 'academic gaze' both within a range of existing disciplines and in the 'new' discipline of youth studies, which functions both to underpin and to articulate youth discourses. In her examination and critique of the construction of knowledge of adolescence, youth studies scholar Nancy Lesko suggests that the constitution, meaning and experiences of youth reality 'can be seen as the *effects* of certain sets of social practices across numerous domains of contemporary legal, educational, family, and medical domains' (1996, p. 140). The study of youth is similarly broad, covering 'the fields of education, criminology, economics, cultural studies, sociology and psychology' (Griffin, 2004, p. 13). Investigation and analysis is undertaken using a variety of research methods (for example, ethnographic and empirical studies, textual and discourse analysis), and covering a wide range of issues and topics within domains such as those mentioned above, as well as within the contexts of media, sexuality, body, subculture, peers, marketing/consumption, government, race, class, gender, work, health, religion and leisure.

A dominant 'theme' in much youth research is youth 'transitions', or youth pathways to adulthood. Youth transitions chiefly focus on family, school and work contexts, and on how youth experience across these areas is shaped by or interacts with the elements of race, class and gender. This work also looks at barriers or challenges to what is considered a 'successful' transition to adult life and productive citizenship. As Lesko writes, 'talk about adolescents – their problems, characteristics, and needs – is a central arena for talking about social expectations for productive, rational, independent adults' (1996, p. 142). The boundaries that govern the constitution of teenagers as normal or deviant function to define and limit what is considered normal and socially desirable in the domains of civil society, sexual conduct and rational thought (Lesko, 1996, p. 142). Research in this area is also attuned to how generational change and wider social change affects the meaning and applicability of such boundaries and distinctions as they operate in the notion and experience of transition, and in the outcomes these produce.

The area of youth studies also has a vocational component. 'Youth work' involves training for working with and for young people in areas such as health, juvenile justice, education, training and welfare.

As a professional practice, areas of study include the ethics of working with young people, youth research methods, policy development and implementation, and effective communication. The aim of such work is to improve the situations of young people. For example, the Youth Work programme at RMIT University describes youth work as 'securing young people's wellbeing while recognising their moral status as human beings, their associated rights, entitlements and obligations' (2012, np). Youth work is about working to ensure optimum development for young people and facilitating opportunities for development by identifying areas of need and providing resources to assist youth in realising their potential so that they may 'thrive intellectually, physically, and creatively as human beings' (RMIT University, 2012, np).

What is interesting to note here is how youth studies (to gather under a single term the varied work of a range of disciplines) both operates from *and* articulates – or assumes *and* produces – the youth discourses discussed above. For instance, it is because youth represents the process of transition from child to adult that knowledge of the shape and experience of youth reality is needed. But it is because of this knowledge of young people as different from adults and from children in the possession of certain cognitive, physical and social capacities that a notion of youth transition is 'there' to work from. The knowledge we have of youth is not separated from the means of its production, but the means of its production is shaped by the knowledge we have of youth. Both the Werribee Kings and Gobs 2012 cases shocked the public, yet responses to these 'new' events called on and confirmed already established ideas about youth and their troubling behaviour. This is not to say that ways of thinking about and analysing youth do not change, but frameworks for producing knowledge are responding to knowledge already produced. How is it, then, that youth has emerged relatively recently as an object of academic research? To what extent are specific claims about youth, be they academic or journalistic, organised by a core set of intellectual frameworks? In order to answer these questions, it is necessary to engage with youth studies to get a sense of where these discourses and analytical frameworks have come from and what organises and underlies their intelligibility.

The developmental paradigm

One important conceptual paradigm that serves to underpin youth discourse can be broadly characterised as developmental. I will consider developmental psychology in a moment, but the basis for such a framework for distinguishing youth has its origins in Enlightenment thinking. Coming out of the Middle Ages where no special attention was paid to the circumstances or needs of children as distinct from adults, new ways of thinking about children and childhood emerged with the Enlightenment and its interest in understanding human nature and the role and value of education (Heaven, 2001, p. 9). Two leading figures in this work were John Locke and Jean-Jacques Rousseau. Roger Cox writes that seventeenth-century thinker John Locke was 'driven to face the problems of childhood through his basic concerns with the nature of the human mind and with the proper relationships that ought to exist between adults in civil society' (1996, p. 61). Locke's work in *Some Thoughts Concerning Education* (1693) was a detailed attempt to articulate the kind of upbringing and education that would enable a child to meet the demands of the adult world (Cox, 1996, p. 50). Locke suggests that 'we must look upon our Children, when grown up, to be like ourselves; with the same Passions, the same Desires' (*Some Thoughts*, para.41). He sees the child as being 'of the same nature as the adult, intellectually, socially and politically' but as needing 'to be brought up within some special space protected by parents and teachers' in order for that nature to develop (Cox, 1996, p. 62). Locke writes that 'the great Mistake I have observed in People's breeding their Children has been ... That the Mind has not been made obedient to Discipline, and pliant to Reason, when at first it was most tender, most easy to be bowed' (*Some Thoughts*, para. 34).

Locke's position is that the adult must express, on the child's behalf, the qualities of reason and freedom that are still only potentialities in the 'imperfect state' of childhood (Cox, 1996, p. 62). This is because, according to Locke, '[h]e that is not used to submit his Will to the Reason of others, *when* he is *young*, will scarce harken or submit to his own Reason, when he is of an Age to make use of it' (*Some Thoughts*, para.36). The role of the parents is to be a model of reason for the child until the child is capable of making its own judgements (Cox, 1996, p. 57). Reason therefore governs both parents and child, for parents supply the understanding that the child lacks and which must be 'exercised for the child's own freedom' (Cox, 1996, p. 60).

A desire to articulate what ordered adult life should entail makes it necessary, therefore, to regard children as a 'special case' (Cox, 1996, p. 63). Locke must necessarily define the child as 'incomplete, inadequate and "imperfect" ' in order to conceptualise 'humankind as intellectually self-conscious, critical and autonomous' (Cox, 1996, p. 63). Thus a lesser part or aspect to human nature must be articulated in order to 'get to' this most desired state. This continues to be a dominant and powerful way of thinking about youth. Even though Locke suggests child and adult are of the same nature, there is a fundamental difference between them and thus a need to bring youth to an adult level of reason and self-awareness.

In contrast to Locke's belief that children 'love to be treated as Rational Creatures sooner than is imagined' (*Some Thoughts*, para. 81), Rousseau recommends leaving 'childhood to ripen your children' (1969, p. 58). In his text *Emile* (1762), part philosophical treatise and part novel, Rousseau traces the development of Emile from infancy through to early manhood focusing especially on the nature of his education and upbringing (Cox, 1996, p. 65). Rousseau writes that '[n]ature provides for the child's growth in her own fashion, and this should never be thwarted' (1969, p. 50), which is unlike Locke who is 'looking for the "man" in the child and seeking... to develop the capacity for reason as soon as possible' (Cox, 1996, p. 66). Learning for Rousseau is therefore about making discoveries through direct engagement with the physical environment (Cox, 1996, pp. 66–7). Rousseau notes that '[s]ince everything that comes into the human mind enters through the gates of sense, man's first reason is a reason of sense-experience' (1969, p. 90). To use books as substitute for feet, eyes and hands as 'our first teachers in natural philosophy', Rousseau writes, 'does not teach us to reason, it teaches us to use the reason of others rather than our own; it teaches us to believe much and know little' (1969, p. 90). Emile is only permitted to learn about morality and human life via secondary means during his adolescence, because by then he will be 'self-possessed enough to deal with the opinions of others' having 'learned so far only through experience and not through authorities' (Cox, 1996, p. 68). Underlying this is a belief in childhood innocence that must not be interfered with, but preserved. 'Nature would have them children before they are men', Rousseau writes. 'If we try to invert this order we shall produce a forced fruit immature and flavourless, fruit which will be rotten before it is ripe' (1969, p. 54). Overall, Rousseau is seeking to avoid precocity and ensure that adults do not make judgements about the child's nature and abilities prematurely (Cox, 1996, p. 67).

What Rousseau has established is the notion that children possess their own ways of thinking and that they should therefore be allowed to develop and grow in their own way and at their own pace (Heaven, 2001, p. 10). While Locke defined the child according to the autonomy of the adult (Cox, 1996, p. 63), proposing that the child's mind was 'a blank slate, or *tabula rasa*' waiting 'to be written upon' (Heaven, 2001, pp. 9–10), Rousseau advocates a notion of innocence that assumes its own internal coherence and grants creative potential to the child's mind (Cox, 1996, p. 64). Both, however, set up a concept of youth based on key differences between youth and adult in terms of internal states of being.

Developmental psychology

Since Locke and Rousseau, much theorising worked from and reinforced this conceptualisation of youth. Two names which feature prominently in the recent history of such work are modern adolescent psychologists Erik Erikson and Jean Piaget. In the area of developmental psychology, Erikson and Piaget follow and contribute to this conceptualisation of youth in their concern with what is considered appropriate development. Their work offers an understanding of youth as a life stage determined by physiological growth and development. They focus on theories of cognitive maturation through specific ages and stages of growth, which trace a progressively more complex ability to reason and to integrate the external world with an internal state. Child psychologist David Elkind writes that for Erikson, adolescence is also a time in which a personal identity is to be constructed by bringing together various 'facets of self into a working whole that at once provides continuity with the past and a focus and direction for the future' (1998, p. 16). Erikson describes of this stage as resolving 'identity vs. identity confusion' (McKinney and Vogel, 1987, p. 16). As part of a series of developmental stages across the life span, the development of a personal identity 'is based on the integration...of all previous identifications with both internal endowments and aptitudes based on environmental opportunities' (Elkind, 1998, p. 16); or rather, with having the necessary mental abilities and requisite experiences that, when balanced together, enable transition into future developmental stages.

The particular interest of Piaget centres on the development of adolescent reasoning ability according to 'functional invariants...and stage-specific aspects of cognition' (McKinney and Vogel, 1987, p. 21). An individual progresses through a number of specific and age-appropriate cognitive levels, developing an ability to manage a broader and more complex range of experiences, and to organise these into stable patterns (Lerner, 1987, p. 58). Like Erikson, this theory proposes that adolescence represents 'a qualitatively new developmental level' with specific learning tasks that mark its course and which must be accomplished before the next stage of development can be reached (Lerner, 1987, p. 59). Marking out youth according to structures of cognition and internalised states of maturation shows both theorists delineating clear moments when adolescence begins and when it ends. Thus, developmental psychology theorises a notion of youth transition in terms of charting stages of cognitive maturation and its qualitative expression towards (and defined by) adult-level maturity and mental function.

A key transition, according to Piaget's research, is that at approximately 11 or 12 years of age and through to about age 14 or 15, a form of rationality develops called 'formal operations' (Moshman, 1999, p. 11). This stage, which indicates movement towards adult cognitive maturity, is possible only after the previous stage known as 'concrete operations' is consolidated. According to David Moshman, a concrete thinker is logical and systematic and able to manage multiple facets of a situation based on coherent conceptual frameworks like classes, numbers and the logic of relations. The formal-operations stage, however, signals a more complex adaptation of these conceptual frameworks (Moshman, 1999, p. 11). A formal-operations thinker is able to make sense of reality by thinking about and through 'hypothetical possibilities' (Moshman, 1999, p. 13). People of this age group are thus seen to have a capacity to think in abstract ways and towards propositional meanings that take them beyond the here and now (Elkind, 1998, p. 28).

The difference between concrete and formal thinkers is in their reasoning ability. Concrete thinkers formulate meaning that is most consistent with what is directly observable, whereas formal-operations thinking is characterised by second-order thinking. This type of thinking uses the symbolic systems of language or mathematics, for example, to take a step back and consider what the possible relationship between two variables might be (Moshman, 1999, p. 13). In doing so, formal-operations thinkers go beyond the real and immediate, they perform 'operations on operations' (Moshman, 1999, p. 13), they 'think about thinking' (Elkind, 1998, p. 39). They are thus able to consider and evaluate possible outcomes independent of lived reality but in a way that brings to their reality a sense of the past and future, of the multiple options and choices that go into making their reality knowable, real and liveable (Elkind, 1998, pp. 33–48). The major task of adolescence is thus to achieve an overall sense of identity synthesis via processes of integration. The task, that is, is to bring together the cognitive transformations that have occurred over time and, in response to both experience and maturation, to form a relatively stable character structure that remains consistent through time and across different situations (Lerner, 1987, p. 59).

Developmental psychology grounds 'youth' in physiological develop-ment. Youth is defined as a condition of growth, as part of the *process* of 'coming of age' that has to be physically and socially lived out. This approach also focuses particularly on the construction and consolida-tion of an individual identity in such a process, such that youth is seen as the crucial time for forming one's identity. Youth is conceptualised here as an inevitable part of the life cycle, but one that is eventually passed through on the way to a desired level and standard of social competency enabled by complex cognitive functions. This approach therefore conceives of youth in terms of in-built cognitive capacities and core learning tasks which are then tied to the character traits and expres-sive forms of young people. In this way, a developmental psychology perspective provides a way of describing youth in terms of a fundamen-tal nature which grounds or underpins behaviour. From this perspective, and from within the developmental paradigm more generally, youth is taken to be part of a natural and inevitable physiological and psycho-logical growth process, and the influence of this approach is evident when youth behaviour is discussed in terms of innocence, lack and vulnerability.

For example, such a perspective can be seen in operation in the public furore that erupted in May 2008 in response to the work of Australian artist and photographer Bill Henson. An artist of international acclaim, Henson's photographs of naked pubescent girls and boys became the subject of controversy when, prior to the exhibition of his work in Sydney, 20 photographs were seized by police in response to public com-plaints that the images constituted child pornography[4]. A review of the media coverage of this incident points to the controversy as stemming from the fact that the depiction of minors in a sexualised way brings 'art' into 'the realm of pornography' (Bachelard and Mangan, 2008, np) and, indeed, exploitation. This is a particular problem here because images of pubescent kids as opposed to young children or older teens inevitably involves the depiction of budding sexuality, and yet these children are also considered to be too young to be able to consent to such a depiction of themselves. The implicit assumptions of developmental logic can be identified in this issue over the representation of minors.

Official findings were that the works did not constitute child pornog-raphy, but this did not end debate over the issues of child exploitation and 'the delicate point of consent' for those under 16 years of age ('It is important to get a proper perspective on Henson', 2008, np). Larissa Dubecki, journalist at *The Age* newspaper, argues that Henson's art grap-ples with 'the ambiguity of teen existence' and offers depictions of 'the stormy adolescent interior' (2008, np). But according to psychologist Steve Biddulph, the very depiction of this life stage, 'innocent and beautiful' as it may be, 'takes their [children's] power and their privacy away and lets the world in' (2008, np). From this perspective, the act of capturing innocence ends it or at least risks severely disrupting the natural process of sexual development by prematurely sexualising children and forcing them to deal with situations beyond their mental capacity to handle. 'Teenage children are developmentally fragile', Biddulph writes, 'they try on any number of selves, and they have to be free to do so, without adult predation on their bodies or minds' (2008, np).

Biddulph's position echoes the arguments of all the theorists discussed above: that (late) childhood constitutes a special time and space which involves both cognitive and physical development and which is tied to identity construction. However, these processes leave youth vulnerable while going through them and this is only compounded when parents allow them to be subject to the needs and wants of artists like Henson. From this perspective, youth do not possess the maturity and experience to appreciate the consequences of a decision to pose naked, and by this reasoning cannot make an informed decision to do so. Biddulph believes therefore that it is entirely inappropriate to even ask the question of whether it would be wrong to photograph a minor in such a manner; there can be no question that it is wrong (2008, np). (In Chapter 5 I return to the question of teen sexuality and agency in more detail.)

Developmental principles and assumptions underlie the differing perspectives on this issue. There is a general concern to protect a developmental stage that is by its very nature ambivalent, and some see such a stage as being honoured artistically by Henson, whereas others see it as being violated and destroyed. But what can be noted from this example is that a developmental perspective does not take into account the socially determined meaning of the developmental process it describes. The process is taken as absolute, and the different expressions of that process are taken as indicators of pure being tied to physiological development and its related mental capacity. This suggests that the meaning of such processes should not even be subject to debate, let alone subject to attempts to depict them which leave the representation of a developmental stage – and thus the stage itself – open to interpretation. I deal with the effects of this conceptual grounding in the case studies to follow on filmic depictions of young female sexuality, the development of teen reasoning ability, and challenges to the presumed lack of teen self-awareness in cases of youth violence. In the next section, however, I examine a different conceptual approach that, in contrast to the developmental paradigm, focuses on youth as a socially constructed category.

The critical political economy paradigm

Critical political economy is another conceptual paradigm informing youth discourse. Over a number of publications, education theorist Henry Giroux draws on this perspective in his critical reading of youth as a market-based category defined through commercial discourses. This approach differs from developmental psychology insofar as it is a critical approach to youth and does not treat it as a natural state of being. However, it is via a critical reading of market-based definitions of youth that the assumptions underpinning Giroux's own position on youth, and the limits of these assumptions, can be identified.

According to Giroux, 'beneath the abstract codifying of youth around the discourses of law, medicine, psychology, employment, education and marketing statistics, there is the lived experience of being young' (1996, p. 3). Giroux writes that his own youth was marked by being working class, which meant that he existed outside the privileged social and cultural spaces of the white, middle-class mainstream. 'Class marked us [Giroux and his friends] as poor, inferior, linguistically inadequate, and dangerous', and being part of such a marginalised and disadvantaged class and culture 'penetrated us with a trauma that we could hardly navigate theoretically but felt in every fibre of our being' (1996, p. 8). There is an order of class, but also of race and gender relations in place here that, for Giroux, defines the lived experience of being young (and this signals Giroux's alignment with Marxist thought). Giroux does not treat this system of relations as natural or inevitable, but he nevertheless 'begins' his analysis of youth based on the implicit privileging of the white, male middle class of the developed Western world. As will be noted later, Giroux argues that social investment in the well-being of youth is needed at the level of lived experience, which is defined according to the differentiations of race, gender and class as determined by Western capitalism. These foundational elements of Giroux's approach to youth, while discursively constructed or framed, are taken as the grounding for the experience of being young. Giroux treats these elements as separate from the discourses of capitalism and the free-market economy. In this way, Giroux posits youth as a lived or material experience or state of being according to the foundational orientations of race, gender and class. Placed over this basis are the codifications of youth according to the discourses mentioned above, such as psychology and education, which frame and mediate the experience of race, gender and class in particular ways and thus enable and constrain possible experiences and opportunities for young people. So for Giroux, youth is a state of being but it is also 'a personal, historical, and social construction' that is 'negotiated within and across a range of class, racial, gender, and sexual orientations' (1996, pp. 10–11).

Giroux's framework for analysing various sites and determinations of the meaning of youth is informed by the concerns of a critical political economy perspective. According to Peter Golding and Graham Murdock, critical political economy focuses 'on the interplay between the symbolic and economic dimensions of public communications' (1991, p. 15). Cultural spaces and texts are examined in ways that seek to reveal their organisation in financial terms; how the economic conditions in which cultural production takes place influence what discourses and forms of representation enter the public domain and who has access to them. Critical political economy is theoretically informed by neo-Marxism, and distances itself from the 'liberal pluralist' tradition that accepts the social organisation of the capitalist system as ideal. Instead, it is centrally concerned with examining how power is constituted and exercised within such a system. Critical political economy is thus materialist as it focuses on how people interact with their material environment and on how the symbolic sphere gets shaped in relation to that environment by people who do not have equal access to material resources. In short, critical analysis investigates and describes the dynamics of 'late capitalism' (Golding and Murdock, 1991, pp. 15–17).

Accordingly, Giroux argues that the ascendancy of corporate models of citizenship and the predominance of market discourse has shaped a relationship between youths and adults that produces negative effects for the young. Giroux writes that liberal culture has become 'synonymous with market culture' and that 'the celebrated freedoms of the consumer are bought at the expense of the freedoms of citizens' (2000, pp. 1–2). Giroux believes that this situation threatens both children's well-being and that of democracy. Where the values of democracy are enmeshed with the market, where freedom is defined as a private good, a key tension is lost 'between market moralities and those values of civil society that cannot be measured in strictly commercial terms but are critical to democratic public life' such as 'justice, respect for children, and the rights of citizens' (Giroux, 2000, p. 2).

This kind of critical approach to market-based constructions of youth can be seen in discourses of health and well-being that express a notion of 'kids in crisis' or 'youth at risk'. For example, figures from the Australian Institute of Health and Welfare reveal 'serious problems among adolescents' such as 'increases in self-harm and mood disorders, assaults and injury, obesity and chronic illness' (Miller, 2008, p. 15). Similarly, Michael Carr-Gregg describes today's young women as 'spiritual anorexics' because they lack support from social institutions that provide a sense of tradition and ritual (cited in Marcus, 2008, np). Carr-Gregg argues that kids 'have a hole in their self where they do not believe in anything', or 'come to believe that their worth is derived from the number of possessions they have' (cited in Marcus, 2008, np). Miller writes that according to youth researcher Richard Eckersley, 'fundamental social, cultural, economic and environmental changes' in the Western world 'are damaging young people's health and wellbeing' (2008, p. 15). Factors such as 'increased family breakdown, work–family pressures, heavy media use, materialistic values and dietary deficiencies' (Miller, 2008, p. 15) have 'made it harder for young people to feel accepted, loved and secure; to know who they are, where they belong, what they want from life and what is expected of them: in short, to feel life is deeply meaningful and worthwhile' (Eckersley cited in Miller, 2008, p. 15).

Young people are seen to lack grounding in and recognition of aspects of life – like a secure sense of identity, self-worth and belonging – that should not have a market value but rather exist unmediated by commercial culture. With the internet, peer groups, education and study pressures and increased marketing to children, identity is increasingly drawn from popular culture interactions which are designed for profit over well-being. Critical political economy points to teens that are raised within a commercial cultural system that seeks to quantify self-worth and belonging as being at risk of negative social outcomes. An often heard appeal in response to this kind of framing of young lives is that we need to 'just let kids be kids'. Such a statement was made in response to the Bill Henson photograph controversy by the Australian Prime Minister at the time, Kevin Rudd (Dubecki, 2008, np). The underlying assumption is that youth are being stripped of a natural life they would otherwise freely live out in the absence of commercial and consumption-based pressures and pursuits. Their lives would instead be defined by creative play and agenda-free exploration, perhaps of the order that Rousseau advocates, or of the kind articulated in the Early Years Learning Framework mentioned in the Introduction that suggested that the purpose of children's play was for them 'to simply enjoy being' (Bita, 2009, np). While this play may include emulating the activities of the adult world, at least it would not be the result of a marketing campaign.

These commentators assume an authentic experience of being young that is supported by certain non-commercial social structures that they see as being corrupted or confined by the operations of corporate culture. As will shortly be explained, Giroux's work operates from the same assumptions, but Giroux would take this example of adults arguing for a return to a non-commodified life as actually *belonging* to corporate models of youth. Giroux argues that a market discourse does not mark all youth as 'at risk', only those kids who belong to the white middle class. However, Giroux also suggests that a 'youth at risk' discourse is partly what contributes to a situation where even mainstream youth defined according to commercial discourses comes to be treated as a threat to adult society.

In Giroux's critique, non-white and working-class youth are disadvantaged because of their material environments, and the negative effects of these disadvantages are exacerbated when the predominant discourse through which the elements of race, gender and class are coded is that of corporate culture and market discourse. Giroux argues that this discourse may relate expressions of 'at risk' behaviour by marginalised youth to the disadvantages of their actual lives or material environments, but unlike white youth, the discourse marks them as individually responsible for their actions. As Giroux writes, 'the logic of the marketplace blames kids – especially those who are poor, Latino, or black – for an alleged lack of character while it dismantles social services that help to meet their most basic needs' (2000, p. 6). The effect of this is to position these youth as a risk *to* society. In contrast, 'when privileged white kids mimic destructive adult behaviour, such acts are generally treated as aberrations' (Giroux, 2000, p. 19), or deviant behaviour is blamed on other, external, forces – like popular culture – that are separated from the spaces of white affluence (Giroux, 2000, p. 8). (Both these possibilities for explaining destructive behaviour from white, middle-class youth are considered in Chapter 6.) But according to Giroux, when disadvantaged kids engage in destructive behaviour, they are treated as being the underlying cause of the behaviour as well as its victims. In short, they become a social problem (Giroux, 2000, p. 19).

Giroux is pointing to an implicit assumption in a 'youth at risk' discourse where the life conditions of mainstream (white, middle-class) youth do *not* produce deviant behaviour, hence the need to look elsewhere for explanations for destructive behaviour. In the Werribee Kings case, the adverse influence of the media, peer pressure and inadequate parental authority were all mentioned as possible factors influencing the behaviour of the boys (a 'youth at risk' discourse). But a 'youth *as* risk' discourse can also be seen to operate in aspects of the Werribee Kings case which suggests that the two discourses do not divide along class lines as straightforwardly as Giroux suggests. Comments relating to the working-class roots of the Werribee area and the instability created by recent urban growth tie the behaviour of the group of boys to the disadvantages of their social class (Dubecki, 2006, p. 3). Reports that a number of them had dropped out of their final year of school, due perhaps to the marginalisation experienced within the school streaming system (see Petrie, 2006; Houlihan and Metlikovec, 2006), can also be seen to inform their socially undesirable behaviour. In these explanations, the conditions of the boys' lives are taken to contribute to their deviant behaviour, but they are not necessarily treated as mitigating circumstances. On Giroux's account, making an *explicit* connection between life conditions and threatening behaviour such as this would actually make it easier to treat the boys *themselves* as a threat to the wider community, as no mediating factors – such as violent media – are considered, and a much more direct line of culpability can be drawn. For both mainstream and marginal youth a notion of character and associated behaviour are tied to social location, but this has different effects for each group according to market discourse. This discourse relates socially desirable behaviour to the social locations of mainstream youth and thus looks elsewhere to explain any deviant behaviour by this group, but the discourse attributes the socially undesirable behaviour exhibited by marginal youth directly to their social location.

Returning to a previous point, Giroux suggests that while the codifications of market discourse privilege the already privileged white, middle-class mainstream, those seemingly advantaged by the discourse and who are therefore not blamed for any lack of character eventually suffer the same consequences as non-mainstream youth. This occurs when a presumption of innocence is framed by corporate culture, the effect of which is that the sympathetic responses afforded to white youth turn into a general fear and disdain for *all* young people. Giroux critiques a notion of innocence of the kind produced by the developmental paradigm; a notion of innocence that is taken to reflect 'aspects of a natural state, one that is beyond the dictates of history, society and politics' (2000, p. 2). To treat youth as naturally innocent denies the cultural codes that structure such a notion, and when those codes are that of the market, Giroux argues, 'children are ascribed the right of protection but are, at the same time, denied a sense of agency and autonomy' because they are not taken to belong to society (2000, p. 2). Positioning children as existing outside of politics and society and shrouding them in innocence does not therefore lead to concrete actions to protect them, but abandons them to the dictates of the market. These mentalities, according to Giroux, 'remove the supportive and nurturing networks that provide young people with adequate healthcare, food, housing, and educational opportunities' (2000, p. 2). When market-defined notions of adult responsibility and protection are dominant, the effect is to reduce innocence 'to an aesthetic or a psychological trope that prompts adults to find their "inner child," adopt teen fashions, and buy a range of services designed to make them look younger' (Giroux, 2000, p. 18).

This is not the kind of concern for young people (both mainstream and marginalised) that is attentive to the situated contexts in which youth is lived. Giroux argues that within commercial discourse, the economic and structural elements of the cultural system are rarely questioned or made accountable for their role in appropriating dominant definitions of youth and turning them from 'a historical and social category' into 'a market strategy and a fashion aesthetic' for adult commercial gain (2000, pp. 18–19). Giroux suggests that without any conceptual distance between commercial and public space, adult society offers consumerism as the only available type of citizenship for children (2000, p. 19). For example, education is now defined according to the language of the corporation which speaks in terms of privatisation and standardisation and of private enterprise over public good. This is seen in public schools that lease out space in hallways and cafeterias for business and product advertising, which, Giroux contends, sends 'the not-so-subtle message to students that everything is for sale – including ... identities, desires, and values' (2002, p. 38). Structuring education according to corporate discourses of individual freedom and consumption fails to acknowledge that freedom or an ability to choose is unequally distributed among socio-economic groups. The discourse does not account for the historic and socio-political contexts of student lives. Students are therefore trained to participate in society as individual consumers and without the benefit of social services designed to help them meet basic needs (Giroux, 2000, p. 6; 2002, p. 39). As a result, Giroux argues, 'responses to youth that were unthinkable 20 years ago' are now justified, 'including criminalisation and imprisonment, the prescription of psychotropic drugs, psychiatric confinement, and zero tolerance policies' (2009, p. 19). So when faced with issues of teenage violence or drug use, the predominant response is to stiffen jail sentences and try young people as adults rather than recognise the conditions that facilitated such behaviour in the first place (Giroux,

2000, p. 6). Market principles make it easier individualise social problems, making them a private concern or responsibility, removed from the public agenda, and youth are blamed for their actions as seemingly equal and autonomous participants within a neoliberal system of social relations (Giroux, 2000, p. 6; 2009, p. 2).

Giroux argues that corporate models of culture therefore deny *all* young people the ability to actively construct their own identity positions from their situated social contexts, confusing democratic ideals of freedom and public citizenship with the freedom to consume and notions of individual responsibility. When behaviour is deemed a personal choice and an individual responsibility, differentiations of race, class and gender carry symbolic value and meaning as consumer categories, but the lived-in effects or influences of these elements on behaviour are covered over or ignored. Giroux argues that the effect of this is that public perceptions of young people have altered from their 'being *at risk* in a society marked by deep economic and social inequalities' to being *'the risk'* (2002, p. 35). Young people 'have come to be seen as a source of trouble rather than as a resource for the future' (Giroux, 2009, p. 18). Out of a situation of growing commercialisation of schooling and public space, and a lack of adult investment in their well-being as public citizens, the possibilities for youth enabled by commercial discourse lead to descriptions of 'ultraviolent, predatory, and morally depraved' teens who are the cause, not the symptom, of social unrest (Giroux, 2002, p. 36). Even 'white suburban kids' like the Columbine gunmen (and the Werribee Kings and Gobs 2012 schoolgirls), who are often 'protected by the myth of innocence' and are not considered capable of exhibiting deviant behaviour, are increasingly experiencing the 'wrath of adult authorities, the media, and the state' (Giroux, 2000, pp. 8–9) as a result of adult disinvestment in the conditions of race, gender and class that shape youth reality at a most basic and fundamental level.

Giroux proposes a particular way to address the inequalities and disadvantages corporate discourse produces for all young people. Within a political economy perspective, emphasis is placed on the importance of having an alternative space outside the operations of the market, a 'cultural space that is open, diverse, and accessible' and in which 'all groups in society can recognise themselves and their aspirations as being fairly represented' (Golding and Murdock, 1991, p. 22). Giroux wishes to reinstate a public sphere that is attentive to the problems for youth created by corporate culture by developing a 'radical pedagogy' that would educate young people to be critical readers and participants in culture. It would offer all young people a context for understanding that citizenship is more than a private affair and that capitalism and democracy are two different things, as well as providing the practical tools for maintaining the difference (Giroux, 2002, p. 42). He also advocates for young people to utilise their own social circumstances and produce space for expressing forms of knowledge that fall outside of mainstream curricula or are not considered worthy of serious attention (1996, pp. 19–20). Young people's use of cultural texts is, for Giroux, a key way for them to produce and circulate their own meanings and relationship to the world – which might involve challenging the disadvantages of their lived-in social conditions – as distinct from the identity formations determined by discourses that position them as a threat to adult culture.

Giroux's work thus contributes to youth discourse by providing a critical and interrogative vocabulary when it comes to discussing things that impact on the experience of youth, which in turn signals the assumptions that Giroux makes about youth. Giroux assumes that a robust public sphere can escape the determinations of market discourse. It is a space from which to offer the 'critical attention [that] must be paid to the historical, social and institutional conditions that produce those structures of power and ideology that bear down on youth in their everyday lives' (Giroux, 2000, p. 35). There is an assumption in Giroux's work that when there are certain social and cultural spaces devoted to the development and open representation of ideas, it is possible to freely express oneself, and also to act with an awareness of how such expression is framed according to one's fundamental positioning in culture and society. But would it be possible to exist outside the forces which frame one's positioning in society without being implicitly connected to them? How would it be possible to think outside the determinations of corporate discourse without also calling on the discourse in order to define an 'outside' or alternative sphere to it? While it is possible to conceptualise and operate within a space that is set against the operations of commercial culture, to seek to establish and maintain it as a separate sphere would be to ignore its fundamental reliance on commercial culture for its meaning, purpose and intelligibility. Such dependence would prevent any total or final determination of an ideal or authentic form of youth identity from being made for its very definition would be dependent on that which is deemed inauthentic.

However, Giroux assumes that an 'authentic' youth is that which is experienced outside the mediations of corporate culture. While Giroux does not accept the non-commodified distinctions of race, class and gender as naturally meaningful, he does treat them as constructs that determine one's primary positioning in, and experience of, culture and society in a manner that is consistent with Marxist theory. But again, the experience of such an authentic self must implicitly rely on that which is marked as inauthentic. Thus, to conceive of identity as having an ideal form with certain foundational qualities or aspects requires covering over a fundamental implication with the identity formations offered by commercial culture.

In contrast, Buckingham presents a non-oppositional approach to the relationship between culture and consumerism in conceptualising youth. In the area of cultural studies (which the next section will focus on), there has been a move away from 'judgemental critiques of "consumerism" ' towards 'a more anthropological analysis of what is now termed "material culture" ' (Buckingham, 2000, p. 164). This approach suggests that 'the social and cultural needs that are manifested in our uses of material objects do not exist in some supposedly pure, non-commercial sphere' (Buckingham, 2000, p. 165). Contrary to Giroux's position, such needs are actually articulated and experienced within the context of consumer culture (Buckingham, 2000, p. 165). Instead of assuming an essential human need which either finds itself corrupted or expressed through commodity consumption, focusing on how material goods are used and acquired becomes a way for people to define themselves and their relationships, and so allows for a different construction of identity. With regard to 'youth' it is possible to argue that no inherent or essential identity exists prior to consumption, especially considering the emergence of youth as a market category in the post-war period. When viewed from this perspective, young people are not 'merely victims of a process that lies outside their control or that inevitably works against their authentic interests', but neither is consumer culture a means through which young people's authentic needs 'are unproblematically expressed' (Buckingham, 2000, p. 165). By not assuming the existence of an authentic youth identity that pre-exists consumption, Buckingham acknowledges that mainstream culture does more than simply reproduce a dominant ideology; it is a site that allows for an experience of freedom and autonomy (2000, p. 164). Where Giroux seeks to find ways for youth to appropriate cultural spaces and create texts outside the market sphere, Buckingham points to the possibility of seeing the market as not simply working to impose 'false needs and values', but 'as an infinitely flexible terrain, on which consumers create their own identities, often in diverse and innovative ways' (2000, p. 164).

Giroux's approach, however, posits a view of youth as having a particular grounding or basis that is separate from an adult culture. In this case, adult culture is that of the free-market economy which does not understand actual children and their experiences (Giroux, 2000, p. 6). Critical political economy is a perspective concerned with examining the impact of the economic determinations of society on people's access to symbolic resources and the consequent ordering of power relations in society. While this perspective, in contrast to a developmental paradigm, provides theorists like Giroux with a means of critically analysing the underlying assumptions of certain constructions of youth, it works from its own assumptions regarding what constitutes public good and authentic existence that are not subject to critique. In this way, a critical political economy perspective is similar to the developmental paradigm in that it does not account for the socially determined meaning of its own founding assumptions about youth. Giroux thus posits a notion of youth (all youth) as having a range of authentic formations that are able to be acknowledged when framed within the discourses that shape a public sphere and are set against those formations enabled by market discourse. Giroux's position, in contrast with the perspective on youth described by Buckingham, is constructed in opposition to commercial discourses, and this position is treated by Giroux as the basis of and for youth identity. The effect of this is to presume or 'fix' a certain conceptualisation of youth as ideal, authentic or genuine in a similar way to the developmental perspective's presumption of a natural state of youth tied to physiological development. This constrains other constitutive possibilities for youth by naturalising a particular framework for distinguishing what counts as an essential and authentic youth identity or state of being and what is inessential and inauthentic.

Significantly, however, this means that Giroux's position on youth does not result in escaping or getting outside of the negative influences of corporate culture, but has the effect of keeping them in place. Buckingham shows that a focus on the possibilities for self-definition offered by consumer culture challenges the puritanism of more traditional analyses, however this approach also tends to neglect 'material and institutional constraints on consumption' (2000, p. 164). While Giroux does not neglect such constraints in his work, his ideal notion of youth actually *requires* the continued functioning of market definitions of youth which he sees as disempowering and disadvantaging young people. Alternatively, an analysis of youth identity that is not grounded in any notion of authentic being requires taking into account the processes involved in identity construction. Part of the work of making sense of youth thus involves investigating the manner of operation of the very concepts that are in use – their uses and limits, what they enable and constrain. This allows for a greater reflexivity in thinking about and taking action regarding youth, rather than relying on assumptions that serve to perpetuate the problematic issues that theorists like Giroux are attempting to solve. Indeed, despite the deeply felt concern for young people Giroux shows in his critique, or the urgency of his pursuit to improve their lives, he implicitly relies on the very constructs he seeks to dismantle. I will consider the implications of this problem in the next chapter.

The (sub)cultural paradigm

A conceptual paradigm that demonstrates a greater awareness of how its own conceptual processes contribute to the notion of youth it generates is that of youth (sub)cultures. This paradigm encompasses traditional (and classic) studies of 'spectacular youth subcultures of the post-war era such as skinheads, punks, mods and rockers' as well as more recent 'post-subculture' scholarship (Nayak and Kehily, 2008, p. 12). Early studies of subcultures which came out of Birmingham University's Centre for Contemporary Cultural Studies (CCCS) presented subcultural groups as 'pockets of working-class resistance to the dominant hegemonic institutions of British society' (Bennett and Kahn-Harris, 2004, p. 1). Post-subculture research, however, has strongly critiqued the Birmingham approach, documenting instead the rise of globalised media cultures and consumption patterns that have produced 'fragmented and ephemeral youth groupings rather than full-blown subcultures' (Nayak and Kehily, 2008, pp. 12–13). But this work continues an interest in articulating youth cultural practices and forms of expression whether in material or virtual contexts. I consider both traditional and more recent approaches to youth culture here within a single paradigm because, despite their theoretical differences, both attempt to articulate the meaning of youth culture, identity, experience and forms of expression, whether that occurs within a framework that focuses on class and resistance or according to accounts of the fluid and sometimes fleeting associations facilitated, for example, by new media. Furthermore, despite changes in theory over time, a (sub)cultural paradigm still contributes to a commonsense idea about youth as distinct from other identity categories, as the previous two conceptual paradigms have done.

Introducing the study of youth subculture, John Clarke, Stuart Hall, Tony Jefferson and Brian Roberts write that the term 'culture' means the 'level at which social groups develop distinct patterns of life, and give *expressive form* to their social and material life-experience' (1976, p. 10). They describe the culture of a particular group as a 'way of life', with its values, customs and ideas 'embodied in institutions, in social relations, in systems of belief' (1976, p. 10). The term is also used to describe the 'maps of meaning' which make the social and relational patterns of the group intelligible to its members, and 'through which the individual becomes a "social individual" ' (Clarke et al., 1976, pp. 10–11). Youth culture, Clarke et al. contend, is the outcome of specific social changes in the post-war period that were 'radically and qualitatively different from anything that had happened before' (1976, p. 15). They describe the particular cultural pursuits of young people during the post-war period as 'closely linked with the expansion of the leisure and fashion industries' which became known as the 'teenage market' (1976, p. 15). As such, the term 'youth culture' identifies its members according to 'its most phenomenal aspect – its music, styles, leisure consumption' (Clarke et al., 1976, p. 15). This concept of youth thus finds meaning within commercial discourses that set up a relationship in which youth groups appropriate and reproduce things from the market which are then taken and re-incorporated back into the market (Clarke et al., 1976, p. 16). This differs significantly from Giroux's conception of the relation between youth and the market.

However, these descriptive conditions of youth culture disguise important differences and distinctions like class and the variety of ways young people can be seen to relate to the dominant culture (Clarke et al., 1976, p. 16), which is the basis of Giroux's objection to commercial constructions of youth. Clarke et al. assert that more than one cultural form exists within a society and its dominant ideas, and there are ways for less powerful groups to express themselves from a position subordinate to those dominant ideas. It is the social structures and cultural meanings of the most powerful class, however, that constitutes the dominant order, and other groups ultimately exist in relation to this. In this way, the dominant culture is able to represent itself as '*the* culture' and to be in a position to 'contain all other cultures within its inclusive range' (Clarke et al., 1976, p. 12).

For example, Dick Hebdige's work on the punk subculture in Britain during the 1970s shows how punks 'displayed' their objection to the dominant order 'at the profoundly superficial level of appearances: that is, at the level of signs' (1979, p. 17). Members of the group sought to gain possession of signs and, through them, the meanings they generated within ideology that extended all the way into the most mundane areas of life (Hebdige, 1979, p. 17). So-called humble objects, like the safety pin, for example, were appropriated by punk groups and given 'secret' meanings which were expressed in their 'illegitimate' use on the body (for example, as a piercing), thus establishing 'a form of resistance to the order which guarantee[d] their continued subordination' (Hebdige, 1979, p. 18). By using commodities already available, punks responded to their social conditions at the time – such as growing joblessness, poverty and shifting moral standards – by dramatising them. Using 'stylistic ensembles' including ripped t-shirts, spiked hairstyles, chains and so on to express their genuine anger and frustration, punks represented their opposition in a language that was current and commonly available, yet they remained in a subordinate position. However, by making a spectacle of themselves, punks were able to 'symptomatize a whole cluster of contemporary problems' (Hebdige, 1979, pp. 86–7). What Hebdige calls the 'structured improvisations' of punk culture (1979, p. 104) carried an active and constructive potential within dominant codes, indicating an ability of punks to negotiate their place in the larger social order.

Subculture theorists like Hebdige make use of the 'linguistic turn' in cultural studies to articulate this kind of critical response to the dominant social order. In his introduction to British cultural studies, Graeme Turner explains that language is a basic and foundational concept as it both constitutes and gives meaning to 'a system of relationships; it establishes categories and makes distinctions through networks of difference and similarity' (2003, p. 11). Following Saussure, Turner notes that 'the connection between a word and its meaning is not inherent, or natural, but, in most instances, quite arbitrary' (2003, p. 11). Language does not, therefore, 'fix intrinsic meanings' to a pre-existing reality; rather, 'specific social relations are defined through the place language allocates them within its system of relations' (Turner, 2003, pp. 11–12). This semiotic approach takes account of the arbitrary nature of social and cultural constructs and of the value systems that underlie them as it works to understand the effects these systems produce. Giroux, however, takes a certain social order as a given from which to articulate his notion of youth.

The cultural sphere in a cultural studies perspective thus becomes the site where the meaning of terms such as 'youth' is negotiated and where its lived effects are determined. Turner points out that because different cultures use different language systems, they can in effect inhabit different worlds (2003, p. 12). On this basis, there is significant capacity for movement and change as there is no one 'correct' or underlying way of understanding the meaning of culture and its function. A cultural studies perspective is interested in investigating how individuals and groups, such as young people, as both producers and consumers of culture, are constructed by, and in some instances contest, the repertoire of social contexts and meanings made available to them through dominant systems of signification and ideological codes. In this way, and in contrast to Giroux's position on the limited representative possibilities of commercial culture, the study of youth subculture offers a way of seeing youth as a category with productive potential, and Hebdige's study is one example of this.

However, Hebdige's work also explains how instances of resistance to dominant signs are re-incorporated into the mainstream order and transgression is returned to normality. As the punk subculture's visual and verbal vocabulary became ever more familiar, Hebdige argues, it was increasingly easy to assign it a place within an existing referential context (1979, pp. 93–4). The response of mainstream television or the press, for example, was to take what was striking and different about punk style and place it within an 'acceptable' ideological framework such that 'boys in lipstick are "just kids dressing up" ' and 'girls in rubber dresses are "daughters just like yours" ' (Hebdige, 1979, p. 94). What was a resistive spectacle against a normative order was thus recuperated to become instead 'a diverting spectacle within the dominant mythology from which it in part emanate[d]', and so the 'fractured order [was] repaired' (Hebdige, 1979, p. 94). From a youth subculture perspective, whether via processes of naturalisation and diffusion, or by being positioned as a spectacle, outside of normality altogether, the meaning and significance of disturbing and confronting youth behaviour is determined by the dominant culture. A process of social reparation comes via dominant definitions of difference and cultural distinction.

Despite this, Hebdige still argues for a way of reading youth subculture as having subversive potential. Hebdige writes that punk culture 'stands apart' from everyday cultural consumption as a 'visible construction, a loaded choice' (1979, p. 101). It is a deliberate attempt by the subculture to direct 'attention to itself' and give 'itself to be read' (1979, p. 101). Thus, while punk style represents a culture of consumption, it is 'conspicuous' in that its stylistic choices purposefully reveal its 'identity and communicate ... its forbidden meanings' (Hebdige, 1979, p. 103). By being so 'obviously fabricated' in displaying its own codes, Hebdige suggests that punk style distinguishes itself from the orthodox culture by making specific *use* of commodities (1979, pp. 101–103). Here, the category of youth is marked as distinct via the practices of youth subculture members, rather than through any final meanings that are attached to those practices. Both Hebdige and Giroux share an interest in how young people can find ways to articulate their own experience and identity, but their solutions express a different conceptualisation of youth. For Hebdige, the re-shaping of forms of commodity culture to express a 'valid' or 'authentic' youth identity is possible, while Giroux rejects all market-based forms of culture as oppressive and alien to an 'authentic' youth identity.

However, traditional subculture study, like critical political economy, is underpinned by neo-Marxist concerns, and both seek ways to articulate forms of youth identity against the formations offered by an oppressive adult culture. But unlike Giroux's reading, the youth subculture tradition focuses on the possibilities for resistance to a dominant culture that are provided *by* that dominant culture, rather than by some alternative sphere. And where developmental psychology presumes adulthood to be a natural (not a cultural) state that youth (naturally) desire to enter into, a youth subculture perspective focuses on youth as a cultural category, on politics and power relations, and on the possibility of the subversion of a dominant (adult) culture. This approach, more so than Giroux's critical political economy perspective, takes account of the conceptual moves that provide the grounding for different identity positions, an effect of which is to understand culture (and thus youth) as open to multiple and alternative constructions.

This understanding of culture is carried through but developed differently in post-subculture studies. Post-subcultural theory, as developed in the work of David Muggleton (1998, 2000) and Steve Redhead (1997), as well as, amongst others, Andy Bennett (1999), Sarah Thornton (1996) and Michel Maffesoli (1996), marks a shift away from semiotic and structural analyses of youth culture towards 'sociological research approaches informed by ethnographic and qualitative methodologies' (Weinzierl and Muggleton, 2003, p. 9). Research work is concerned with what individuals 'do' in situated contexts and with how they use texts and cultural objects (Martin, 2004, p. 33). This is not unlike Hebdige's work described above, but this approach focuses less on symbolic systems and more on observing the situated, real-time social interactions of real people (Martin, 2004, pp. 30–35). Similarly, post-subculture theory is critical of the concept of 'subculture', particularly its connotations of 'homogenous groups with clearly bounded memberships' (Martin, 2004, p. 23)[5]. In response, it engages a conceptual vocabulary that emphasises the fragmented, globalised, mobile and diffuse nature of culture and of youth cultural experience and expression. A post-subcultural discourse thus offers a way of understanding youth that is not necessarily defined by place or class or by any claimed opposition or resistance to a parent culture, as was characteristic of the 'Gramscian-semiotic approach' adopted by the Centre for Contemporary Cultural Studies (Weinzierl and Muggleton, 2003, p. 5).

For example, Andy Bennett and Keith Kahn-Harris write that the term 'tribe' is used to illustrate 'the increasingly fluid and unstable nature of social relations in contemporary society' (2004, p. 12). Tribal associations, such as those found in dance-club settings, enable 'expressions of "togetherness" based on articulations of fun, relaxation and pleasure' (2004, p. 12). Another favoured term is 'lifestyle'. This term relates to an individual's desire to actively make and remake their identity and, more so than the term 'subculture', it allows for the interpretation of 'shifting identity politics and stylistic associations of contemporary youth' (Bennett and Kahn-Harris, 2004, p. 13). A further term used in post-subculture analyses of youth, particularly with regard to music, is 'scene.' The term is used to describe more organised spaces or sites for the production and consumption of music (Bennett and Kahn-Harris, 2004, pp. 13–14).

Furthermore, David Chaney highlights the fact that contemporary culture has fragmented and is now constituted by a plurality of lifestyle choices and preferences, which applies to people generally, not just the young. As such, an assumed distinction between a 'sub' and 'dominant' culture no longer holds true (Chaney, 2004, p. 47). When public culture is seen as fragmented and diverse, it is more difficult (and not entirely necessary) to identify cultural practices as belonging to any particular dominant or marginal group.   Instead, it makes sense to appreciate that identities and cultural groupings are reflexively constructed and enacted in multiple ways (see, for example, Bennett and Hodkinson, 2012). In this way, post-subculture theory offers a vocabulary for describing youth that does not reduce it to an expression of class location or oppositional ideology. Identities are negotiated, and culture acts as a resource for everyone in this process rather than an 'inheritance' (Chaney, 2004, p. 42).

However, activity in this area of youth studies does not deny the ongoing influence of macro social structures on forms of identity. Peter Martin argues that a sociological focus on the ways in which cultural objects are used in real situations by real people does not mean neglecting the social structure and its patterns of power and inequality

(2004, pp. 23 & 33). But this approach is wary of the tendency of structuralist interpretations of such conditions, be they semiotic or Marxist, to over-determine meaning (Carrington and Wilson, 2004, p. 77). Martin writes that conditions of power or social structure 'must be understood as the *outcomes* of the activities of real people in real situations, *and the ways in which these are represented*' (2004, p. 23). It is important, then, according to Martin, to emphasise that 'while individuals may thus be seen to "make" their identities, and their "worlds," this does not mean that they have the ability to define meanings or construct themselves just as they please' (2004, p. 35). Rather, self-formation occurs in relationship between the individual subject and macro social structures (Martin, 2004, p. 35).

Taking these two phases in the theorisation of youth culture together, the influence of a (sub)cultural paradigm is evident with regard to popular discourses about youth when attempts are made to understand and explain youth behaviour, cultural expression and resistance, and, in some instances, to bring these to order. For example, the Werribee Kings and Gobs 2012 cases demonstrate youth resistance to and subversion of dominant values and expectations, and, recalling Hebdige's remarks about how punk style was able to be incorporated back into the mainstream or placed outside normality entirely, responses to these events have tried to both normalise and demonise the conduct of the participants as a means of reasserting a dominant social order.

For instance, in terms of normalisation, the behaviour of the Werribee Kings boys was variously attributed to systemic social disadvantage and to familiar circumstances of youth like peer pressure and parental authority. It was also reported that some of the parents of the boys had described their behaviour as 'just a bit of fun' ('Father's plea', 2006, np). Similarly, after the Gobs 2012 incident, social commentator Duncan Fine suggested that, far from being a new phenomenon, 'this problematic area of children and sex has been around forever' (cited in 'Teens think sexting is normal', 2012, np). The main difference between now and earlier periods, he believes, is that young people's sexualised behaviour is more visible thanks to the prevalence of mobile phones and social media. Other responses highlight the abnormality of the teens' conduct. One article on the Werribee Kings case quoted a child psychologist likening the behaviour of the 'mob' to Nazi prison camp guards because 'somewhere along the line they have not learned to have a social conscience and to respect the dignity of human beings' (Cheetham cited in 'DVD mob "like Nazi camp guards"', 2006, np). Cyber-safety expert Susan McLean disputes Fine's view on youth and sex arguing instead that kids are becoming more sexualised and that the kinds of things young people are doing and experimenting with is very different from 50 years ago. McLean reports that GPs are seeing girls with 'injuries sustained as a result of trying to emulate [sex acts that] they've seen online and what their boyfriends have seen online and asked them to do', which is something not seen in the past (cited in 'Teens think sexting is normal', 2012, np).

Alternatively, a (sub)culture discourse may be employed to make sense of how young people use and engage with cultural texts and objects. The textual tradition, characteristic of subculture scholarship, as well as the post-subcultural concern with understanding what people do in situated contexts, allows for consideration of how young people make use of cultural conventions, symbolic material and media discourses to represent themselves. In both cases discussed above, and at the beginning of the chapter, the teens demonstrate some level of conscious and reflexive play with a range of conventions and discourses. Their intent may be to rebel, antagonise, parody or to simply have fun, and, whether through a notion of self-conscious display or through ideas of 'tribe' or 'lifestyle' which emphasise active image construction that is fluid rather than fixed, youth have the opportunity to offer their own accounts of themselves within this paradigm.

However, this potential can also be limited by the very structures that facilitate it. A (sub)cultural approach, in both its stages considered here, is not premised on the notion that there is a true nature or meaning of youth, instead appreciating that 'youth' is 'made'. 'Youth' names a series of discourses, practices, relationships, and social and institutional places and spaces in which many youth subjectivities can speak in the social world. As such, efforts to explain youth are always socially and theoretically situated, and notions of youth are socially constructed. However, this also means that accounts of youth subcultures (or indeed youth 'scenes', 'tribes' or 'lifestyles') will not necessarily match how a particular individual or group understands its own cultural formation. If it is understood that observing youth or giving an account of their experiences is not a transparent activity, but is instead mediated by discourse and circumscribed by the research practices employed, then a potential effect of this approach to youth is to situate youth realities as independent of attempts to articulate them.

This is partly due to the relationship between subject and researcher. According to Simon Frith, early subculture theorists were clearly different from their subjects, but at the same time an ambiguity existed between them and their subjects – were 'youth subcultures being explained from the inside out, or anatomised from the outside in?' (2004, p. 175). Frith suggests that these scholars were certainly 'outside the spectacular subcultures that interested them' but that 'they did not draw on any sense of cultural superiority' (2004, pp. 175–6). Rather, subcultural phenomena were distanced from researchers because the discursive approach taken served to abstract youth from its everyday social construction and practice (Frith, 2004, p. 176). For scholars employing ethnographic techniques instead, working from the 'inside out' seems possible, but even here Frith sees a tendency in post-subcultural scholarship to still 'make youth somehow *different*' by looking for 'evidence of resistance and transgression' even when researchers themselves were once *of* the cultures they now mark as different (2004, p. 176). According to Frith, scholars seeking to access youth culture (whether via semiotic or ethnographic means) 'seem to freeze youth into a particular moment of consumption and display' when at the same time youth as a social category is understood to represent a transitional phase rather than a stable social role (2004, p. 177).

This paradigm demonstrates greater awareness of the effects of its conceptual processes than either developmental psychology or critical political economy, but its methods also constrain thought about youth. This approach seeks to understand young people from within their own worlds but it also needs to circumscribe the category in order to say something meaningful about them. The effect is to create a conceptual distance between actual young people and available knowledge about them. The next chapter outlines how a deconstructive reflexivity can work through such limits.

Contributions to dominant youth discourses

In summary, the three conceptual paradigms examined here offer different constructions of youth. The developmental paradigm defines youth according to physiological growth and development in relation to adult-level mental function and physical state. The critical political economy paradigm defines youth as a state of being or lived experience that is marked according to the distinctions of race, gender and class under capitalism. The (sub)cultural paradigm defines youth as a cultural category according to relations of class, style and consumption (traditional subculture scholarship), and in terms of diverse constructions of taste and lifestyle preferences (post-subculture theory).

Developmental theory is concerned to define standards of appropriate development to ensure the achievement of a coherent identity. This theory assumes youth behaviour and activity to be a natural expression of their developmental stage and presumes a direct correlation between youth identity and physiology. This relationship is used to determine the features, function and characteristics of youth. However, this approach is not open to acknowledging the culturally defined meanings of such features, functions and characteristics. Instead, it takes them to be inherent and naturally apparent or self-evident.

In contrast, Giroux, informed by critical political economy, posits an ideal youth that he sees as being corrupted by the commodification of culture and education. Giroux argues for ways to allow young people to express themselves free from the impediments and perceived injustices of corporate culture. But Giroux limits the possibilities of youth by presuming an ideal form of being-youth and a range of identity markers that are moralistically set against forms of youth identity enabled (or constrained) by market discourse.

Where developmental theory and critical political economy posit an ideal youth, (sub)culture theory does not work from such a definite grounding, appreciating instead the process of reality construction as an effect of everyday conduct, language practices, ideological codes and structural determinants. This perspective allows for questions of youth agency, and for youth to speak for themselves, even if this voice is circumscribed by larger and more powerful ideological forces. A focus on youth agency also risks locating the expressive practices of youth cultures outside the positioning made available to them by others. The effect of this is to affirm a youth reality that remains inaccessible to attempts to articulate it, and also perhaps to over-emphasise the agency of youth.

Each perspective also makes a distinct contribution to youth discourses, manifesting in contemporary events in a number of ways. The influence of a developmental psychology perspective is perhaps the most dominant in public and media discourse on youth. It is evident in the Werribee Kings and Gobs 2012 cases in comments that relate to how young people are adversely influenced by violent and sexualised media due to a lack of self-awareness and ability to understand the implications of their behaviour. It is also evident in the Bill Henson case regarding the issues of youth sexualisation, exploitation and consent. Comments that relate to the role of media in the premature ending of innocence and the need to protect vulnerable youth from exploitation are also informed by a developmental perspective. Similarly, the interrogative approach to youth developed by Giroux, which assumes an authentic form of being-youth, is evident in discussion on how young boys are being corrupted by violent media and young girls exploited by a hyper-sexualised commercial and consumer-driven culture. The media is taken as a corrupting influence on the 'proper' childhood or adolescence that exists outside the media sphere. It is seen as taking young people away from real life, and this position assumes a need to return to a 'natural' order which feeds back into, and relies on, a developmental framework. But Giroux's approach connects with discussion about the promise of media use as a means of self-expression outside privatised and corporatised cultural environments. (Buckingham also argues this potential, but not in opposition to commercial culture.) Youth (sub)culture theory may be called on when considering the behaviour of the boys in the Werribee Kings gang as an effect of their social location, as an act of resistance and subversion, and also in terms of their perceived level of self-consciousness about their behaviour, as seen in the way they rejected explanations for their actions. This is also evident in the Gobs 2012 case where the girls attempt to subvert a social action discourse. (Sub)culture theory informs discussion of youth choices and accounts of youth agency and conscious intention that offend against social norms and expectations, such as when one of the Werribee Kings refused to be remorseful for his actions or how the Gobs 2012 girls used the premise of offering oral sex to parody the Kony 2012 campaign.

Approaching youth identity

Although these approaches to youth specify youth differently and thus contribute differently to discourses on youth, there is, however, a point of commonality among them. All these approaches work to articulate the identity of youth. For developmental psychology, youth identity is inherent in their physiology and the meaning that is attached to youth physiology is determined by the ideal state of development that adults have attained. For Giroux, youth identity is defined according the foundational elements of race, gender and class that offer different identity positions to young people according to the ideological formation of the adult culture. For (sub)culture theory, youth identity is a product of cultural interactions and is expressed in style, language, practices of consumption and in everyday activities. Whether grounded in biology or culture, and whether seen as essential or contingent, what is common to all three approaches is that they are all concerned with the articulation of youth identity, and this is done by differentiating youth in culture and in its relation to and difference from what is 'adult'.

What does it mean, then, to discuss youth identity 'directly' or as a distinct category? As far as being able to study youth and take concrete action in response to 'real world' issues and events concerning young people, such a move would seem necessary. But it also seems possible that an approach to youth that 'begins' from or relies on youth as a distinct identity or category might direct thinking in ways that reinforce seemingly fundamental distinctions which do not acknowledge the conditions that underpin and enable such a notion in the first place. I see the effect of this as allowing for an essentialism of identity to develop.

I draw this connection, and treat it as a cause for concern, because I see a similar treatment of youth identity to that identified by feminist and postcolonial theorists concerning the identities of women and racial others. These identity categories have been subject to significant challenge and review by feminist and postcolonial theorists who have made use of deconstructive theory. The concern in these areas is with the status and meaning of authentic identity and the issue of what it means to speak for oneself when one's speaking position is determined as secondary to a dominant speaking position. Similarly, the meaning of youth, while conditioned by specific modes of conceptualisation (as natural or as constructed), and by various limitations, comes from a primary relationship of difference from something else (adult, dominant culture). I turn in the next chapter to consider some of the analytical strategies and points of argument developed by feminist and postcolonial theorists that challenge this key intellectual framework on the notion of identity. I look at where dominant frameworks come up against their own limits and thus cannot adequately address the speaking position of 'secondary' subjects even though they claim to. This raises a question regarding the reflexivity of dominant identity frameworks, and also, therefore, a question of their ability to account for the effects that they produce. I look at what an approach similar to that provided by postcolonial and feminist theorists might offer a discussion of the meaning of youth identity, and how this might enable a more reflexive approach to constructions of youth and responses to youth behaviour.

3
Deconstruction and the Question of Identity

This chapter introduces deconstructive theory and asks what it means to conceptualise youth identity when it comes from and through a primary relationship with an 'adult' culture and identity. I do this by looking to postcolonial and feminist theorists who have utilised deconstructive methods in questioning this notion of identity as it operates in race and gender discourse. As a model for approaching a similar questioning of youth discourse, I examine work from Edward Said, Homi Bhabha, Judith Butler and Gayatri Spivak that addresses the identity positions of women and racial others. They focus not only on the dominant conceptual conditions through which such identity positions are produced, but also on how the voices of women and racial others are constrained and subordinated. These theorists work to displace the grounding assumptions of identity as distinct and directly accessible to oneself and offer a means of thinking beyond frameworks that posit dominant and marginal identities as natural and inevitable. Bhabha, Spivak and Butler, in particular, make use of deconstructive techniques to reveal how the dominant identity positions of men and of the West are actually dependent on a subordinated identity category. In doing so, they demonstrate why it is problematic to seek to have marginal identities 'speak' themselves from within such an order as a way to address or overcome their subaltern status.

Following an elaboration of their work, I consider how frameworks informing youth discourse involve similar issues, and turn directly to the question of what deconstruction has to offer a reading of youth. Specifically, Spivak's discussion of the subaltern subject effect and Bhabha's discussion of racial stereotypes and the notion of mimicry offer a way to understand how dominant discourses constrain the possibilities of youth. Their analyses reveal the ways in which the operations

51

of colonial discourse create unintended effects due to the misrecognition of the conceptual grounding of the discourse. This connects with my overall concern to develop ways to bring greater awareness of the effects of youth discourses to the work of making sense of youth, and this chapter establishes a theoretical basis for undertaking such work. In considering why it is important to open up to other conceptual possibilities for youth, this chapter looks beyond ways of thinking that centre on and proceed from a notion of identity as presence. The case study chapters that follow (Chapters 4, 5 and 6) then take this up in relation to a range of specific youth issues and events.

Postcolonial and feminist identities

Postcolonial theory investigates the Western imperialist tradition and its silencing of certain groups and cultures. Theorists work on displaying oppositions within this tradition and articulating critical positions against it in order to open up ways for colonised people to speak for themselves. In *Orientalism*, the text which inaugurated the field of postcolonialism, Edward Said writes that the term 'Orientalism' represents 'a Western style for dominating, restructuring, and having authority over the Orient', rather than a means for articulating the Orient, or the nations and cultures located in the East, as 'a free subject of thought or action' (1978, pp. 3&5). Said asserts that 'the Orient' is one of Europe's 'deepest and most recurring images of the Other' (1978, p. 1), as it places 'the Westerner in a whole series of possible relationships with the Orient without ever losing him the relative upper hand' (1978, p. 7). Hence, the Orient is based 'more or less exclusively upon a sovereign Western consciousness out of whose unchallenged centrality an Oriental world emerged' (Said, 1978, p. 8).

To illustrate this, Said presents two colonial figures of the early twentieth century. Arthur James Balfour, a member of the British parliament, and Lord Cromer, the representative of England in Egypt, employ metaphors of the child in articulating their privileged knowledge of 'Oriental civilisation' (1978, p. 35). 'There are Westerners, and there are Orientals', Said explains: 'the former dominate; the latter must be dominated', because for Cromer, 'subject races did not have it in them to know what was good for them' (1978, pp. 36–7). In defining the Oriental in these ways, Said writes that Balfour and Cromer used specific descriptive terms for the Oriental such as 'irrational, depraved (fallen), childlike' and 'different'. It is hardly surprising that they should thus consider the European to be 'rational, virtuous, mature' and 'normal'

(Said, 1978, p. 40). Further comparisons link the Oriental to Western society by way of their childlike identity: they are 'rarely seen or looked at', but instead are 'seen through, analysed not as citizens, or even people, but as problems to be solved or confined or...taken over' (Said, 1978, p. 207). In another instance, Said notes that against the superiority of Western scholarship and power, the Orient, like the child, or indeed, youth, is 'always in the position of both outsider and of incorporated weak partner for the West' and only able to be judged from 'the Orientalist's grander interpretive activity' (1978, p. 208). Also, owing to their inherent 'primitiveness', Orientals are not granted independence as their general ignorance of self-government means that 'they had better be kept that way for their own good' (Said, 1978, pp. 228–231). In this way, Said argues, 'being a White Man' during this time 'was a very concrete manner of being-in-the-world, a way of taking hold of reality, language, and thought' (1978, p. 227).

Such terminology resonates with many of the ways of thinking about youth raised in the previous chapter, linked perhaps most directly to the perceptions and assessments of Locke and Rousseau and those that a developmental psychology perspective offers. In developmental psychology's focus on reason as the ideal state of (adult) maturity, according to which young people and their growth is judged, such descriptive terms as noted above carry connotations of presence, completeness and wholeness for the Westerner/adult in comparison to either a lack of or at least a developing reasoning ability in the Oriental/youth. Development occurs in a linear and seemingly 'natural' order of developmental stages that are defined by certain expert observers (see Chapter 2 on Piaget and concrete/formal operations). This knowledge is consequently used to order social relations and discourses around youth as 'transitional', 'incomplete', 'in between', 'less than' or 'lacking' in their mental, social and physical capacities and therefore as being in need of protection and guidance in order to ensure that they become adults in the 'proper' way at the 'proper' time. An alternative way of seeing this, as Said does, is to recognise that such descriptions of Orientals means that they are most comprehensively *contained* by 'dominating frameworks' that depict them as objects of study, and something to be judged and disciplined (Said, 1978, p. 40), which is not to get to who or what Oriental people really 'are'.

Feminist scholarship similarly deals with the forces of exclusion (and also containment) that define the female subject. Judith Butler writes that the 'exclusionary matrix by which subjects are formed...requires the simultaneous production of a domain of abject beings...who form the constitutive outside to the domain of the subject' (1993, p. 3). It hardly needs saying that under patriarchy the female subject emerges as secondary and inferior to the male subject. Discussions about their respective characteristics reflect the values of the dominant social order: reason over emotion, mind over matter or the body, and culture over nature. The masculine is associated with the former aspect and the feminine the latter. Here, as with colonised others, women function as the 'constitutive outside' of masculine subjectivity as it is through the male subject's consciousness that the category of woman finds meaning.

The question of what it means to know the identities of those who are articulated via a dominant subject (Westerner/man) can be extended to a discussion of youth. The most fundamental distinction and basic definition of youth is that it is not adult. That the description is not the other way around (adult as 'not youth') is not simply a matter of word choice. It reflects a very particular power structure and conceptual history as seen in the previous chapter in the work of Rousseau and his stages of development towards rational adulthood, and through to contemporary views and theoretical debates about youth as a symbol and signal of the future health (or otherwise) of society. This manner of definition also reflects the idea that adulthood can be reflected upon, whereas youth remains something of a mystery because young people lack the ability to be self-reflective. The fundamental distinction of youth as not adult therefore orders youth according to a series of binary oppositions which are already familiar from the preceding discussion: culture/nature, knowledge/innocence, reason/unreason, all of which stem from the key binary: presence/absence. It is at this point that the terms of deconstruction can be introduced as a means of intervening in this conceptual order.

Deconstruction and presence

For Jacques Derrida, the term 'metaphysics' refers to a history of thought in which the notion of a centre or fundamental governing principle is understood to designate an 'invariable presence' (1978, p. 279). Concepts such as essence, truth, identity and consciousness function as a grounding force (Culler, 2007, p. 93). The metaphysical tradition thus designates presence as a 'first or original instance' (Lucy, 2004, p. 102) that is 'normal, pure, standard, self-identical' (Derrida, 1988, p. 93) from which it is then possible to think a secondary and subordinate order of concepts that are derivative, impure, determined on the basis of their perceived lack, deficiency or defects (Wortham, 2010, p. 104). This tradition produces hierarchies such as masculine/feminine, nature/culture, speech/writing, which are based on an opposition of presence to absence. The first (and superior) term in the each pair is characterised in terms of its 'purity, plenitude, originality or self-sufficiency', in other words, 'its presence' (Wortham, 2010, p. 104). This 'metaphysical gesture', according to Derrida, 'has been the most constant, most profound and most potent' in terms of both enabling and inscribing the limits of intelligible reality (1988, p. 93). Here, then, the meaning of adult, male and colonial identities lies in their presence or self-presence defined by virtue of qualities that are thought to inhere within them. The thought of youth, women and racial others therefore depends on the prior thought of adult, male and coloniser and they are thus defined as non-self-present. It follows, then, that youth, women and racial others are seen as fundamentally lacking or incomplete. So what is it to discuss or know the identity of someone directly or in positive terms when a notion of their selfhood is conditioned by and dependent on the prior conceptualisation of a dominant Self which positions them as Other?

Gayatri Chakravorty Spivak takes up this question in her key postcolonial text, 'Can the Subaltern Speak?' She asks after 'the consciousness of the subaltern woman' but does not try to 'find' it as such; rather, in looking for ways 'to keep the ethnocentric Subject from establishing itself by selectively defining an Other', Spivak studies the conceptual barriers preventing satisfactory definition of subaltern identities (1988a, p. 292). Her work thus focuses on 'the benevolent *Western* intellectual' who claims to be able to hold a position of ideological transparency in reading non-Western identities, and to thereby be in a position to 'disclose and know the discourse of society's Other' (1988a, p. 272). Spivak suggests that in the intellectual's desire to 'intervene in the struggle of the subaltern for greater recognition and rights', he or she instead comes to speak *for* the subaltern (Moore-Gilbert et al., 1997, p. 29). This is because, according to Spivak, the intellectual's claim of being in a transparent position means systematically ignoring 'their own implication in intellectual and economic history' (1988a, p. 272). They are in fact unable 'to escape the determinations of the general system of exploitation of the Third World – in which Western modes and institutions of knowledge ... are deeply implicated' (Moore-Gilbert et al., 1997, p. 29). Western scholars therefore operate within an ethnocentrism hidden behind claims of impartiality.

This is something to be noted with regard to research into youth experience and self-knowledge. Via ethnographic study, for example, or following Henry Giroux's belief in an authentic youth reality and thus the need for non-commodified social space to express it, capturing youth voices means accessing central indicators of 'true' youth experience and reality and 'presence'. The issue raised by Spivak, and here explained by youth, gender and cultural studies scholar Angela McRobbie, is that such an approach treats

> the voices of young people ... as transparently meaningful and as evidence in themselves, rather than as complex social constructs which are the products of pre-given discourses, in effect 'written' in advance as scripts made available by dominant culture for their teenage speakers.
>
> (1994, p. 180)

It is only through such constructs that the very notion of youth becomes knowable, from which it is possible to imagine what 'true' youth identity or consciousness or presence 'looks like' and thus attempt to get to it outside the conditions which are thought to prevent its true expression, true being. But what is being suggested here is that to speak oneself as youth is to reflect how one has been spoken to, spoken about or spoken for. While the aim is to give priority to youth voices and cultures and experiences – which may be situated against a dominant social order, or, for Giroux, a corrupting commercial sphere – actual youth voices are still framed by how youth are first spoken about. How they speak themselves, therefore, is not free from these constraints, these limits. Even the most sympathetic readings or emancipatory gestures, such as Giroux's radical pedagogy, necessarily make use of conditions of oppression such work is trying to escape or overcome. In other words, youth speech is not strictly its own (something that will be discussed further in Chapters 5 and 6). Even an outright rejection of available frameworks is still conditioned by them, and so connected to them.

Similarly, Dick Hebdige comments on this problem of speaking for the other in his study of youth subculture, suggesting that there is a tendency to go too far in accounting for the reality of those being described. Hebdige believes that it is unlikely that members of the subcultures he describes in his study would recognise themselves in the work, and that it would be even more unlikely for subcultural members to welcome the attempts of researchers like him to understand them (1979, p. 139).

Hebdige suggests that he and other researchers 'threaten to kill with kindness the forms which we seek to elucidate' and that

> we should hardly be surprised to find [that] our 'sympathetic' readings of subordinate culture are regarded by the members of a subculture with just as much indifference and contempt as the hostile labels imposed by the courts and the press. In this respect, to get the point is, in a way, to miss the point.
>
> (1979, p. 139)

Interestingly, and as noted in Chapter 2 regarding the limits of a (sub)cultural studies paradigm, these comments affirm 'real' youth knowledge and reality, but concede that accessing or reading it is not a direct process or activity, but one that ultimately confirms the 'distance between the reader and the "text"' (Hebdige, 1979, p. 140). For Hebdige, this means that 'if we penetrate the object, we liberate it but destroy it; and if we acknowledge its full weight, we respect it, but restore it to a state which is still mystified' (Barthes cited in Hebdige, 1979, p. 140). The status of authentic speech is both put in question and affirmed here.

With similar concerns, the post-structuralist feminist project of challenging the patriarchal order does more than just seek to reverse the unequal binary opposition between men and women. Butler writes that a deconstructive critique 'brings into question the foundationalist frame in which feminism as an identity politics has been articulated' (1999, p. 189). So, as in Spivak's writing, a feminist post-structuralism is about more than looking for a 'pure' or unified feminine voice or space, and about more than seeking to articulate what such a space would or should look like. It asks questions about the positions women occupy and about the 'political operations that constrain and constitute the *field* within which positions emerge' (Butler and Scott, 1992, p. xiv). By using this approach, the foundational notions that traditionally ground a feminist identity politics and centre structures of meaning, such as the 'materiality of bodies', 'experience' and 'the unified self' (Butler and Scott, 1992, p. xiv), can be more productively read as constructed elements that work to silence as well as marginalise certain groups and other feminisms defined by class, ethnicity, nation, race and sexuality (Crosby, 1992, p. 131). This is because a reliance on foundational notions paradoxically serves to fix and constrain the subjects a feminist politics is actually seeking to liberate (Butler, 1999, p. 189). This brings into question any notion of cause or origin that 'presumes a fixed or ready-made subject' (Butler and Scott, 1992, p. xiv).

In a similar way, Spivak argues that 'the problem of the muted subject of the subaltern woman' will not be 'solved by an "essentialist" search for lost origins' (1988a, p. 295), or a belief in an untouched, complete and 'true' subaltern consciousness that could be accessed independently of colonial discourses (Moore-Gilbert et al., 1997, p. 31). This is the basis of Spivak's critique of the Subaltern Studies group: a group of historians attempting to 'recover expressions of subaltern consciousness in the colonial period', by stressing 'the role of the subaltern as historical agent' (Moore-Gilbert, 1997, p. 87).

Spivak explains that

> to investigate, discover, and establish a subaltern or peasant consciousness seems at first to be a positivistic project – a project which assumes that, if properly executed, it will lead to firm ground, to something that can be disclosed.
>
> (1988b, p. 202)

However, attempts by the group to establish a foundation for understanding identity independently of the colonising force it is linked to means that the group fails to recognise that the subaltern is a constructed social category and subject position (Moore-Gilbert, 1997, pp. 87–8). In Spivak's view, the group mistake a notion of a 'consciousness-in-general' with 'subaltern consciousness' (1988b, p. 203). The effect of this is that while they 'rupture' the dominant discourse in their attempt to uncover the 'real' subaltern, the group also 'repeats' the knowledge structure which they criticise, namely, Western humanism. They do this by assuming that subaltern consciousness can be fully grasped and see themselves as being in a position to offer privileged insight into it. In a similar way to the Western intellectual noted above, the group position themselves outside the discursive field, or as having unique access to it (Spivak, 1988b, p. 202). In other words, they perform a 'repetition-in-rupture' in that a 'reversal of the dominant discourse ... involves remaining within a logic defined by the opponent' (Moore-Gilbert, 1997, p. 85). It is Spivak's view that while a reversal is necessary, the terms in opposition must also then be displaced, because a directly counter discourse risks cancellation or reappropriation by the dominant (Moore-Gilbert, 1997, p. 85), as was the case for the punk subculture in Hebdige's study discussed in Chapter 2.

The structurality (or supplementarity) of presence

Instead, a particular problematising move can be used to address the feminist and postcolonial challenge to the notion of identity as presence, the problems associated with knowing and accessing those who are not positioned as such, and a desire to avoid simply replicating the same exclusionary framework. In his paper, 'Structure, Sign and Play in the Discourse of the Human Sciences', Derrida argues that a notion of centred structure – of an originary presence governing a structure of thought – requires a prior conceptual move in order to be thinkable as such. As I will go on to explain, Derrida's claim has implications for understanding the operation of social orders that posit a dominant and fixed Subject and its Other.

In the history of Western philosophy, on Derrida's account, the notion of an originary presence or centre has always been thought of as 'that very thing within a structure which while governing the structure, escapes structurality' (Derrida, 1978, p. 279). As Derrida puts it:

> structure – or rather the structurality of structure – although it has always been at work, has always been neutralised or reduced, and this by a process of giving it a centre or of referring it to a point of presence, a fixed origin.
>
> (1978, p. 278)

This centre or originary presence cannot be substituted or subject to the variations of form that the structure it governs may take, otherwise it is not the centre but an effect of the structure, governed by the structure. So if the centre of the structure must escape structurality, then

> the centre is, paradoxically, *within* the structure and *outside it*. The centre is at the centre of the totality, and yet, since the centre does not belong to the totality..., the totality *has its centre elsewhere*. The centre is not the centre. The concept of centred structure – although it represents coherence itself... – is contradictorily coherent.
>
> (Derrida, 1978, p. 279)

This means that even as it governs a structure, it is not possible to conceive of such a centre *other* than as something non-identical with the structure, hence as non-identical with itself. Derrida writes that 'the concept of centred structure is in fact the concept of a play based on a fundamental ground, a play constituted on the basis of a fundamental immobility and a reassuring certitude, which itself is beyond the reach of play' (1978, p. 279). The classical concept of structure must therefore conceive of a centre *before* the play, or as underpinning the play of elements *within* the structure, and not as itself subject to play. For

Derrida, however, because 'the centre is not the centre' it is not identical with itself and is thus 'other' before it is 'itself', before it is named as the centre (1978, p. 280). It is 'a central presence which has never been itself, has always already been exiled from itself into its own substitute', only 'the substitute does not substitute itself for anything which has somehow existed before it' (Derrida, 1978, p. 280). Derrida argues that there is already a 'play' at the centre of structure, which is why the centre is able to receive 'different forms or names' (1978, p. 279). He writes that the 'history of the concept of structure... must be thought of as a series of substitutions of centre for centre' (1978, p. 279), and this proliferation of names for the centre – essence, consciousness, God – thus evinces the fact that the centre that supposedly governs the play of elements within the structure is nevertheless subject to that play of elements (1978, pp. 280).

This is to say that the centre does not take the form of a 'present being' and it has no 'natural site' (Derrida, 1978, p. 280). Rather than seeing the centre as a 'fixed locus', Derrida suggests that it is necessary to think of it as 'a function, a sort of nonlocus in which an infinite number of sign-substitutions' come into play (1978, p. 280). And if any system is always one in which 'the central signified, the original or transcendental signified, is never absolutely present outside a system of differences', then 'the absence of the transcendental signified extends the domain and the play of signification infinitely' (Derrida, 1978, p. 280). It is therefore not possible to 'determine the centre and exhaust totalisation'. A sign that is used to take the place of the absent centre, to supplement it, occurs as an addition or a surplus. The sign adds something, and this does not result in completion but produces a situation where there is 'always more' (Derrida, 1978, p. 289).

On this point, Derrida argues that 'if totalisation no longer has any meaning, it is not because the infiniteness of a field cannot be covered by a finite glance or a finite discourse, but because the nature of the field – that is, language and a finite language – excludes totalisation' (1978, p. 289). The field of signification, of language, excludes totalisation – there is 'always more' – because rather than being inexhaustible or too large, it is missing a centre which grounds the play of signification (Derrida, 1978, p. 289). This makes the field 'in effect that of *play*, that is to say, a field of infinite substitutions only because it is finite' (Derrida, 1978, p. 289). Derrida calls the play that is permitted by the lack of a centre 'the movement of supplementarity' (1978, p. 289).

A notion or concept of originary presence must therefore be supplemented in order to function as such. For instance, a notion of 'purity' or 'naturalness' actually contains its opposite form, when, in order to be thinkable, it must necessarily rely on that which is considered unnatural or impure (Lucy, 2004, p. 136). The perceived or the assumed purity of the concept of originary presence is therefore less than complete, less than pure, less than itself; there is 'self-difference at its very origin' (Wortham, 2010, p. 204). For Derrida, this originary lack needs to be supplemented in order to appear as whole, pure, complete; however, a supplement 'is not simply added to the positivity of a presence' but has the function of *producing* it as such in the first place (1997, p. 145). For example, Niall Lucy writes that the purity and naturalness of the human form represented in sculpture is often seen supplemented by a piece of drapery. While this cloth is added to the work and is taken to be external to the object's innate beauty, completeness or totality, as an 'enhancement' to the piece, the cloth also functions to augment its purity. This signals that the sculpture's perceived wholeness is not inherent, for how can something be added to what is already complete and total, and what need would there be to do so? (Lucy, 2004, p. 136). The totality of the form turns out to be incomplete, there is something lacking which must be 'filled' or supplemented before it can appear as total and whole. This means that the supplement (drapery) is added, but it also replaces the seeming plenitude, truth or essence of the form it supplements. There is no perceived conceptual purity without the movement of supplementarity, but this makes whatever is constituted to be originary or self-present already other than itself. This process thus displaces the purity and priority of a primary concept because it is thinkable only in its difference from itself, and so is therefore defined by an 'originary difference' rather than a pure, self-sustained presence (Lucy, 2004, p. 88).

It is on condition of the movement of supplementarity that the possibility of thinking in terms of a presence/absence binary and its appearance as natural, given or true is opened up, but in the same moment it is also necessarily upset. According to Derrida, deconstruction makes 'enigmatic what one thinks one understands by... "presence"' (1997, p. 70) because it is not possible to think it without also thinking the notion of absence. What is thought to exist independently and of itself is actually dependent on that which it is opposed to, such that presence is 'breached' or 'split' by absence. This approach renders the inside–outside relationship of binary pairs 'undecidable'; their difference is not assumed to be pre-determined, pure or absolute, but rather an *effect* of a signifying or supplementary process. The 'prior conceptual move' mentioned above is to recognise the 'play' that is the condition of conceptuality which opens up seemingly fixed distinctions to discussion of what constitutes them and, significantly, to different meanings altogether.

So, looking again at Spivak's work, rather than seeking 'a record of an authentic voice corresponding to a Western notion of speech as the expression of a full subjectivity' (Young, 1990, p. 164), Spivak writes that she prefers to 'read the retrieval of subaltern consciousness as the charting of what in post-structuralist language would be called the subaltern subject-effect' (1988b, p. 204). By abandoning a sense of a fixed self (an originary presence), Spivak invites thinking in terms of the multiple elements that makes the self intelligible. The critical concept of a subject effect first understands that 'a subject may be part of an immense discontinuous network ... of strands' such as 'politics, ideology, economics, history, sexuality, language, and so on' (Spivak, 1988b, p. 204). It is these strands, in 'different knottings and configurations', and 'determined by heterogeneous determinations', that 'produce the effect of an operating subject' (Spivak, 1988b, p. 204). Things get interesting, however, when (and echoing Derrida's remarks) this operating subject requires 'a continuist and homogenist cause for this effect and thus posits a sovereign and determining subject' (Spivak, 1988b, p. 204). The key point Spivak makes is that such a notion of the sovereign subject is actually 'the effect of an effect', but one that seeks substitution 'of an effect for a cause' in order to function (1988b, p. 204). Put another way, what is thought to be originary about subjectivity is in fact an outcome of the heterogeneous and discontinuous determinations of discourse, which means that any discussion of a sovereign will as it applies to non-dominant groups 'is no more than an effect of the subaltern subject-effect' (Spivak, 1988b, p. 204). But Spivak's work shows that by calling on concepts such as 'origin' and 'the subject', critics inevitably cover over their fictional nature as discursive effects (Moore-Gilbert, 1997, p. 99).

The framing of youth as a problem that needs to be 'fixed' reflects a similar process of covering over the condition of grounding assumptions as discursive effects. The positioning of youth as an external threat to social order when discussing things like young people's seemingly irrational decisions (Chapter 4), their precocious sexuality (Chapter 5) or their violent behaviour (Chapter 6) signals a lack of awareness that their framing as such is a discursive effect. Similarly, by failing to recognise the conditions of intelligibility of the adult subject as an effect of discourse as well, its appearance as natural and dominant works against itself. In order for the adult subject to function as natural and dominant, it must be acknowledged that this subject is not naturally apparent or self-grounding, but rather that it emerges in a difference from itself. However, the adult subject cannot continue to make sense as a sovereign determining subject by doing this. For the adult subject to maintain such a position, its other, youth, on which it depends for its intelligibility, must be situated outside of itself as an equally determining or authentic subject. This ensures that any action taken against youth as an external threat perpetuates the positioning of youth as threat because this is the only way the adult subject can be maintained in its perceived internal coherence. Any corrective action therefore only serves to require *more* corrective action (more research into the teen brain, more regulation of teen sexuality, more treatment of youth dysfunction). In the end, what is thought to be being artic- ulated about the full consciousness of youth, or what is thought to mark the expression of youth as a distinct identity category, is actu- ally a mis-naming of the effect of the process of self-identification of adult presence. Youth only appears to be inherently disruptive in nature because of the assumption of an adult self-presence. To rearticulate the basis of identification of both youth and adult in terms of a 'subject- effect' framework could break this cycle by reframing what counts as a 'youth problem' and in a way that does not necessarily risk the coher- ence of either subject position in order to do something about it. This is something I take up further in the following chapters.

With similar concerns to Spivak, postcolonial theorist Homi Bhabha presents the notion of the 'stereotype' and how it produces 'ambivalence' in colonial discourse. 'The objective of colonial discourse', Bhabha writes in *The Other Question*, 'is to construe the colonised as a population of degenerate types on the basis of racial origin, in order to justify conquest and to establish systems of administration and instruction' (1996, p. 41). In adapting the psychoanalytic terms of fetishism to colonial discourse, Bhabha argues that the stereotype of the colonised other as depraved and degenerate produces ambivalence for the coloniser because, like Derrida's supplementarity, it is a mode of identification that requires the 'articulation of modes of differentiation' against a desire to maintain 'the myth of historical origination' (1996, pp. 43–44). From Freud, Bhabha writes that fetishism 'is that repetitious scene around the problem of castration' (1996, p. 44). It occurs when 'the recognition of sexual difference' (that 'some do not have penises') creates an 'anxiety associated with lack' to the point where that lack or difference is disavowed by 'fixation on an object that masks that dif- ference and restores an original presence' (Bhabha, 1996, p. 44). The 'stereotype as fetish' involves a similar process of recognition and dis- avowal by the coloniser. In seeking to ' "normalise" the multiple beliefs and split subjects that constitute colonial discourse', racial others are brought into a familiar and accepted space: that of Western 'racial purity' and 'cultural priority' (Bhabha, 1996, p. 44). Because of this, however, differences of 'race, colour and culture' have to be undermined because they threaten that pure space, even as such racial purity and cultural priority is made knowable only *after* an encounter with, and realisation of, these differences (Bhabha, 1996, p. 45). In other words, Bhabha's application of the terms of fetishism, which reflect the movement of supplementarity as described by Derrida, suggests that the coloniser has 'access to an "identity" which is predicated as much on mastery and pleasure as it is on anxiety and defence' (1996, p. 44). The 'desire for a pure origin' is 'always threatened by its division', for the act of disavowal, or fixation on the stereotype, must be repeated in order to prevent the threat of difference from the other from splitting 'the soul and whole, undifferentiated skin of the ego' (Bhabha, 1996, p. 45).

This repetition of the stereotype has further implications with regard to how it troubles the concept of identity. As Bart Moore-Gilbert argues, 'the regime of the stereotype' does not evidence 'the stability of the "disciplinary" gaze of the coloniser, or security in his own conception of himself', but rather 'the degree to which the coloniser's identity (and authority) is in fact fractured and destabilised by . . . the colonised Other' (1997, p. 117). Any belief in the unity or essential nature of identity is marked as already incomplete by the very manner of its identification as essential; it is undermined as it is asserted (Moore-Gilbert, 1997, p. 119). For Bhabha, the need to repeat 'the *same old* stories' about the colonial subject (and, indeed, youth), in order to maintain what the coloniser believes to be essentially different about them, reveals that both their identities are not unitary, stable and distinct, but rather are defined by a diversity of positions (1996, p. 47). Bhabha takes this to be 'a *productive* ambivalence' in the work of challenging colonial discourse (1996, p. 38) because it means that when colonial discourse is asserted, it is also 'always slipping, ceaselessly displaced, never complete' (Young, 1990, p. 143). This also means that the process of identity formation for both coloniser and colonised continuously transgresses attempts to narrowly fix or close down its meaning.

Along these lines, it is possible to observe how attempts to define youth based on a similar assumption of a fundamental difference between youth and adult also produces effects that transgress conceptual boundaries thought to be stable and distinct. A developmental framework, for instance, ends up signalling its own explanatory limits when, as I'll discuss in Chapter 4, a founding (and adult) rationality is posited as something that is *grown into* even as this rationality is taken as the prior authority underpinning and governing the positioning of youth as lacking reason. In Chapter 5, an expectation that youth 'come of age' requires that young people move out of the distinctions of youth, so the function of this notion actually hinges on the limits of youth being transgressed.

Bhabha's discussion of the concept of mimicry further illustrates the ongoing displacement of identity against attempts to define it based on an assumption of fundamental or essential difference. As 'a new term for the construction of the colonial Other in certain forms of stereotyping' (Young, 1990, p. 147), but with the potential to further disrupt colonial authority, 'colonial mimicry is', according to Bhabha, 'constructed around an *ambivalence*'; that is, 'the desire for a reformed, recognisable Other, *as a subject of a difference that is almost the same, but not quite*' (1994, p. 86). Moore-Gilbert writes that mimicry can be understood to 'express the "epic" project of the civilising mission to transform the colonised culture', so a desire for a subject that is the same means that 'the colonised subject' should 'adopt the outward forms and internalise the values and norms of the occupying power' (1997, p. 120). This, however, cannot wholly occur, because to mimic in this way is to repeat or copy the original – the coloniser's culture – and to copy it is not to be identical with that original culture. Consequently, this process of cultural translation and adaptation actually produces a lack which destabilises the original because it requires the slippage or displacement of meaning for both the notion of 'originality' and the possibility of its replication to even occur (Moore-Gilbert, 1997, p. 119).

Mimicry therefore describes a process where, in Robert Young's words, the 'colonial subject...will be recognisably the same as the coloniser but still different', and so 'is only a partial representation of him' (1990, p. 147). A confrontational effect of this is that the coloniser is presented with a grotesque, displaced image of himself for the imitation has subverted the identity that is being represented (Young, 1990, p. 147). As a partial presence, this move by the colonised not only ruptures the discourse but transforms it into an uncertainty (Bhabha, 1994, p. 86). Bhabha contends that 'the *menace* of mimicry is its *double* vision which in disclosing the ambivalence of the colonial discourse also disrupts its authority' and its narcissistic demands (1994, p. 88). The coloniser undertakes certain strategies so as to maintain power, to fix the colonised as an object of knowledge, but in doing so is confronted 'with a returning gaze of otherness' that threatens 'its mastery, its sameness' (Young, 1990, p. 147). Bhabha suggests that here 'the observer becomes the observed and "partial" representation rearticulates the whole notion of *identity* and alienates it from its essence' (1994, p. 89). As such, 'a miming of the very operation of domination' goes beyond 'a process of identification and disavowal' to a point where both 'the identity of the coloniser [or adult] and colonised [or youth] becomes curiously elided' (Young, 1990, p. 148).

The notion of mimicry has implications when discussing what youth is supposed to do: become adult. The process of taking adult form involves, to adapt Moore-Gilbert's phrase, adopting the outward forms and internalising the values and norms of adult society. This, however, requires the transgression of the basic notion of youth as 'not adult', thus threatening the coherence of the structure which produces such a notion of youth and relies on it for the structure's own renewal and continuation. The process of mimicry, while a key part of what youth must 'do' to become adult, distorts that which is being 'copied' or 'repeated' and returns an image that subverts the original. The core task of youth operates at odds with itself when following through on what it is supposed to do displaces the order it is moving towards or into. The social order that dominant explanatory frameworks for youth support is confronted with the ambivalence of the figure of youth in working to reproduce itself as something whole, complete and discrete. One particular example of mimicry is explored in Chapter 6 regarding the struggle to adequately explain the behaviour of the boys responsible for the Columbine massacre given the way they self-consciously made use of adult speaking positions to negate a range of possible explanations for what happened.

Investigative possibilities

What has been revealed thus far is the dependence of dominant subject positions on their subordinated, marginalised and disavowed others and the possibility that as long as this dependence goes unrecognised, such identity positions will continue to be troubled by their subordinated others and will fail to recognise that the trouble and the tension is actually their means of self-definition. Such antagonism is what dominant subjectivities want and need from their subordinates in order to appear as though they themselves are self-present, self-sufficient and originary. In Butler's words, the 'abjected outside' of the dominant subject is actually ' "inside" the subject as its own founding repudiation' (1993, p. 3). But what can actually be done with this insight? What does it enable that will be of use in analysing youth identity? This is not about simply reversing the binary terms to overcome a conceptual problem; something else has been suggested that alters the terms in use and that changes the grounding from which the work of identity proceeds for everyone (dominant and marginal): identity comes out of a *difference* from itself.

As Young argues, and to reiterate earlier remarks on the supplementarity of presence, if identity as a concept is thought of as 'absolute sameness' and 'individuality', it therefore has to be 'specified by being different', in fact, 'it can only be defined by difference from others' (2000, p. 199). Identity thus always and immediately summons up its opposite and so it is not originary, it cannot be totalised or thought other than through a constructed relationship based on 'difference' (Young, 2000, p. 199). Here, identity is decentred; it is not an intrinsic and self-sufficient state of being, it is non-essential and able to be changed (Young, 2000, p. 201). Indeed, the very possibility of identity being thought is characterised by ambivalence, by the 'slippage' or 'undecidability' of meaning. The consequence of this, however, is that the object of analysis evades attempts to secure its meaning, thereby disrupting the authority of those doing the theorising to the point of there never being a point of resolution or completion. Yet a conceptual crisis such as this actually means becoming *more* aware of what is at stake in understanding identity. This process requires undertaking 'a persistent critique of what one cannot not want' in the production of, and in attempts to privilege, certain truths about identity (Spivak cited in Moore-Gilbert, 1997, p. 112). That is, a notion of stable or dominant identity cannot avoid nor do without the disavowed other in its own constitution. As Lucy writes,

> once it is accepted that every binary opposition…is already in deconstruction, there can be no going back to a way of understanding that requires the terms of any binary pair to be seen according to an absolute and a priori difference.
>
> (2004, pp. 12–13)

The notion of identity is subject to a reversal and displacement of binary structure in order to be thinkable as self-present, contained and complete. How things seemingly 'are', therefore, is actually already other than what they are thought to be. Thus it is necessary to think differently if key identity structures are to continue to find meaning, and deconstruction provides a means to do this.

A turn to deconstruction in analysing youth discourse is not about replacing a flawed logic, nor is it a nihilistic move or one that advocates the free play of meaning (criticisms often levelled at deconstruction). Deconstruction actually offers something affirming and enabling insofar as addressing conditions of conceptuality and being responsive to the effects these conditions produce provides a means of offering other – more productive – possibilities for dealing with the problems these effects create. For example, Spivak seeks a way of 'speaking to' and 'learning from' the other by not relying on a belief in a true, authentic subaltern consciousness, nor by denying that their reality as subaltern is constructed or imposed from an outside (1988b, p. 135). A 'constitutive paradox' characterises all attempts at thinking about subordinated identities because for there to be something to argue about or for at all is dependent on the identity category of 'subaltern' continuing to be arguable, and thus it remains within the discourse that conditioned its emergence. In this way, 'the subaltern cannot speak' (Spivak, 1988a, p. 308) when 'the subaltern is...only heard through the mediation of the non-subaltern' (Moore-Gilbert, 1997, p. 108). It is their silence that makes the West possible and so makes them possible to be thought and spoken about at all. But neither can the subaltern be spoken for because any articulation on their behalf could not escape the language system that first conditioned their intelligibility as subaltern. Spivak does, however, acknowledge that whether or not subaltern women recognise themselves in the terms used by Western critics, they still speak from a place conditioned by their relationship to a colonising force (Moore-Gilbert, 1997, p. 108; Spivak 1988b, p. 135). A similar kind of critical awareness can also be extended to understanding the positioning of youth.

Likewise, Butler suggests that a critical examination that comes from viewing the natural as constructed requires taking existing terms of reference like 'the body', 'the subject' and 'experience', and continuing to use and repeat them but in a subversive way, so as to 'displace them from the contexts in which they have been deployed as instruments of oppressive power' (1992, p. 17). Indeed, a post-structuralist analysis demands the reuse of these terms because it recognises that there is no space in which to challenge the authority of the terms other than within the space that they produce and occupy (Butler and Scott, 1992, p. xiv). By exposing a traditional representation of fixity, such as the body, as contingent and non-originary, there is an initial 'loss of epistemological certainty', but Butler makes the crucial point that 'this loss of certainty does not necessarily entail political nihilism as a result' (1992, p. 17).

A post-structuralist feminist reading or a postcolonial reading of identity does not seek to render key terms useless or deplete them of meaning; their repetition via a critical intervention in fact 'provides the conditions to *mobilise* the signifier in the service of an alternative production' (Butler, 1992, p. 17).

So with regard to youth, the aim of the analytical work to follow is to continue to think 'youth', but to 'mobilise the signifier' differently. I am concerned with the possibility of how to keep the idea of youth intact given that it cannot not be used in making sense of the identity structures it serves. I seek to develop ways of thinking and speaking about youth that are responsive to the contingencies of its conceptualisation and the effects of this. I look at how this might inform discussions around and questions about youth development, reason, sexuality, youth violence and youth media use and, in particular, the perceived problems associated with these things. Crucially, though, I am concerned with how to do this without necessarily casting youth as a threat or danger to society as the only means of keeping existing explanatory structures intact. As previously noted, this merely perpetuates the need to cast youth in such a way. My exploration into such a possibility begins in the next chapter on the teen brain.

4
Reasonable Unreason: The Limits of Youth in the Teen Brain

This chapter presents a deconstructive analysis of a developmental narrative operating in a neuroscience discourse. The analysis implements the deconstructive framework outlined in the previous chapter and follows my analytical purpose, which is to develop a way of conceptualising youth that is responsive to the effects of the manner of its discursive construction. The particular object of my reading is a growing body of scientific research on the teen brain. Popularised by feature stories in magazines such as *Time* (Wallis, 2004) and *National Geographic* (Dodds, 2011), in television documentaries (for example, 'Inside the Teenage Brain', 2002; 'Teen Brain', 2005) and in publications such as Barbara Strauch's *The Primal Teen* (2004), research in this area is concerned to understand adolescent brain maturation, its structure and function, and how this shapes mental capacity in young people. (An outline of teen brain science follows in the next section, however see also Phillips [2007] for a detailed overview.) Much of this research is particularly concerned to uncover why teenagers behave in irrational ways and engage in risky behaviour (see Reyna and Farley, 2007; Casey et al., 2008; Fischhoff, 2008; Gerrard et al., 2008; Reyna and Rivers, 2008; Rivers et al., 2008; Steinberg, 2008; Sunstein, 2008). This work has gained large-scale public and political acceptance as it appears to finally offer solid evidence for troubling teen behaviour, and the possibility that adults can now seek to more effectively manage teens' behaviour and in doing so protect them (and others) from unnecessary harm.

However, a number of scholars have presented thoroughgoing critiques of this science. Michael Males (2009; 2010) argues that it is bio-determinist, Judith Bessant (2008) critiques its 'scientism' and Robert Epstein (2007a, 2007b) argues against the 'myth' that brain maturation 'causes' teen turmoil and chaos, focusing instead on teen capability. Howard Sercombe raises methodological questions for the research field and notes a tendency to over-interpret the data, 'taking a fragment of information' about teen brain activity and 'reading off some generalisation about the nature of all young people' as to why they are lazy or take risks (2010a, p. 75). Sercombe also emphasises how discourses on adolescence provide the conceptual 'atmosphere' that youth researchers breathe, but that often this is unrecognised in a cognitive neuroscience context where interpretation is assumed to take place in a 'neutral discursive environment' (2010b, p. 41). Similarly, Peter Kelly notes how particular scientific knowledge practices produce evidence about teen brains which takes on the status of natural truth, and which achieves a high degree of support in public and policy domains (2012, p. 946). Kelly highlights that such scientific truth relies on 'taken-for-granted-assumptions about adolescence as a near universal experience of a particular time in life; and of the figure of the adolescent as the irrational, impulsive, risk taking Other to the figure of the rational, considered, prudent adult' (2012, p. 946).

Males, Sercombe, Bessant and others argue that this work ignores the influence of socio-economic context on teen behaviour, Males suggesting that poverty is a much more accurate predictor of risky behaviour among young people (2009, pp. 12–16). Omitting these considerations makes it easy (and convenient) to blame young people (and their brains) for their bad behaviour, thus pathologising them, rather than attending to the social problems and inequalities from which such behaviour stems (Males, 2009, p. 16). These critics argue that brain science is being used to confirm popular prejudices against young people as inferior to adults due to natural, essential or innate cognitive limitations. Furthermore, these prejudices work to justify increasingly restrictive policies against young people (Males, 2009, pp. 6&18).

The emerging field of 'critical' or 'cultural neuroscience' is attentive to these problems and limitations (see Choudhury, 2009; Choudhury et al., 2009). Work in this area seeks to offer a 'reflexive scientific practice that responds to the social and cultural challenges posed both to the field of science and to society in general by recent advances in the behavioural and brain sciences' (Choudhury et al., 2009, p. 62). Taken together, these critical analyses and perspectives point to how the availability of new technology in mapping teen brain development does not attend to or resolve the issues that are raised by the culturally specific meaning attached to mental function. As Kelly writes, the processes of knowledge production about brains, minds and young people are never just about science, technology and evidence. These processes involve social, cultural, economic and political assumptions/presumptions about young people, their development and the challenges of growing up in the industrialised democracies at the start of the twenty-first century.

(2012, pp. 945–6)

With this in mind, I too take a critical approach to this science, but apply a different analytical lens. Following Derrida's logic of supplementarity, his reading of Descartes and Foucault on the history of reason and madness, and his discussion of Freud's work on the written character of psychic content, I analyse the underlying assumptions of the neuroscience discourse with regard to the development of reasoning ability. The analysis reveals the discursive effects which serve to undermine the aims and findings of the science by putting in question the very meaning and distinction of what counts as human subjectivity. Accordingly, this deconstructive reading remains aware of the consequences of a particular conceptual framework in order to avoid contradictory expectations about how youth 'become adult'.

The physiology of reason

Advances in non-invasive brain-imaging technology have given neuroscientists unique access to the adolescent brain as it grows and develops. For example, as part of a US National Institute of Mental Health longitudinal study, Dr Jay Giedd has used magnetic resonance imaging (MRI) to scan participants (aged 3–27 years) every two years, building up records of their brain development, tracing and tracking how different parts of the brain mature (2008, p. 335–6). (Other imaging technologies include functional MRI, which measures patterns of brain activity, and diffusion tensor imaging, which indexes the connectivity of white matter fibre tracts [Casey et al., 2008, p. 65].) In the past, and under the influence of such theorists as Jean Piaget whose concept of formal operations suggested that adult-level cognitive ability was reached by age 12, it was commonly believed that brain development was complete by late childhood. However, MRI technology is showing that this is far from the truth, with evidence to suggest that extensive structural change occurs in the brain's gray and white matter beyond puberty and into early adulthood (Wallis, 2004, p. 48).

There are two phases to this structural change – 'nerve proliferation' and 'nerve pruning' – and two key phases in the lifespan when this occurs – just before birth, and from late childhood through to the early 20s (Wallis, 2004, p. 49). The process of nerve proliferation and pruning is where an excess of neural connections are built up, generating new nerve pathways and connections, followed by a period of elimination in which unused connections are pruned away (Wallis, 2004, p. 49; Dodds, 2011, p. 43). Wallis reports that 'the thickening of all this gray matter – the neurons and their branch-like dendrites – peaks when girls are about 11 and boys 12½', after which 'gray matter is thinned out at a rate of about 0.7% a year, tapering off in the early 20s' (2004, p. 49). As this thinning process occurs, the brain's white matter thickens. Axons are insulated with myelin (or white matter), a fatty substance that protects and enhances nerve signals, making their transmissions faster and more efficient (Wallis, 2004, p. 49; Dodds, 2011, p. 43). The result of this process, says Giedd, is that 'you get fewer but faster connections in the brain' (cited in Wallis, 2004, p. 49). So what is lost in the pruning process is a raw learning potential and a better chance of recovering from trauma, but what is gained is efficiency in brain function, which is of vital importance in having optimum adult-level brain function (Wallis, 2004, p. 49).

In the cognitive science tradition this focus on development is central, and it is worth pausing here to note (and to reiterate from Chapter 2) the predominance of this type of work in the area of youth studies. In developmental terms, 'each stage of the life span has its own developmental tasks which involve motor, physical, social or emotional aspects of behaviour', and these tasks must be mastered in order to successfully move on to the next stage (Heaven, 2001, p. 5). While changes in society and environment influence what things are considered critical to a person's social and psychological growth – such as preparing for family and working life in the early twenty-first century – development, for everyone, follows a set sequence of stages that occur in the same order and at roughly the same time. This process is linear and cumulative, and the end result concerns the integration of these many different aspects so that identity, or a stable sense of personhood, can be said to have been 'achieved' (Heaven, 2001, pp. 19, 20&29).

The discursive parameters that this concern with development establishes in discussions about youth are powerful (although not universal). The influence of a developmental discourse is apparent when reference is made to young people's perplexing and bewildering behaviour, their emotional volatility, and their maturing and therefore somewhat dangerous bodies. The discourse informs discussion on how young people occupy social space, issues of education, parenting, welfare and policy, to name a few. It is also found in scholarly or research contexts, in the popular media, and in everyday discussion. All these areas turn on the issue of young people's perceived intellectual, emotional, social and physical competencies, or more particularly, on the fact that youth are *not* fully developed in these areas. As mentioned above, Piaget is foremost in the research on teenage cognitive development, and even as this recent research on the teen brain advances on past assumptions established by his work, it works, nonetheless, according to the parameters set by it. These are a concern with charting and tracking development across the teen years, which is a time understood to 'mark a significant qualitative change in reasoning ability' (Heaven, 2001, p. 21).

Accordingly, the final part of the proliferation and pruning process occurring in the late teens is most critical as it concerns the development of 'some of our highest mental functions' (Wallis, 2004, p. 49). Located at the front of the brain is the prefrontal cortex which is responsible for executing high-level functions such as 'planning, setting priorities, organising thoughts, suppressing impulses, weighing the consequences of one's actions' (Wallis, 2004, p. 51). The prefrontal cortex is the last part of the brain to reach its adult dimensions, following the pruning of neural connections located at the rear of the brain that interpret and coordinate sensory functions like vision, movement, hearing and touch (Wallis, 2004, pp. 49&51; Dodds, 2011, p. 43). Giedd states that not only is the frontal lobe responsible for the above-mentioned higher skills and abilities, but (and recalling from Chapter 2 the discussion of formal-operations thinking) it is the 'part of the brain that allows us to conduct philosophy and to think about thinking and to think about our place in the universe' (2002, np). As such, it is 'the part of the brain that has changed the most in our human evolution' and is what, in a manner of speaking, 'most separates man from beast' (Giedd, 2002, np). So during this time of proliferation and pruning teenagers have an excess of connections, which is inefficient when it comes to executing higher-order mental functions, but the plasticity of the brain that comes with this excess means having a greater overall potential to learn. However, a capacity to think and act with reason is the sign of a more mature (but also a smaller) brain.

The idea that a mature brain is capable of thinking about thinking and of reflecting on the nature of the self can be understood as belonging to a history of thought that Jacques Derrida calls logocentrism or the 'epoch of the logos' (1997, p. 12). This 'founding metaphysical authority', writes Niall Lucy, to reiterate ideas introduced in the last chapter, began with Plato and conceives of presence as prior to everything else – knowledge, history consciousness (2004, pp. 70–1). 'The *logos* expresses the desire for an ultimate origin, telos, centre or principle of truth which grounds meaning' (Wortham, 2010, p. 89), and which can be known of itself, independent of any form of representation (Lucy, 2004, p. 70). This history determines the meaning of being as presence or self-presence (Derrida, 1997, p. 12). In addition, and to signal a notion that I will be returning to later in the chapter, within logocentrism there is also a phonocentrism. Thought and speech, or voice and being, are understood to be absolutely proximate to one another, such that the truth or essence of being originates with spoken (not written) language (Derrida, 1997, pp. 11–12; Lucy, 2004, p. 71). As Christopher Norris explains, 'in spoken language...meaning is "present" to the speaker through an act of inward self-surveillance which ensures a perfect, intuitive "fit" between intention and utterance' (1982, p. 23). Through speech, 'an inward and immediate realisation of meaning...yields itself up without reserve to perfect, transparent understanding' (Norris, 1982, p. 28).

This conceptual history can be related to research on the teen brain in two key ways. First, the investigative techniques of the science are structured according to a particular way of conceptualising the self: that there is such a thing as a naturally apparent truth or essence that can be uncovered or accessed (using imaging technology), so the research is working to establish the 'essence' of youth. This is consistent with the metaphysics of presence that assumes that it is possible to know the origin or truth of the self and to have pure and unmediated access to it. As Bessant notes, the science operates from an assumption that using MRI scans makes it possible to directly observe our thoughts and experiences (2008, p. 351). The second aspect is that by tracking the development of teen brains, a path to 'the self-presence of the cogito' (Derrida, 1997, p. 12) is traced, while at the same time, the pre-existing truth of the cogito is implicitly relied on as the source of meaning and context of interpretation for the science. This is due to the fact that by being within the 'epoch of the logos', there is simply no other position from which to think. The reason that makes this science intelligible at all is presumed to the point of being invisible. Yet this presumption is the key thing that would see the project collapse from within its own logic, because what is thought to be foundational about the self is something that the science suggests is *grown into*. The findings indicate that the exercise of reason (which is also an indicator of self-presence) only comes fully 'on-line' *in* the prefrontal cortex, so the science is working on the basis of grounding and founding assumptions at the same time as it is 'revealing' how they develop.

Accordingly, what is 'discovered' about the nature of youth by following the logic of the science is at odds with the very notion of 'essence'. If based in presumed physiological and biological fact, then the essence of youth would be its very *development* towards a certain level of cognitive ability, such that youth is not so much a state of 'being' as it is a process, or a 'state' of being in process. When the most basic questions asked about the teen brain are to do with its development towards something, youth is, in its essence, something other than itself. And while what youth is developing towards could easily be called something other than 'adult', this does not change the fact that this concept of youth has no meaning or function independent of this process.

This calls for a consideration of how the nature of being and of reason might be understood in a way that 'no longer issues from a logos' (Derrida, 1997, p. 10). While it is seemingly logical to posit youth as becoming present, and to understand that this formation of youth proceeds from (rather than comes before) the metaphysical notion of presence, this notion of youth is actually already outside the scope of possibility the science is working to and within if, in proceeding from this notion of presence, youth represents a growing *into* this state of being. By not recognising that the terms of intelligibility of the science are other than what they are thought to be, the findings of the research, while consistent with the objectives of the science, work against or exceed the science, which necessitates *not* acknowledging the notion of youth that is produced in order to keep a logocentric order of reason intact. Interestingly, and as already discussed in the previous chapter, Derrida suggests that there is a prior opening that comes before the notion of undeconstructible presence. Although this prior opening can itself be understood as a governing presence or centre, the problem identified here concerning how a youth/adult relation operates based on a supposed path from absence to presence is actually secondary to this prior opening. This is to say that *there is something going on prior to the grounding from which this research proceeds*. Something has to 'happen' before it becomes possible to conceive of the possibility of looking directly at absolute presence and then to conceive of what is other to it.

With regard to the teen brain research, what therefore leads to the point where analysis can begin on the conceptual contradictions noted above is recognising the supplementarity of the grounding assumptions of the research. It is from this recognition that it is possible to first conceptualise youth in the ways described above, even though the contradictions raised here go unseen, and the ways of thinking youth that a cognitive science approach produces persist as the dominant way of thinking. The analysis of the teen brain research below therefore continues with the key assumptions in place. From here it will be possible to more fully explain the significance of reading this material deconstructively later in the chapter, and to address how to conceptualise a notion of youth beyond these limits.

Genetics and experience

A further element involved in the neural pruning process, and one that is thought to have a significant bearing on how the frontal lobe develops, is 'experience'. Wallis writes that 'most scientists believe that the pruning process is guided both by genetics and by a use-it-or-lose-it principle' (2004, p. 48). In other words, it is guided by a nature/nurture relationship in which the brain both determines experience and is itself determined by experience (Sercombe, 2010b, p. 34). With regard to experience, Giedd's research recognises the co-determining relationship of brain and environment during this time. He states that

> how the teens spend their time seems to be particularly crucial. If the 'use it or lose it' principle holds true, then the activities of the teen may help guide the hard-wiring, [the] actual physical connections in their brain.
>
> (2002, np)

According to Giedd, certain activities might therefore be preferable over others. Giedd continues:

> If a teen is doing music or sports or academics, those are the cells and connections that will be hard-wired. If they're lying on the couch or playing video games or [watching] MTV, those are the cells and connections that are going to survive.
>
> (2002, np)

What is indicated then is that, in the brain, 'experience becomes flesh' (Wallis, 2004, p. 48).

Genetics is the other key factor affecting the 'road' to the frontal lobe. While the specific triggers for the myelination or pruning process are not yet understood (Sercombe, 2010b, p. 39), what is known is that the pro-liferation and pruning process proceeds in gradual stages from the back of the brain to the front. Basic and fundamental brain functions are consolidated first, and areas capable of complicated thinking and pro-cessing are consolidated last (Wallis, 2004, p. 49; Dodds, 2011, p. 43). That this process happens for all people and is what should happen in a 'normal' brain suggests that it occurs irrespective of one's experience. Interestingly, these discoveries about the timing of teenage brain devel-opment are prompting questions about the onset of mental illness and cognitive disorders. Choudhury writes that 'youth is the stage in life in which mental disorders are often thought to begin' and 'it is increas-ingly speculated that the maturing brain may be of causal significance' (2009, p. 160). For instance, researchers are finding links between the period of neural proliferation and the appearance of such disorders as attention deficit hyperactivity disorder and Tourette's syndrome (Wallis, 2004, p. 52). Rapid tissue growth in early childhood may be the cause of hyperactivity and tics (Wallis, 2004, p. 52), whereas 'developmental events' during the maturation of the prefrontal cortex may be involved in the development of schizophrenia in late adolescence (Choudhury, 2009, p. 160). This suggests that it is the process *itself* that causes these problems to occur or to become manifest. While there is speculation over whether schizophrenia has prenatal origins or is caused by an abnormal or even an excessive pruning process (schizophrenics lose as much as 25% of their gray matter compared to an average teenager who loses only 15% [Wallis, 2004, p. 53]), what seems unquestionable here, despite the variables that could lead to illness, is the inevitability of the process itself.

The reason of physiology

What is interesting to note here is not so much the research findings themselves, but how they are offered without any disturbance to our acceptance of the 'truth' of physiological or biological processes. Science enjoys a privileged position in terms of constructing truths. As Kelly notes, 'sciences have rules for producing evidence and truths', and while the social and philosophical study of science demonstrates that this is not the same as revealing an ultimate truth, this difference is not always made apparent in discussion about it (2012, p. 73). Additionally, neu-robiological explanations for behaviour are often assumed to supersede social or psychological perspectives (Choudhury et al., 2009, p. 73). The assumption underlying this research is that there is a truth about brain function that is waiting to be revealed, and, thanks to recent advancements in brain imaging technology, we can now say that 'this is what is *really* going on in the teen brain'. The notion that there is a complete truth to find or discover that is 'out there' (or 'in here' as it concerns our internal bodily processes) remains intact, despite how we are led to certain ideas and understandings about that truth based on what our means and method of investigation are at any one time. A belief that, even with variations in environment and experience, there is a natural order that follows an internally coherent developmental schedule remains intact here. This is what the research, in all its past and future stages, is trying to identify and isolate as this is where a governing presence or ultimate truth about the brain development of youth resides.

However, if experience becomes flesh and flesh (meaning our genetics) has a determining influence over experience, then over time (and over generations) the composition of the flesh, on which analysis is based, should also change[1]. Giedd mentioned previously that the frontal lobe, the centre for reason, has changed the most in our human evolution. Yet here, there is still the assumption that the proliferation/pruning process itself is controlled by something outside one's experience; an as yet unspecified 'trigger' within the brain or the body that has an independent function above and beyond any particular meaning that may be attributed to it by a discourse. This assumption also ensures that the developmental processes of specific parts of the brain can be seen to occur despite exposure to both enabling and inhibiting environmental factors ('use-it-or-lose-it'). To some degree, therefore, reason is able to be pre-determined not only in its physical location but in its specific expression.

But is the capacity of different parts of the brain – cerebellum, corpus callosum, prefrontal cortex, amygdala – to change and grow *before* any specific experience a biological (genetic) determinant or an experiential one? Can the function of both experience-based and genetics-based brain regions, such as the cerebellum (experience) and corpus callosum (genetic), be known *outside* of their growth and change which happens *through experience*, which is always contextual and therefore irreducible to absolute nature? Would the various brain regions and their presumed 'in-built' capacities still sub-serve the prefrontal cortex if external – experiential – conditions are somehow insufficient? What happens if these regions do not get enough of the kinds of experiences (or nurturing) that would enable their in-built capacities to be activated in forging a connection with the frontal lobe, first through proliferation, then in the consolidation of those connections through nerve pruning?

If the proliferation and pruning process itself cannot 'happen' in the absence of experience, if the process is only made 'operative' through experience, and if that experience is made meaningful only through a discourse, then it is actually not a given or a natural imperative. The implication of this fact is that without context there can be no way of knowing what the process 'is' or how it operates, and no way to actually have it happen at all. Giedd poses the question of whether brain development paths are influenced by nutrients or by parenting or by genes (2002, np), but the question cannot really be answered according to the way the question is asked if the question is framed in terms of the pre-determining function of genes. This is because, technically, genetic factors are just as contextual as environmental ones. This is not only because genetic composition changes over time, but because the function that is attributed to genes has no meaning outside context.

By questioning the governing structure of the research which, I argue, can be seen as a form of logocentric reason, we become conscious of its structurality, or the manner of its constitution, and also then its constitutive limits. At work here is a structure of thought that assumes an outside-context or an interior and governing truth that is able to be accessed. But what this deconstructive reading allows us to 'see' is that this truth is actually one specific '*instance* of a general structure' of meaning that is thought to be the '*origin* of that structure' (Lucy, 1995, p. 61). As noted in the previous chapter, to think in terms of a structure of thought whose origins can be pointed to leaves unregistered and thus unseen the general (supplementary) structure that makes such a notion possible at all. In other words, there is a non-recognition of the conditions of intelligibility. To therefore work from this general structure enables us to see that a discussion of origins 'begins' from a place that is already contextual (it structures the notion of absolute origin), which unstructures the truth of the origin as absolute at the same time. As such, a notion of origin which is thought to be elementary, a given, turns out to be dependent and derivate, deprived of its authority as constituting a pure presence (Culler, 2007, p. 94). The effect of this is that a nature/nurture distinction is blurred and we are instead subject to a general (meaning 'enlarged' concept of) experience. In other words, what is thought 'natural' and hence pre-determining is actually 'nurture' specific; it is an effect of experience.

'Feral children'

Two cases of so-called feral children provide an interesting illustration of the constitutive limits of logocentric reason and how the notion and logic of brain development is subject to a general experience. The label 'feral child' is given to children who have grown up with little or no human contact. Some feral children are raised by animals; others survive alone. In other cases, such children have been physically confined and experienced total social isolation (Ward, undated, np). The 2006 case of Oxana Malaya belongs in the former category. Elizabeth Grice reports that Oxana spent five years as a young child living with 'a pack of dogs on a rundown farm near the village of Novaya Blagoveschenka in Ukraine' (2006, np). What is thought to have happened is that when Oxana was three 'her indifferent, alcoholic parents left her outside one night and she crawled into a hovel where they kept dogs' (2006, np). No one came looking for her, 'so she stayed where there was warmth and food – raw meat and scraps' – and, in time, forgot 'what it was to be human', lost 'what toddler's language she had', and learned 'to survive as a member of the pack' (Grice, 2006, np).

A television report on Oxana presented by journalist Tara Brown contrasts her story with the earlier case of Genie, who fits in the latter category of 'feral child'. In the 1970s, Genie's mentally unstable father locked her away in his home in Los Angeles where she endured near total sensory and social confinement for 13 years. Genie was strapped to a potty chair during the day and tied to a bed at night, and consequently she developed no verbal skills, could not walk and was not toilet trained (Brown, 2006, np). Brown states that 'conventional thinking was that language would be impossible' for her, 'but early on Genie confounded the scientists' (2006, np). Linguist Susan Curtiss, who worked with Genie in the years following her discovery, says she learned many words and developed a large vocabulary, but her comprehension of language did not progress any further than this (Brown, 2006, np). In the end, Genie was institutionalised and scientists working with her were barred from any further contact (Brown, 2006, np). Oxana, too, learned language and other basic skills like walking upright and eating with her hands, and she now lives in a home for the mentally disabled (Grice, 2006, np).

What is interesting is that these feral children are reported to have had the potential to develop normally, but due to their neglect, that potential was lost. Dr Bruce Perry suggests that as Genie was without an adequate opportunity for the acquisition of language, the 'neurosystems responsible for speech and language' did not get stimulated 'and because they weren't stimulated, they got smaller and less functional and disconnected', which resulted in actual physical changes to her brain (cited in Brown, 2006, np). Her brain shrank, and not in the way it does in order to have reason emerge, but through lack of use to the point of disability, or at least an incapacity or severely limited capacity for language. Genie was certainly not able to develop to the point of being able to contemplate the nature of her existence; that is, to a point that would satisfy the standard implied by the teen brain research. Yet Curtiss says of Genie: 'she was not mentally deficient – her lights were on, and everyone who worked with her...knew that she was not retarded' (cited in Brown, 2006, np). For Oxana, psychologist Lyn Fry says that while she has an odd language style in that she speaks without any inflection or rhythm in her voice, she does have 'a sense of humour. She likes to be the centre of attention, to make people laugh' (cited in Grice, 2006, np). Grice reports that Oxana's mental capacity has been determined as that of a six-year-old, and six-year-olds certainly have a sense of humour. What Oxana cannot do, though, is 'read or spell her name correctly', and 'she can count but not add up' (Grice, 2006, np). Similarly to Genie, Oxana has fragments of language but no integration of them and therefore no comprehension beyond these fragments, which is the key to intellectual growth. The final assessment is that Oxana 'has learning difficulties, but she is not autistic, as children brought up by animals are sometimes assumed to be' (Grice, 2006, np).

However, Fry mentions that 'the question that's always been asked by people who have studied these children in the past is about what does it really mean to be human' (cited in Brown, 2006, np). Fry suggests that a notion of humanity is associated with language development and that it is generally accepted that language acquisition needs to occur by age five or it doesn't happen at all (Brown, 2006, np). Both Genie and Oxana missed out on developing language during that vital period. In addition, Grice notes that while Oxana's time with the dogs must have included seeing other humans from a distance, she did not belong with them. Now, of course, Oxana does have a degree of language and is orientated towards people (Grice, 2006, np), but, crucially, Perry says, speaking of feral children in general, because they 'have not had the experiences that help their brain organise systems to make sense of the world, the world never makes sense' (cited in Brown, 2006, np), or at least, not *human* sense.

With regard to the issue of brain development, this would seem to confirm that there is no naturally occurring organisation in the brain that is knowable outside someone's experience (and outside a general context for experience). If these feral children have areas of brain shrinkage yet they manage to have some language, then presumably their neural connections were not consolidated beyond the detached elements that provide their basic-level abilities. Or, on the other hand, if a full pruning process *had* taken place, there would have been a severely limited range of connections to secure. So while there may be frontal lobe function in these cases, the intellectual and behavioural outcome would not be much different than if a full pruning process had not taken place. Either way, the function of the frontal lobe, and therefore reason, is specific to experience. But by implication, this would also suggest that language is a decidedly uncertain marker for defining what is human, when a capacity for language may be 'in-built', but when its activation is environment dependent. In other words, the very designation of both the capacity and the developmental process as *natural* presupposes the continued, normal functioning of a process (or set of processes) of *socialisation* as though the latter were likewise a natural phenomenon.

It is perhaps not surprising, then, that Tara Brown's story finishes by affirming Oxana's humanity. Oxana chose to be reunited with her father even after his terrible neglect of her, prompting Brown to suggest that despite her suffering and the fact that it has damaged her brain, Oxana has 'an undeniable spirit and the truly remarkable human gift of forgiveness'. The suggestion made here is that no matter what one's parents may do, the desire for comfort from them prevails over the essentials for survival; it is something we have 'been hard-wired' to do (Brown, 2006, np). So Oxana's humanity is not put in question despite her lacking other desired demarcations of it. This is a comforting thought given that her 'inhumanity' was to some extent forced on her, but it adheres to a notion that something intrinsic and therefore pre-existing her experience is ultimately in charge of who she is. Yet once again, this inner humanity could not be known outside of Oxana's experience or outside of the experience of the rest of us because it is only within a specific context of and for experience that it is possible to conceive of such a notion as a pre-existing humanity or inner state of being. And even if that inner humanity could be known, what would it be if it has no means of expression, no language, if someone is not able to think about themselves *as* human *in* specifically human ways?

Consequences for defining and assigning personhood

The problem highlighted here is that reason, which is defined through and as language, as speech, is still the frame of reference for how growth, development and maturation are not only understood but also calculated. This now also has a direct bearing on how we assign personhood. But in the absence of reason, what counts as belonging to the order of the human? In 2005, the US Supreme Court case *Roper* v. *Simmons* considered whether the death penalty should be applied to people under 18 years of age. The court received and reviewed summaries of neurological evidence showing that the teenage brain is not fully developed, and it finally ruled that juveniles should be exempted from capital punishment (Ross, 2009, p. 183; DeLisi et al., 2010, p. 25). The rationale used by the court in this case was similar to that used in a previous landmark case – *Atkins* v. *Virginia* (2002) – which exempted the mentally retarded from receiving capital punishment (DeLisi et al., 2010, p. 26). Under consideration in both cases were questions of neurological capacity (both cognitive and socio-emotional) and that of 'impaired judgement or reduced ability to appreciate the wrongfulness of one's conduct to the degree that one could ultimately be condemned for that conduct' (DeLisi et al., 2010, p. 26). Noteworthy here is that for some people, a disability or diminished capacity is *normal* and for others it signals abnormality, disease or illness, and for others still, like the feral children, it signals a now-unrecoverable normality. Also, the first of these possible interpretations is used on a scale of *potential* for reason and as a marker of maturation, and the other two are used as a marker of *limitation* and inability to acquire fully functional reason. However, no one option is any more a given than the others, since one is no more obvious or determinable than the others. As Choudhury et al. suggest, 'evaluating mental states as "normal" or not is a task that relies on fragile assumptions and contested criteria' (2009, p. 70), for even if the brains 'look' different on an MRI scan, whether as damaged or just immature, none can be used as the 'control' case, beyond question, especially when reason is experience-dependent (that is, dependent upon a process of socialisation for its establishment and reproduction). In the absence of reason in its ideal and fully developed (adult) form, normal and abnormal therefore share a certain kind of equality.

This lack of distinction will be addressed again in Chapter 6 concerning attempts by authorities in the wake of the Columbine massacre to distinguish between youth behaviour that indicates criminal intent and youth behaviour that constitutes a 'normal' or expected level of teen maladjustment. To continue with the current line of investigation, though, a further point to make is that what counts as diminished capacity is not even diminished if we consider that it also constitutes someone's total brain capacity. Whether or not that is seen as an expanding totality – as a series of successive stages of total ability that accumulate over time towards full prefrontal cortex function – does not alter the fact that of or within itself, the brain is not missing anything. But is someone any less of a person because of this? Can we think in terms of a scale of personhood, or of a coming or becoming of the self, based on this?

Elizabeth Roudinesco considers this issue in a dialogue with Derrida. She expresses concern over the issue of granting human rights as opposed to animal rights to great apes

> based on the idea that, on the one hand, great apes are endowed with cognitive structures enabling them to learn language in the same way as humans, and on the other hand, they are more 'human' than those humans suffering from madness, senility, or organic illnesses that … deprive them of reason.
>
> (cited in Derrida and Roudinesco, 2004, p. 62)

Roudinesco argues that proponents of this project

> trace a dubious border between the human and the nonhuman by relegating the mentally handicapped to a biological species no longer belonging to the human kingdom, while also placing the great apes within another biological species integrated into the human.
>
> (cited in Derrida and Roudinesco, 2004, p. 62)

An equally dubious border is being traced, though perhaps not deliberately, with regard to young people and the question of their humanity with the force of scientific 'truth' behind it. Derrida's response to Roudinesco is that 'the "question of animality" is not [just] one question among others' as it

> represents the limit upon which all the great questions are formed and determined, as well as all the concepts that attempt to delimit what is 'proper to man', the essence and future of humanity, ethics, politics, law, 'human rights', 'crimes against humanity', 'genocide', etc.
>
> (cited in Derrida and Roudinesco, 2004, p. 63)

Given the decision in *Roper* v. *Simmons* on demarcations of criminal culpability, this list of what is 'proper to man' should include 'human responsibilities' as well. Derrida continues: 'the modern concept of right depends massively on the Cartesian moment of the *cogito*, of subjectivity, freedom, sovereignty, etc.', and 'to confer or to recognise rights for "animals" is a surreptitious or implicit way of confirming a certain interpretation of the human subject' based on this moment (cited in

Derrida and Roudinesco, 2004, p. 65). So granting human rights to great apes by necessity means excluding the mentally ill (Roudinesco cited in Derrida and Roudinesco, 2004, p. 67), and also youth and anyone who is deemed inadequate to reason. As Roudinesco remarks, 'the entire rhetoric depends on a claim . . . of an alleged passage from the human to the nonhuman that would be linked to the existence of neurological or cerebrally degenerative illnesses' (cited in Derrida and Roudinesco, 2004, p. 67). Given teen brain research, this passage can be linked to *generative* processes as well. This 'certain interpretation of the human subject' is a very narrow one, and leaves only a narrow window for its 'achievement'.

This issue has not gone unremarked upon in the literature on teen brain science. Sarah Spinks comments that 'knowing more about the *structure* of the brain does not necessarily tell us more about the *function* of the brain' (2002, np). While it makes sense to suggest that immature brain structures will translate into immature behaviour, the notion of function is more complicated than this (Spinks, 2002, np). For Kelly, technologies enable us to represent brain activity and processes but 'it does not follow that this simulation of brain activity provides evidence that these regions of the brain do, indeed, determine the nature of consciousness, of reason, of irrationality' (2012, p. 954). Similarly, Sercombe argues that images of the brain that show areas of activation in response to stimulus are not someone's thoughts. 'To go from there to judgements about limitations in capacity requires a great deal of interpretive work which takes place against a backdrop of what we think we already know about young people' (2010a, pp. 74–5). Philosopher John Bruer is also critical of the simple notion that teens exhibit difficult behaviour because of the immaturity of their frontal lobes. Bruer contends that

this notion [that] there's going to be some easy connection between counting synapses or measuring white matter and the kinds of behaviours people display or we want them to display is one we're going to have to do a lot more work on before it's science.

(cited in Spinks, 2002, np)

Reason cannot 'come'

Such cautionary words pick up on issues already discussed but also point to the need for a further unpacking of the teen brain research concerning the links between teen physiology, their 'difficult' behaviour and what that means for definitions and demarcations of humanity. If we continue for a while longer to accept the neural pruning process as pre-determined, and also therefore the ultimate location and character of reason in the brain as neurological 'fact', then to speak of teens' unreason or irrationality, even intermittent reason, is not just to imagine it as 'faulty' or 'false' reason, it is to speak of something that has no relationship to reason at all, precisely because reason is not 'there' yet. As purely a matter of 'counting synapses or measuring white matter', the presence of reason is about what connections are firing where and what parts of the brain have been through the pruning process and are for all intents and purposes 'set in their ways'. So reason cannot 'appear' until the frontal lobe is fully functional: reason does not, cannot, have a scale of function *and* still have a specific totality.

But how does one grow *into* reason when its proper and only function is specific to the activity of the frontal lobe? What would be the point, for example, of teaching an adolescent to think and act reasonably when they literally lack the ability to do so? It would make more sense to wait until they are 25 when they have consolidated all their brain functions, except that, by then, it would be too late to make any permanent changes due to the loss of brain plasticity. Adolescence *is* the time to teach and to become reasonable (and responsible, and mature, and able to control impulses and avoid risks, and so on), but it is also the time when the brain is not prepared to fully do this.

This is borne out by research that suggests that risky behaviour occurs because the cognitive processes responsible for impulse control and risky decisions mature at different rates (Casey et al., 2008, pp. 63&65). Psychologist Laurence Steinberg contends that 'risk-taking increases between childhood and adolescence' due to the development of what he calls 'the brain's *socio-emotional system*' that leads 'to increased reward-seeking, especially in the presence of peers'. Risk-taking then 'declines between adolescence and adulthood because of changes in ... the brain's *cognitive control system*' which is responsible for a capacity to self-regulate and which develops 'gradually over the course of adolescence and young adulthood' (2008, p. 83). The difficulty is that these changes work to different timetables. Teens engage in risky behaviour because the brain's processes concerning pleasure seeking and assessing risk versus reward mature sooner than the brain's cognitive control system that is capable of moderating that behaviour. As such, Steinberg suggests that mid-adolescence is 'a time of heightened vulnerability to risky and reckless behaviour' (2008, p. 83).

This mismatch between the developmental timing of these brain systems is speculated to have an evolutionary purpose. Thrill seeking, for instance, promotes exploration and develops independence (Wallis, 2004, p. 51). Dodds writes that 'anthropologists have found that virtually all the world's cultures recognise adolescence as a distinct period in which adolescents prefer novelty, excitement and peers' and these traits work to produce 'a creature optimally primed to leave a safe home and move into unfamiliar territory' (2011, p. 55). The ability to adapt to new environments is and has been vital to human survival, and teens are ideally placed to do this. What is not universal, however, are the activities young people engage in. In a contemporary Western context such a natural exploratory drive includes drinking alcohol, smoking, reckless driving, taking illicit drugs and practising unsafe sex. These behaviours are considered very risky, if not life threatening. This is all the more frightening because the brain's cognitive control system is yet to fully mature. In fact, Giedd thinks that it's 'a particularly cruel irony of nature . . . that right at this time when the brain is most vulnerable is also the time when teens are most likely to experiment with drugs or alcohol' (2002, np). While it doesn't take much to point out that conceptions of risk and risky behaviour are time and culture specific – so it is a mistake to assume that teens are *naturally* drawn to drugs, alcohol and unsafe sex – it is a lack of coordination between emotional and cognitive control systems, and the illicit temptations offered by Western cultures, that leads Steinberg to suggest that teens actually constitute a 'public health problem' (2008, p. 79).

Research also indicates, however, that teens are not unthinking – as in, impulsive and spontaneous in a purely reactive sense – but actually think *more* than adults when making decisions about risk. Rivers et al., (2008) offer an alternative to conventional assumptions that teens are overly emotional and impulsive, which makes them prone to making rash and poor decisions. They suggest that 'instead of assuming that development progresses from hot intuitive thinking to cold calculation bypassing emotion', studies show that 'intuition is developmentally advanced and that emotion is integral to intuition' (Rivers et al., 2008, p. 108). What the authors call 'fuzzy-trace theory' focuses on how 'people represent, retrieve, and process information when they make decisions, and how decision making changes with development' (Rivers et al., 2008, p. 108). In this theory, adult-level thinking is characterised as 'gist-based intuition' (which is considered a 'fuzzy' style of reasoning) in which the core meaning or bottom line of a situation or a decision is intuitively assessed; an ability that reflects an adult's level of knowledge, understanding and experience (Rivers et al., 2008, pp. 109&116). This is contrasted to a 'verbatim style of reasoning' that is attributed to youth. This kind of thinking is deliberative and analytical and relies on learning facts and committing details to memory in order to make a decision (Reyna and Farley, 2007, p. 65). According to this theory, mature thinking actually appears to be more 'irrational' because it doesn't necessarily involve a deliberate or conscious analysis of risk and reward. But being able to filter out unnecessary detail and to quickly assess the meaning of information or a situation is considered a sign of expertise (Rivers et al., 2008, pp. 109&117). Immature thinking may therefore be described as involving a greater amount of thought, and Reyna and Farley state that 'when it comes to risk', studies show 'that teens actually tend to *overestimate* rather than underestimate the true risks of potential actions' (2007, p. 63).

However, while teen thinking may be described as more calculated, even more rational, the problem is that this translates to 'suboptimal choice behaviour' (Casey et al., 2008, p. 63) or 'unhealthy risk taking' (Rivers et al. 2008, p. 108), and as such requires preventative action and intervention. Dodds writes that 'teens take more risks not because they don't understand the dangers but because they weigh risk versus reward differently' (2011, p. 54) and that is due not to a dominance of affect over thinking, but a lack of coordination between affect and thinking (Steinberg, 2008, p. 97). If teens' socio-emotional systems are more developed than their control regions at the front of the brain, then the perceived benefits of a risky action (like receiving admiration from one's mates for jumping off a roof) will likely outweigh the perceived risks (like that of serious injury or even death). Reyna and Farley suggest that a way to address unhealthy risk-taking in teens is to incorporate gist-based thinking into teen behavioural intervention programmes; that is, train teens to think more intuitively and less logically (2007, p. 64). Steinberg suggests 'limiting opportunities for immature judgement to have harmful consequences' (2008, p. 99). He advocates that raising the driving age, increasing adolescent access to mental health and contraceptive services, and developing tighter regulations on the sale of alcohol would prove more effective in limiting risk taking than 'attempts to make adolescents wiser, less impulsive, or less shortsighted' (2008, pp. 99–100).

But to lower exposure to risk, to manage teens' experience of risk and make risk 'safer', is to limit the scope for developing gist-based intuition and for actually developing the prefrontal cortex. Sercombe argues that 'taking risks is precisely the experience that develops the pre frontal cortex', so to prevent young people from taking risks could therefore mean 'consigning them to a conservative and fear-driven adulthood that does not know how to assess and manage risks healthily' (2010a, p. 76). Similarly, Bessant contends that 'if we accept that emotions and experience are essential to rational thinking, "good judgement" and "normal social behaviour" ', then protective/prohibitive measures such as increasing voting age, drinking age and the age of legal liability and sexual consent 'will actively work to prevent or inhibit young people from having the encounters they need to develop intuition, insight and perception' (2008, p. 358).

Exactly what is being expected of teenagers here is unclear: respond to an evolutionary call to explore one's environment but do not take unhealthy risks or be exposed to serious risk. The possibility for serious risk needs to be contained, but an ability to control oneself in risky situations needs to be developed for long-term survival. How realistic are these expectations, given teens' level of brain maturation? Do teens actually possess the neurological capacity for it? If intuitive, gist-based reason is considered a superior form of intelligence to a verbatim style of reasoning, and if we accept the notion that a fully functional reason (or responsibility or moral accountability or impulse control) has a specific totality (so to be 'less than' is to not be 'it' at all), then it is only possible to judge teens as being in 'error' when held to a notion of reason (as intuitive and gist-based). But teens are also doing what is normal and necessary from an evolutionary perspective; they are not in error at all, their brains are in fact doing the 'right' thing: preparing for adult-level function. On this basis, reason cannot come if teens are inhibited or prevented from doing what comes 'naturally' to them because such behaviour constitutes unacceptable risk. Furthermore, reason cannot come if 'true' (and ideal) reason exists only when there is consistent frontal cortex function, and if the ability to exercise reason constitutes the key boundary in determining what makes us human. We must therefore define teen brains in terms of deficiency and lack, even as this undermines how youth develop requisite cognitive skills for mature reason, and even as this implies that a growing brain (and a diseased brain) is technically an inhuman brain (that is, for any science or metaphysics that equates humanity with *complete* reason, with a final and total reason). These parameters for reason also implicitly put in question the primary nature and authority of the cogito. If the cogito comes first, how can it be grown into, based on these conceptions of brain development?

Another issue to contend with here is that current neurological theory positions teens as actually being more in touch with their senses than adults. They engage in verbatim thinking rather than intuitive thinking. The baser, sensory-controlling and emotion-driven areas of the brain go through neural pruning first, while the neural connections that interpret and manage these systems and senses are still developing. This means that teens are, in one sense, too rational, but in another sense, they have an underdeveloped capacity to doubt their senses (as in, knowing that something is too risky despite how it may appear). Hence, teens have an underdeveloped capacity to effect a distance between the truth of the senses and the truth of the self, a distance which is required if reason is to come.

Madness within reason

It is this lack of distance, a lack of mediation between the senses and the self, that is the problem here. This reflects the work of René Descartes and his establishment of the certainty of the self in the cogito. Derrida writes that Descartes sought to 'rid himself of all the opinions in which he had hitherto believed' but which turned out to be false (1978, p. 45). Descartes sought to do so, on this account, by deliberately doubting all his opinions, beginning with those established via the most natural foundation of knowledge: sensation. Descartes reasoned that if his senses could deceive him sometimes then they could deceive him all the time so he therefore submitted to doubt all knowledge originating from sensation (Derrida, 1978, p. 45). This work of doubting all that which it is possible to doubt, from his body to the sanity of his own thoughts, led Descartes – in 1642 – to the ultimate certainty of the cogito (I think, therefore I am) and to the dominance since then of Cartesian reason over unreason or madness. As indicated at the beginning of this chapter concerning logocentrism, what cannot be doubted is the presence of the being who is able to think the possibility that everything might be false. On the basis of this reasoning, Descartes can therefore question everything, including whether he might be mad. But that one is able to think whether or not one is deceived by one's senses means that one is not mad because 'reason provides grounds for doubting everything' (Lucy, 1995, p. 52). But on Derrida's reading of Descartes' argument, it also means that 'reason is madder than madness... and... madness is more rational than reason' (Derrida, 1978, p. 62). Reason reaches towards 'nonmeaning and oblivion' whereas madness 'is closer to the wellspring of sense'

(Derrida, 1978, p. 62), but it is also a 'state of not being in doubt' (Lucy, 1995, p. 52).

This division between reason and madness is similar to how youth is understood according to fuzzy-trace theory. As noted above, this theory suggests that young people exhibit a greater degree of logical thought than adults; their decisions are based on the deliberate assessment of information available to them from their immediate environment. But due to the immaturity of teens' cognitive control mechanisms compared to their socio-emotional systems, they will often fail to accurately assess the potential risks of a situation. While teens engage a verbatim form of reasoning, they fail to doubt their senses, which often results in 'sense-less' behaviour. In contrast, adults do not wholly rely on the 'truth' of their senses to grasp meaning, but will draw on a reserve of previous knowledge, experience and a fully developed frontal lobe to ascertain the 'gist' of a situation. This may involve doubting what the material circumstances of a situation appear to be – which may not seem like a logical thing to do – but intuitive-style thinking produces more rational behaviour.

This division of reason and madness also shows how the difference between youths and adults is commonly thought of in terms of a binary opposition between innocence and knowledge (the operation of which is examined in relation to the issue of young female sexuality in the next chapter). However, this binary implies that in our (adult) capacity to reason intuitively, we cannot presume to know what the reality of someone who is not working from their frontal cortex 'looks like' because anything we might come up with would belong to an order that (Cartesian or logocentric) reason makes possible, which is not where they are. But of course, not to judge youth as being in error, or as being in a state of lack, means risking the privilege and priority of reason, its necessity, as well.

Rather than this inability to access youth reality leading to an impasse, Derrida reads in Descartes a non-absolute separation of reason and unreason that is most useful in picking up and dealing with the problems raised here concerning the coming of reason in the teen brain. According to Derrida, Michel Foucault saw Descartes' reason as leading to the exclusion and objectification of madness, which is why Foucault wrote a history of madness before its capture and internment by reason (1978, pp. 33–4). For Foucault, the silencing of the language of madness in the mid-seventeenth century had to occur in order for reason to become the primary form of human knowledge in the Western world (Lucy, 1995, p. 49). But Derrida's own reading of Descartes as a response to Foucault argues that the latter's project is flawed because, by definition, the absolute silence of madness as Foucault sees it is unable to be articulated and is thus irretrievable in and of itself (Lucy, 1995, p. 55). Foucault's project is also flawed, on Derrida's account, because Descartes never specifically excludes madness from his understanding of reason (1978, p. 55). Instead, Derrida writes, 'if discourse and philosophical communication (that is, language itself) are to have an intelligible meaning...they must simultaneously in fact and in principle escape madness' (1978, p. 53). This is 'an essential and universal necessity from which no discourse can escape, for it belongs to the meaning of meaning' (Derrida, 1978, p. 53). Before any determined history of reason or madness is posited, 'to make a sentence is to *manifest* a possible meaning', and 'by its essence, the sentence is normal. It carries normality within it, that is, *sense*, in every sense of the word' and this is the case 'whatever the health or madness of him who propounds it' (Derrida, 1978, p. 54). This means that madness can only be invoked 'from the *interior* of thought' and only in 'the realm of the *possible*', which is language. It also means that madness is for that reason not senseless (Derrida, 1978, p. 54).

From this, Derrida argues that it is possible to understand that the logos is a reason with a history, but also that a madness-in-general, 'beyond any...determined historical structure', that is, silence, is what opens up '*historicity in general*' (1978, p. 54). Here, Derrida notes that beyond 'a determined silence, imposed at one given moment...silence plays the irreducible role of that which bears and haunts language, outside and *against* which alone language can emerge' (1978, p. 54). So without this general absence or silence, specific determinations of reason and unreason would not be able to be made at all. The implication of this is that the lack of mature, intuitive reason that is here attributed to youth is 'only one *case* of thought (*within* thought)' (Derrida, 1978, p. 56). Furthermore, Derrida argues, the certainty of the cogito need not imprison a notion of madness, not only because the cogito is determined from within madness, but because 'it is valid *even if I am mad*' (1978, p. 55). In other words:

> even if the totality of what I think is imbued with falsehood or madness, even if the totality of the world does not exist, even if nonmeaning has invaded the totality of the world, up to and including the very contents of my thoughts, I still think, I am *while* I think.
>
> (Derrida, 1978, p. 56)

So with regard to the death penalty, for example, it is not simply a matter of deciding if youth are responsible or not, because there would always be 'method in the madness', so to speak. The research cited in the previous section suggested that a quantitative, calculative and deliberate assessment process defines teen thought. But the death penalty is premised on a responsibility that is based in a reason that emerges from the full function of the frontal cortex. It is a reason that speaks on and thinks about the self in a logocentric way and one that has to think that madness has no method otherwise the death penalty could never be justified because we would never be able to make a decision (beyond reasonable doubt) on whether someone did not have reason. Hence we would never be able to exempt young people from a responsibility for their actions under reason.

Reason cannot *not* 'come'

The point here is that there is no outside to a general reason (or general experience). As Derrida argues, silence is the 'limit and profound resource' of meaning and so, because it is inaccessible in itself, non-meaning does not reside in any 'outside' that could be determined (1978, p. 54). While teens may be thought to lack high-order, gist-based reasoning ability, because they have language, they are within a general reason. This means that reason cannot *not* come because there is no truth of youth that could be known that is not already of the order of reason in general. This is to suggest that we are not missing out on anything with regard to youth; there is nothing 'out there' that we cannot touch about their true natures. Lucy writes that since Descartes offered a separation of reason and madness in the definition of the cogito, reason was installed as the only means of attaining knowledge. To attempt to think outside reason is therefore possible only from within a space that is produced by reason (1995, p. 54). This means that even if young people's senses, perceptions and therefore their reality is not the same as that of adults, this can only be analysed from within the limits of reason.

On this basis, it would therefore be *unreasonable* to think or to suggest that teens do not have or do not belong to reason, that they do not belong to its order of presence and all the things that make us human. There is of course no suggestion in the literature that teen subjects do not belong to the order of the human, but it is implied in the non-recognition of the general structure of reason in which teen brain researchers are already working. The problem is that without an awareness of this general structure, there is no thinking beyond the demarcations of a 'reason in particular', and so too what counts as 'unreason in particular'. However, if Derrida's argument holds, to be without recourse to a certain conceptualisation of reason does not leave us without reason at all; rather, it leaves us with the capacity to generate other conceptualisations of reason. But what this lack of recourse does do is problematise reason and the cogito as exclusively belonging to the prefrontal cortex. Except that if reason is not located here, then where?

The answer is that reason *is* of the brain if mind and matter are understood to be inseparable. Derrida claims that in the traditional speech/writing opposition, 'the voice', as 'producer of *the first symbols*, has a relationship of essential and immediate proximity with the mind' (1997, p. 11). Therefore, 'all signifiers, and first and foremost the written signifier, are derivative with regard to what would wed the voice indissolubly to the mind' (Derrida, 1997, p. 11). As such, speech requires no outside or additional signifier for its own expression. But, given the teen brain topic, teen 'speech' is not granted the same status as the notion of speech Derrida is discussing here with regard to the metaphysics of presence. Teen speech has been shown to be wholly matter-bound insofar as teens' capacity for thought is understood to be in direct relation to their neuronal function and the coordination of different cognitive regions. However, even if locatable in the brain, reason supposedly transcends such limitations because it allows for one to think abstractly, propositionally and beyond direct sense impressions. In this way, adult speech may be matter-based, but it is not matter-bound. But what Derrida points to that would mark teen speech as comparable to adult speech – that would mark speech, as the privileged marker of presence, as physical – is that there is a temporalisation of the cogito in the moment that thought becomes aware of itself (1978, p. 58). This means that where logocentrism assumes that immediate and spontaneous intuition is possible, the physical nature of speech (or mind) can be taken as the mediating factor between thought, word and truth.

The textuality of reason

Derrida examines this notion of the temporality of speech through Freud and his work on the graphic representation of psychic content. According to Derrida, Freud understands the nature and quality of the psyche to come about because of a 'breaching' that first opens up a path to perception and memory – and therefore to consciousness – through the different characteristics of neurones; their contact, force and resistance. Some neurones are permeable and don't retain any trace of impression, whereas other neurones do retain an imprint, and Freud attributes psychical quality to the latter (Derrida, 1978, pp. 200–1). On this basis, Derrida writes that it is the 'difference between breaches which is the true origin of memory, and thus of the psyche' (1978, p. 201). But a determination of quality or of content is not found 'in' the trace or impression itself; rather, the initial imprint is what opens up a path to meaning (Derrida, 1978, p. 201). Derrida suggests – on his reading of Freud – that it is because of the trace that there is thought, but thought is dependent on an initial deferral (impression). Accordingly, thought has a temporal quality rather than an immediate proximity and self-presence and to think of the self is to work from this place of difference.

Derrida contends that this temporality of consciousness gives it a written character. In the way that writing is thought secondary to or derivative of self-present speech in the speech/writing opposition, Derrida suggests that an expanded notion of writing actually conditions the possibility of speech. If 'life must be thought of as trace before Being may be determined as presence', then there is 'differance at the origin' (1978, p. 203). Derrida uses the term 'differance' to refer to the operation of the trace in language. Something 'is' in its difference from all other things, so to be what it 'is' it must be deferred from itself, a 'deferred presence' (1982, p. 9). A sign 'represents the present in its absence' and 'the circulation of signs defers the moment in which we can encounter the thing itself' (Derrida, 1982, p. 9). This means that 'the concept of *primariness*' is crossed out and defined instead as a 'theoretical fiction' (Derrida, 1978, p. 203). Derrida argues, however, that to differ and defer does not mean 'to retard a present possibility, to postpone an act, to put off a perception', but to enable it (1978, p. 203). What further confirms the written quality of the psyche, on Derrida's account of Freud's work, is that the quality of consciousness requires an environment for it to be determined. While there are many sensations, their difference, in Freud's words, 'is distinguished... according to its relations with the external world' (cited in Derrida, 1978, p. 204). Thus, 'even before being determined as human... or nonhuman, the *grammè* – or the *grapheme* – would thus name the element' (Derrida, 1997, p. 9). For Derrida, this naming issues from a trace, and even as the trace itself is unable to be marked with a meaning or a presence, it has its basis in matter. So the self emerges from a space of (both physical and metaphysical) differance. However, differance is something that logocentric reason cannot contain or account for and still be itself, yet reason is dependent on differance for its very possibility.

This formulation of the self can be used to address the call for a rationality which 'no longer issues from a logos'. Derrida's work suggests that it is our limited reason that demands we find a point of absolute origin in explaining reason and presence. While it may seem unreasonable to suggest that there is no locatable point of origin for reason (because what would be the point to anything if there were no good reason for it?), if Derrida is right, then we could never know such a point of origin *and* operate from it. Operating from such an origin would require that the centre or origin be 'of' the structure it posits rather than what grounds the structure and what is therefore outside it. To point to the centre could only be done from within the structure, so what is pointed to would not be what its origin 'is'. Derrida contends that the origin is only ever a substitution or supplement, albeit the only 'centre' we can use, think or work from. In other words, there 'is' differance (textuality, contextuality) from which it becomes possible to *think* the mind/body, human/non-human, reason/unreason, genetics/environment distinctions. And if the primary or privileged term in the pair is itself 'secondary' to the originary trace, then, as argued in Chapter 3, it depends on the secondary term for its meaning, which is to say that the secondary term is what actually conditions the possibility of the so-called primary one. In this formation, the determined meanings of each as deployed in research on the teen brain and from within the metaphysics of presence no longer have a fixed status, so what constitutes the 'absence' of youth can be made differently, even as it must remain other to whatever constitutes 'adult'.

Moreover, in this conceptual order, the 'priority' of youth over adulthood no longer represents the antithesis of reason. As Derrida argues, 'from the moment that there is meaning there are nothing but signs. We *think only in signs*' (1997, p. 50). Any notion, word or concept that refers to a pre-contextual origin or unified presence 'is *always already in the position of the signifier*' as opposed to being that originary thing itself (Derrida, 1997, p. 73). To use Derrida's key phrase: 'there is nothing outside the text' (1997, p. 158). Or in other words, 'everything begins then in representation, *as* representation, and can never leave this behind' (Lucy, 2004, p. 89).

On this basis, while reason is ultimately *of* the brain (the neuron as originary trace) it is also not strictly *in* the brain. In Kelly's words, 'the brain provides the architecture for consciousness, but it does not determine consciousness, reason, irrationality' (2012, p. 954). If the actuality of reason as it is understood in teen brain research has no presence outside representation, then it cannot be pointed to other than as a representation. In this work, the MRI scan and other types of brain imaging have been used as the tools for representing the teen brain, for observing it, for locating reason within the brain and for providing proof of how and why teens behave the way they do. But, on Derrida's account, actuality 'comes to us by way of a fictional fashioning' (2002, p. 3). If, as noted above, everything begins as representation, then actuality is not given but made – it is 'actively produced', such that the MRI scan does not provide a transparent perception of the teen brain that is 'stripped of interpretation' (Derrida, 2002, pp. 3&5). Rather, interpretation on the brain will have always already begun because all meaning is contextual. So whatever the scan may show, whatever overall picture of the brain is produced from it, what it means is not intrinsic to either the scan or to the growing brain it depicts.

This insight supports arguments from Kelly (2012), Sercombe (2010a, 2010b), Bessant (2008) and Males (2009; 2010) that scanning technology does not provide direct, discourse-free, values-neutral evidence to explain youth behaviour. It also supports claims from critical neuroscience and its call for a *'reflexive turn'* in the neuroscientific field (Choudhury et al., 2009, p. 65). Choudhury et al. write that

> studying how certain social, political and economic factors push a particular topic under the scientific gaze, and support certain explanatory narratives, allows us to understand why a certain question about the brain gains significance over others at any one time.
>
> (2009, p. 64)

As concerns questions about teen brain development, what constitutes the actuality of reason, what demarcates 'youth' and 'adult' in relation to this, and what constitutes the actuality of unreason and mental illness, comes as a result of a decision-making process which takes place under a certain set of social, political and economic conditions. Articulated from a deconstructive perspective, reason is a textual effect and, as such, there is no already 'right' answer as to what reason is or means or how it develops that is grounded in undeconstructible presence. Such a notion is itself only thinkable from within a contextual field; it is an effect of an originary difference, or double movement, where what structures the notion of presence is also what unstructures it.

To operate with an awareness of the supplementary status of reason, or to be reflexive about how knowledge about the self is being produced, thus opens the way for taking responsibility for its effects, rather than being undermined by them because they exceed the limits of what is taken to be a naturally apparent or self-evident truth. As argued here, an attempt to explain how teen brains develop that uses a developmental discourse grounded in assumptions of logocentric reason ends up signalling the limits of the explanatory logic that is in use. This logic produces effects that exceed or cannot be contained by the order from which they proceed. The effect of this is to put teens' humanity in question, which in turn risks the humanity of the rest of us by putting in question the very logic with which we make such determinations.

There is only so much to be 'discovered' about youth brain function if an interpretive order produced and legitimated by a notion of logocentric reason, truth and presence is taken for granted. In order to keep the notion of (adult) rationality intact, the teen brain research can do no more than assert that teens behave in baffling, inconsistent ways, and confirm the 'enduring stereotype' of youth as a time of 'turbulence, exuberance and passion' (Heaven, 2001, p. 24). Given these discursive parameters, this is all there would be to 'find'. Indeed, despite research findings that suggest that teens are not unthinking, such research could not find teens to be anything but irrational (and all the kinds of behaviours associated with this) otherwise the very meaning and distinction of reason would be lost.

It is perhaps not surprising, then, that for all the claims that this kind of research offers unprecedented insight into the teen brain and has the potential to revolutionise our understanding of youth, the research findings adhere to what is already well known about youth. Giedd tells us that 'the more technical and more advanced the science becomes, often the more it leads us back to some very basic tenets of spending loving, quality time with our children' (2002, np). He admits that 'sometimes it's even disappointing to people that, with all the science and all the advances, the best advice we can give is things that our grandmother could have told us generations ago' (2002, np). While this may well be good advice, it's not all that unexpected that this advice should be offered given the implicit assumptions of the interpretive context.

What is enabled, however, by applying Derrida's work is a way beyond the limits of thinking grounded in assumptions of presence and scientific truth. By recognising the supplementarity of the grounding assumptions of the research, it is still possible to seek to understand why teens behave the way they do and how reason develops, but without an assumption that teen behaviour is determined by their absolute nature. Instead, it is possible to see that teen behaviour is framed by the discourses in use that *structure* a notion of absolute nature. As highlighted by Sercombe at the beginning of the chapter, the dominant discourse of adolescence provides the contextual 'atmosphere' for researchers. This discourse posits youth as a universal life stage that is 'inherently troublesome and difficult' (Sercombe, 2010b, p. 43). But, for Sercombe, if commentators are not actively aware of the discourse and its dominance over other ways of thinking, if they do not work to notice its 'gravitational pull', then they will be led to mark young people as pathological in accordance with these assumptions about youth (Sercombe, 2010b, p. 44). In other words, teens behave the way they do because of what dominant discourses make possible or allow and also what they limit or constrain. At present, the notion of reason that is in use in attempts to map teen brain development cannot account for how that notion of reason develops physiologically.

What this deconstructive reading is pressing towards, then (and in support of the aims of a critical neuroscience), is not just the possibility but the *need* to think differently about how this research contributes to and calls on youth discourse in conceptualising and understanding youth. The critique performed here suggests that, when it comes to questions of youth development, not attending to youth at a conceptual level would lead to a need for more research, because the findings could only confirm the ideas about youth this particular body of research began with – irrational, dangerous, immature teen behaviour. And unfortunately for young people, these ideas are often prejudicial. For Bessant, the teen brain entails prejudicial assumptions similar to those associated with 'the "Jewish brain," the "female brain" or the "Negro brain"' which have been used to explain these groups as both problematic and different (2008, p. 357). But, as mentioned above, by considering the textuality or contextuality from which the science proceeds, instead of affirming 'prejudices and taken-for-granted assumptions while offering authoritative scientific explanations for those views' (Bessant, 2008, p. 357), it is possible to *decide* what different brain regions do and mean and therefore decide the demarcations of 'youth' and 'adult' in relation to it. This allows for consideration of the effects or consequences of such decisions and, if necessary, for different decisions to be made. In doing so, a way of thinking is opened up which would enable a youth/adult distinction and an order of reason to remain intact but in a way that would not necessarily make demands of itself that it could not meet. Such a conceptual move would allow youth to follow through on what they are 'supposed' to do: become adult. It is this issue – how youth 'come of age' – that is taken up in the next chapter.

5
Presumed Innocent: The Paradox of 'Coming of Age' and the Problem of Youth Sexuality

The previous chapter examined the effects of a developmental discourse operating within cognitive science, revealing its limitations in explaining the development of reasoning ability in young people. This chapter continues my concern with the way 'youth' is conceptualised as a 'problem' and the need for greater reflexivity in accounting for the conditions of this conceptualisation. With respect to extreme public concern about the sexualisation of culture and its harmful impact on girls and young women, I argue here that part of the 'problem' of youth sexuality is the very function of the concepts of youth that are called on to make sense of it. Specifically, this chapter analyses three films that foreground questions of young female sexuality in order to deconstruct the discourse of 'coming of age'. This is a different way to approach the problematic nature of young female sexuality than that offered by contemporary debates on the sexualisation of youth, which predominantly focus on the negative impact of media culture on young girls' development. However, as this is a formative context for discussing female sexuality, I will briefly outline the phenomenon of sexualisation and some of its scholarly explanations in order to further explain and situate my approach.

The sexualisation of youth

Concerns about the sexualisation of youth (and of culture more generally) came to prominence with the release of reports from the American Psychological Association (APA, 2007), papers from the Australia Institute on so-called corporate paedophilia and the sexualisation of children (Rush and La Nauze, 2006a, 2006b) and a later report from the United Kingdom (Bailey, 2011). Rush and La Nauze define sexualisation as 'the act of giving someone or something a sexual character' (2006a, p. 1), and the APA report suggests that 'when children are imbued with adult sexuality, it is often imposed upon them rather than chosen by them' (APA, 2007, p. 1). Rush and La Nauze argue that contemporary media culture is putting pressure on children to adopt sexualised 'appearance and behaviour' in a way that prematurely advances an otherwise 'slowly developing sexuality' (2006a, p. 1). They suggest that the sexualisation of children is a problem because the advertising and marketing industries encourage precocity, pushing children to develop too soon and in unhealthy ways (2006a, p. 3). These papers, along with a range of books on the issue (see, e.g., Olfman, 2008; Oppliger, 2008; Durham, 2009; Levin and Kilbourne, 2009; Tankard Reist, 2009; Dines, 2010; Walter, 2010), articulate the alarming ways in which girls and their otherwise slow, natural sexual development is being insidiously compressed, exploited and downright abused by the marketing and advertising industries and the mainstreaming of pornography. As a result, it is believed that irreparable damage is being done to children's mental, social and emotional development.

The literature on the sexualisation of children, youth, and of culture more broadly, suggests that across film and television, literature, magazines and music and in celebrity culture contemporary versions of femininity (as empowered), female sexuality (as on display and always available) and ideal physical appearance (as slim, toned and waxed) are presented in terms of girls' and women's freedom, empowerment and choice to be themselves. However, it is argued that these terms do not denote the realisation of gender, political or economic equality or any kind of genuine choice or means of self-expression. Rather, they translate to a reinforcement of a narrow and deeply patriarchal heteronormativity, which is implicitly white and middle class, as well as being grounded in consumption as a means for constructing the self (Tasker and Negra, 2007, pp. 2–3). Young women 'freely' choose to express themselves in ways that maintain their positioning as objects of the male gaze. They act 'for themselves', they manage their own bodies and actions for their own pleasure, but that pleasure mostly involves receiving male attention and approval and inciting male sexual desire.

This freedom of consumption and self-production aligns contemporary femininity and sexuality with the ideals of neoliberalism. Rosalind Gill and Christina Scharff write that 'the autonomous, calculating, self-regulating subject of neoliberalism bears a strong resemblance to the active, freely choosing, self-reinventing subject of postfeminism' (2011, p. 7). As young women take individual responsibility for their bodies and sexualities, as they self-manage, regulate, monitor and discipline themselves in relation to cultural messages about what is desirable, so they become the 'ideal subjects' of neoliberalism (Gill and Scharff, 2011, p. 7). That is, they act according to ideals of individualism rather than notions of the social or political, and do not acknowledge the ways in which individuals are subject to external influences, pressures and constraints (Gill and Scharff, 2011, p. 7).

In this context of female sexual freedom and individual choice, the era of 'postfeminism' is thus also named. While 'postfeminism' is a contested term with multiple meanings and forms of usage (Gill and Scharff, 2011, p. 3–5), one key deployment of the term has been to describe the 'pastness of feminism' (Tasker and Negra, 2007, p. 8). As Angela McRobbie argues, feminism is invoked in contemporary culture to point out that it is no longer needed (2007, p. 33). As freely choosing subjects, 'there is no exploitation' when young women and girls willingly, and, more importantly, *knowingly*, offer their bodies and sexualities up for display and consumption by men (and other women) (McRobbie, 2007, p. 33). A striptease or a lap dance is an avowed enactment of a girl's liberty and freedom to be herself, her control over her body and choices and sexuality. McRobbie suggests that 'by means of the tropes of freedom and choice that are now inextricably connected with the category of "young women", feminism is decisively "aged" and made to seem redundant' (2007, p. 27). In the words of Yvonne Tasker and Diane Negra, 'postfeminist culture works in part to incorporate, assume, or naturalise aspects of feminism', so its 'success' renders it irrelevant for contemporary culture (2007, pp. 2&8). In its place 'the figure of the woman as empowered consumer' is installed (Tasker and Negra, 2007, p. 2).

Alongside these articulations, ethnographic research is producing insight into how young women are themselves making sense of and negotiating this 'hyperculture of commercial sexuality' (McRobbie, 2007, p. 34)[1]. This kind of work complicates any simple assumption that the cultural trends described above are uniformly bad for all girls, teens and women because it renders them complicit in their own oppression and exploitation. Research by Emily Bishop (2012), for example, shows that young women in fact negotiate contradictory discourses on gender and sex in the context of sexualisation or 'raunch culture'. Bishop's work demonstrates that young women take up a diversity of positions and means of interacting with discourses of sexualisation and do not simply conform to the messages and expectations assumed by the raunch culture thesis. Similarly, research conducted by Sue Jackson and Tiina Vares looks at how tween girls engage the word 'slut' in relation to female celebrity dress codes as a way of producing and negotiating subjectivities. The girls in this study are in fact critical of the styles of dress, behaviour and sexuality offered in popular culture. They do not make sense of these representations within discourses of 'sexually empowered freedom' but instead harness the notion of 'the slut' as a way to regulate the boundaries of 'conventional "good girl" femininity' (Jackson and Vares, 2011, p. 144). While this serves as a means of resistance to sexualised images, Jackson and Vares also point out that it relies on 'old gender binaries' between 'good' and 'bad' girls which brings its own set of problems (2011, p. 145). Nonetheless, this research offers a much more complex picture of young women's engagement with popular culture than mainstream media depictions suggest.

It is clear even from this brief review that the sexualisation of culture has initiated the production of a diverse body of literature, and one which continues to develop as scholars begin to ask challenging questions as to the meaning of and assumptions that underpin discourses of sexualisation, postfeminism, agency, empowerment and media literacy[2]. Common across much of the literature, however, is not just concern for girls and for their well-being but with the problematic nature and status of young female sexuality. At issue are questions of what is normal, natural, healthy and safe for young women to do and think and 'be', and what is pleasurable and genuinely empowering for them. Implicit here also is a notion of the normal course of female sexual development, which governs use and understanding of the terms of female sexual health. What young women are doing 'now' is therefore also about what they will go on to do and become. In other words, their behaviour is framed and interpreted in terms of what it signals about the future and their future (adult, sexual) selves.

Public sentiment is similarly reflective of a concern for young women and how to best ensure the protection of their well-being and normal sexual development. Popular discourses on sexualisation, however, rely more on traditional and Romantic assumptions about childhood and youth in responding to sexualisation debates, seeing them as naturally innocent and therefore as rightly lacking sexual knowledge. This approach is regularly rehearsed in the media sphere when people react with shock when young girls do outrageous things (like start a foundation for giving 'gobs' [see chapter 2]), or when parents complain about sexy clothing options for pre-teen girls and the sexualised posing and mimicry this promotes, and when media commentators duly pronounce on a lack of teen awareness as to the consequences of their actions. In short, the sexualisation of youth is deeply offensive to a commonly held and indeed cherished belief in childhood innocence[3]. The underlying message at the level of public discourse (and in much of the academic literature as well) is therefore that a change in media culture is needed towards more 'healthy' and 'age appropriate' representations of young female sexuality. We need to respect childhood (and youth) as a special time that ought to be protected (from sex) for as long as possible. While this may appear to be a reasonable argument, I suggest that such a position can only perpetuate the problem it seeks to resolve.

Approaching the 'problem' of young female sexuality differently

This chapter's interrogation of the discourse of 'coming of age' shows how the discourse actually contributes to making youth sexuality a problem, which signals a need to imagine youth differently. Young people are called to 'come of age', yet I argue that this concept of youth is grounded in a contradictory logic that produces conflicting aims: a desire to preserve the innocence of youth and a simultaneous expectation that they 'grow up'. By using techniques of Derridean deconstruction, specifically the notion of undecidability, I intervene in this logic and point to where key aspects of 'coming of age' – based on a binary opposition between innocence and knowledge – can be seen to contradict what the discourse sets out to determine. That is, the discourse creates a set of expectations for young people which, once carried out, actually transgress the limits of the discourse. While the natural response is to seek to correct this transgression by reaffirming the limits of the discourse, in doing so the circumstances for those limits to again be breached is recreated. In other words, the discourse produces a notion of youth that breaches the boundaries of that discourse, so invoking it to restore those boundaries does not resolve the issues the discourse creates but in fact serves to keep them in place.

I demonstrate this via analysis of two films that attracted widespread controversy for their subject matter – female sexual precociousness/ abuse in *Lolita* (1997) and teen rebellion in *Thirteen* (2003). A third film, *Towelhead* (also titled *Nothing is Private*, 2007), is examined alongside *Lolita* for it depicts some of the same issues in a particularly discomforting way. Despite containing much controversial material, due to its non-mainstream release, this film did not achieve the same level of public notoriety as the other two. All three films are useful, nonetheless, because what they depict, the issues they raise, their contexts of production and the responses they generated provide an opportunity to engage with the conceptual limits of the discourse of 'coming of age' and how this works to produce female youth sexuality as a 'problem' and as a threat to the 'proper' development of young women. This focus is distinct from situating the problem of youth sexuality as caused by the sexualised, commercial and consumption-driven media environment. However, this analysis adds a vital dimension to debate about the impact and influence of this environment given that arguments about it are often grounded in the assumptions of a 'coming of age' discourse.

Many other films, of course, deal with a 'coming of age' discourse. Recent releases like *An Education* (2009), *Easy A* (2010) and *Juno* (2007) depict, in quite different ways, young women negotiating their sexual and social identities at school, at home and in personal relationships as they mature towards adulthood. These films, however, were all commercial and critical successes and did not attract controversy even though they involve precisely the kinds of things that incite public fear and moral panic about young women: teen sex (all three films), unwanted pregnancy (*Juno*), becoming a 'slut' (*Easy A*), being seduced and exploited by an older man (*An Education*), and the risk or ruin of reputation and life chances (all three). That these films didn't generate controversy for this content may well be due to the age of the central female characters. These protagonists are post-pubescent – aged 16–18 – whereas the films I have chosen to analyse feature lead characters aged 12 and 13 (who, except for the lead actress in *Towelhead*, are all depicted by actors of a similar age). These characters may more readily be described as 'tweens' – as in, 'in between' child and teen. More specifically, they occupy a 'moment' of first becoming 'adult like', as marked by the emergence or 'arrival' of physical sexual maturation and the opening up of its attendant emotional, social and psychological components. All six films mentioned here can be placed within what Sarah Hentges defines as the mainstream 'coming of age' film narrative. The films are about 'finding oneself or overcoming adversity', and while they may challenge aspects of both adult and teen cultures, the fundamental structures of these cultures remain intact (Hentges, 2006, p. 60). However, there is particular anxiety surrounding tweens in the literature on the sexualisation of girls and in the wider community, which is something that sets apart the films I have chosen from the other examples. Tweens cross the boundaries of both child and teen, they are 'on the threshold of becoming sexual' (Lumby, 2010, np), and must negotiate this in a cultural context that wants to both accelerate and commodify their sexual maturation. So as a particular site of concern, I too focus on this developmental 'moment'.

Specifically, the following analysis will indicate where the paradoxical elements that define the discourse of 'coming of age' remain unseen in attempts to make sense of this life stage as it relates to the issue of paedophilia/sexual abuse in *Lolita* and *Towelhead*, and the problem of teenage rebellion in *Thirteen*. I look at responses from critics to these films and show that how they make sense of them in fact works to reproduce the conditions that create the discursive conflict outlined earlier. So while notions of appropriate and timely development inform much of the discussion on sexualisation and how to respond to its presumed negative effects, this reading aims to reveal how these notions work against themselves and cannot provide the solutions they promise. However, dealing with this conceptual problem is not simply a matter of rejecting this discourse in favour of another. The deconstructive reading performed here reveals that it is the contradictory underpinnings of the discourse of 'coming of age' that *enables* youth to be thought at all; the paradox of 'coming of age' actually marks the continuation of the concept. In recognition of this, at the end of the chapter I attempt to pursue a more productive, non-paradoxical, way of conceptualising youth in response to the perceived threat posed by media representations of sex and sexuality in relation to young people, and most especially girls.

Coming of age: Key tensions

The discourse of 'coming of age' articulates a process of maturation that young people go through in preparation for adulthood. In Western society, it involves the development and internalisation of standards of social, sexual, emotional and physical conduct. It is a time when such values are at their most visible and also at their most unstable and vulnerable, being open to rejection even as mainstream society seeks to have them consolidated in specific ways in each new generation of young people. A lot of attention is given to this time, and much is at stake when adolescent growth and development points towards a future that is yet to come. With this in mind, youth studies scholar Nancy Lesko writes that 'coming of age' is accompanied by such phrases as 'teenagers are "at the threshold" and in "transition to adulthood"', which imply a process of 'evolutionary arrival in an enlightened state after a lengthy period of backwardness' (2001, p. 3). Here, teenagers are natural beings located beyond social influences, but there is a point when they enter into, arrive at, or in Lesko's words, 'get dropped down into various social and historical contexts' (2001, p. 3). There are two competing ideas at work here which will be addressed: that 'coming of age' is a lengthy and gradual process of development, but that 'arrival' means to be 'dropped' into society and adulthood from 'outside', from a state of nature.

Understanding youth according to the discourse of 'coming of age' also marks young people as distinct from adults and ultimately as fundamentally different from them. This relationship is, in a wider sense, founded on core Enlightenment values of reason and progress, and the ideal, self-governing individual of modern Western society whose inner qualities social scientists and psychologists can reveal and therefore regulate (Lesko, 2001, p. 9). These ideals place great importance on teenagers' proper preparation for the transition from 'backwardness' to a state of enlightened 'awareness'. In tracing the work of early and key developmental psychologists such as G. Stanley Hall, Lesko writes that an ideal adolescence involved the protection and control of the young person because, it was thought, any adult-like behaviour would mean the loss of vigour once adulthood was reached (2001, p. 62). 'A slow, steady coming of age' guarded against precocity in the young, keeping them in a more manageable state of ongoing preparation and of prolonged dependency so that their eventual entry into the social order would enable them to realise their 'full potential' (Lesko, 2001, pp. 63&88). In addition to this, Christine Griffin notes that for Hall, realising the full potentialities of young people also required developing self-control and discipline which, once achieved, would serve to maintain the economic, ideological and political order of Western society (2004, pp. 11–12). This dominant system of reasoning has since naturalised a developmental schema for youth – understood as stages of cognitive, pubertal or psychosocial growth – which also functions as a universal or essential truth (Lesko, 2001, p. 7). Indeed, this has been the foundation for arguments on the negative impact of sexualised imagery on youth in debate about the sexualisation of culture.

Put another way: 'youth cannot live in the present'; rather, they can only exist within a discourse of 'growing up' and hence as a *future* presence (Lesko, 2001, pp. 137&189). It is their 'becoming' social, which also equates to youth being seen as inherently unstable, in a state of lack, as effectively 'absent', that makes youth fundamentally different from adulthood. Furthermore, to consider the notion of identity as it relates to 'coming of age' is to place it on the side of presence; as that which marks the achievement of full-personhood and therefore as something that is stable and enduring.

However, Lesko calls attention to 'the difficulty of...securing "identity" when youth are contained within an "expectant mode"' or in a state of 'perpetual becoming' (2001, pp. 63&123). This key tension between a demand to secure an identity and being in a state of 'becoming' constitutes what might be called the paradox of 'coming of age'. The discourse of 'coming of age' describes something that is *supposed* to happen given the values and structures of modern society, but which at the same time is *prevented* from happening by those very same structures. The problems this creates for making sense of youth – and young female sexuality – can be identified using deconstruction. I have chosen filmic examples as the basis of my analysis but this is not to the exclusion of 'real world' experiences. In fact, as will later be demonstrated and further discussed in the next chapter, the two are inextricably linked.

Regarding youth as 'becoming', rather than 'being', and therefore as lacking a stable identity, points us towards what the discourse of 'coming of age' privileges: presence. As already introduced in Chapters 3 and 4, it is this concept that Jacques Derrida questions, and what his deconstructive logic enables us to see as working against its own stated aims. The specific problem to be addressed here, however, and similar to the issues raised in the previous chapter, is that the dominant logic of 'coming of age' maintains a belief that knowing youth is the same as knowing their *essence* or presence. Lesko writes of how youth is understood according to developmental stages understood as biological 'fact' and therefore as 'naturally occurring', but approached deconstructively, this is not the same as youth being in a state of nature. On this account, that nature is knowable and thinkable within language makes it always already cultural, hence nature is not self-evident but an effect of language, and so too is the presumed self-presence or full-personhood of adulthood. The play of presence and absence within language, or 'the lack at the origin that is the condition of thought and experience', *enables* thought of a stable adult identity against an unstable (yet natural, essential) youth, even as the ideal of 'arrival' at a total or final (adult) presence is prevented from ever being possible, from ever being 'found in its full being' (Spivak, 1997, p. xvii). With nothing to mark the difference between nature and culture in any absolute way, and with what counts as presence being conditioned by its relationship to absence, what we actually have is the ongoing deferral of presence. This means, recalling the point made in Chapter 3, that the ideal of presence is 'contradictorily coherent' (Derrida, 1978, p. 279).

The implications of this condition with regard to the notion of innocence is an important element in this chapter's discussion of young female sexuality. Innocence implies purity; a state of being that is unworldly, untouched, enclosed, and therefore unknowing. This is a well-established and powerful notion in discussions about youth as seen in the work of Enlightenment thinkers, coming out of developmental psychology, in much of the sexualisation literature, and, of course, in community opinion. But if innocence is thought to be something absolute, a state of pure being, then it is actually indifferent to any power we may attribute to it and it cannot be directly known. To presume to know what that pure state is or looks like is, however, consistent with the metaphysics of presence and I have already noted what this assumption covers over in discussing the supplementarity of the notion of presence in Chapter 3. Similarly, as explained in Chapter 4 regarding research on the teen brain, a lack of reason is considered to be a normal, natural state of being but also 'not enough' if the goal is to become adult. Youth is both 'less than' and 'complete' at the same time. Based in innocence, (female) youth is here idealised and rendered inadequate at once, so it is always going to work against itself and be a problem, which only ends up compromising the foundations of the structure that posits it. In other words, innocence is something to revere and to seek to preserve and protect in its 'wholeness' at the same time as it must be left behind or 'cast off' (Faulkner, 2011, p. 8) if adulthood is to come. Innocence is therefore a state of being that is less than whole in relation to adult presence. But when and how does the leaving of innocence occur? As it concerns 'coming of age', I argue that it can only ever be 'too soon' given binary logic. This brings about the 'problem' of youth sexuality, as I will shortly explain.

But first, it is important to note that in recognising and working within this contradictory logic, we will not and cannot do away with thinking through conceptual oppositions. Derrida argues, recalling Butler's comments at the end of Chapter 3, 'there is no sense in doing without the concepts of metaphysics in order to shake metaphysics' (1978, p. 280). We cannot pronounce 'a single destructive proposition which has not already had to slip into the form, the logic, and the implicit postulations of precisely what it seeks to contest' (Derrida, 1978, pp. 280–1). So in deconstructing the metaphysics of presence as it operates within 'coming of age', we are 'at once conserving and annulling inherited conceptual oppositions' (Derrida, 1997, p. 105). In order to analyse why this dominant way of thinking about youth is problematic and why we need to think differently or more responsively, Derrida suggests that we must stand 'on a borderline: sometimes within an uncriticised conceptuality, sometimes putting a strain on the boundaries, and working toward deconstruction' (1997, p. 105). In applying this approach, there are three additional elements that comprise the first and overall tension of 'coming of age' that the following discussion of *Lolita*, *Towelhead* and, later, *Thirteen* will articulate.

Lolita and *Towelhead*

The 1997 remake of *Lolita* directed by Adrian Lyne and the 2007 film *Towelhead* directed by Alan Ball provide excellent examples of this strain of working both within and against dominant concepts. These films depict what in recent times is considered one of the most dangerous threats to youth: paedophilia (and, by implication, underage/premature sex). Based on the novel by Vladimir Nabokov and following Stanley Kubrick's 1962 film version, the 1997 version of *Lolita* tells the story of middle-aged Englishman Humbert Humbert, a professor of French poetry, who travels to New England in 1947 to take up a new teaching post at Beardsley College. During the summer before he is due to start, he boards with widow Charlotte Haze and her 12-year-old daughter, Dolores (Lo, Lolita, Dolly). We are told in a prologue sequence of Humbert's first love at 14, and how he loses her to typhus four months after meeting her. 'The shock of the death froze something in me', he says in voiceover, 'the child I loved was gone, but I kept looking for her, long after I'd left my own childhood behind'. Humbert describes his desire as a poisonous 'wound' that 'wouldn't heal', and on first seeing Lolita, falls 'madly, hopelessly in love' with her. The film details their five-year relationship both as stepfather and daughter, and as lovers. Their sexual relationship moves from one of playfulness and consent on Lolita's part, to one of manipulating him and scheming against him. Lolita eventually leaves Humbert to be with the only man she was 'ever really crazy about', the mysterious and devious Clare Quilty, who, due to his betrayal of both Humbert and Lolita, is brutally murdered by Humbert at the end of the film. Humbert is utterly destroyed by his love for Lolita, torn apart by her 'escape' from him and for his part in her 'corruption'. Yet despite his anguish he, right to the very end, wishes for her to return to him and be with him forever: 'I was in paradise. A paradise whose skies were the colour of hell flames, but a paradise still'.

Towelhead (or *Nothing is Private*) depicts another relationship between an older man and a young girl but this time from the girl's perspective. It is based on the 2005 novel of the same name by Alicia Erian, and set in the US during the first Gulf War. The film tells the story of 13-year-old

Jasira, an Arab-American struggling to come to terms with her newly developed body, her sexual curiosity and the adult male attention she attracts. Jasira's mother, Gail, refuses to allow her to shave, and when she finds out that her boyfriend Barry has shaved Jasira's bikini area for her, Jasira is immediately sent to Houston to live with her father. 'Listen to me, ok?', Gail says to her crying daughter. 'This whole thing is your fault, alright? The way that you walk around with your boobs stuck out it's impossible for him [Barry] not to notice'.

Jasira's father, Rifat, demonstrates perfect manners in public but in private is often cruel to Jasira both verbally and physically. Jasira defies many of her father's rules including not wearing tampons ('tampons are for married ladies'), not seeing her African-American boyfriend, Thomas ('if you continue to visit that boy's house, no one will respect you') and above all, not having sex ('you're just a child. You have a foul mouth and a foul mind'; 'you don't live in the moral universe. The things you do are not normal'). For her behaviour, Jasira is locked out of the house, yelled at, slapped and beaten.

Her new neighbour, army reservist Mr Vuoso, takes an interest in Jasira. She babysits for his son, and one afternoon he and Jasira discover Vuoso's collection of porn magazines. Sitting in a chair with her legs crossed, Jasira absent-mindedly swings her upper leg as she looks at the pictures. Becoming aroused by the pictures and by the movement of her leg she unexpectedly has an orgasm. Vuoso catches them both and is intrigued that Jasira is interested in the magazines. She continues to masturbate after this and approaches Vuoso in his front yard. 'I miss looking at your magazines', she tells him. 'Why?', Vuoso asks. 'They make me have orgasms', she replies. He leaves a magazine on her doorstep.

Vuoso visits Jasira one night, angry that she hit his son, Zach (who called her 'towelhead' amongst other racist names). Grabbing Jasira by the shoulders to force her to go and get the magazine he gave her, he stops, smells her hair, and embraces her tightly from behind. Jasira tries to break free but he continues to hold and touch her. Undoing her pants he digitally penetrates her, causing her to bleed. Jasira tells him to stop, that he's hurting her, and Vuoso panics when he sees blood. 'I'm sorry, I didn't mean it. I swear to God I'm sorry'. She tells him not to go but he recoils from her and runs out the door. Later in the film Vuoso tells Jasira that he's been called up to serve in Iraq (even though the war is now over) and uses the threat of him leaving to again have sex with her. Jasira does what he says only to see him the next morning going about his usual business.

Another neighbour, Melina, offers Jasira the kind of motherly support she is lacking. Melina is pregnant with her first child and becomes increasingly concerned about Jasira, offering her home as a respite and refuge from her father and Vuoso. After one particularly severe beating by her father (he finds the pornographic magazine Vuoso gave to Jasira), Jasira runs to Melina's house and doesn't leave. Whilst in Melina's care Jasira comes to realise that Vuoso in fact raped her and coerced her into sex and eventually admits this to Melina, her father and her boyfriend in an angry confrontation. Vuoso is arrested and charged. Jasira admits to Melina that she didn't want to sleep with Vuoso the second time but did it anyway because she thought she was supposed to. Melina explains that a grown man knows that even if he wants to do it, sex with anyone under the age of 16 is rape. 'I feel sorry for him', Jasira says. Melina tells her to never feel sorry for him.

Thomas tells Jasira that it's not right for them to sleep together anymore, 'not after what that asshole did to you'. Jasira thinks for a moment and replies: 'I don't want to stop. I like having sex with you. I don't what to lose that because of what Mr Vuoso did'. After this, Rifat allows Jasira to live with Melina and her husband. 'Jasira will stay will you. That will be much better. She's a good girl'. The film ends as Melina gives birth with Jasira by her side, happy at the prospect of living with a loving family.

Both films contain very difficult material and they are not easy to view for this reason, but their depictions of the sexual activity of young teenage girls goes right to the heart of the paradox of 'coming of age'. Both examples represent obvious cases of sexual abuse, and they can be easily explained according to discourses of sexualisation. Here, adults (men, in this case) impose their sexual desire onto girls, imbuing them 'with adult sexuality' (APA, 2007, p. 1), or, as in *Lolita*, express a desire *for* young girls *as* girls. But this is not all there is to say about the films. What is also depicted here is the kind of sexual curiosity that accompanies young people's 'self-motivated sexual exploration', which is not defined as sexualisation by the APA taskforce (2007, p. 1). These films present both discursive possibilities. That is, Jasira is raped and coerced into doing things she doesn't want to do. But she also makes some choices for herself (as does Lolita), which may not necessarily be attributed to a disturbed sense of self caused by premature sexual activity or by sexual violation.

It would be acceptable to suggest that the girls' behaviour is the result of having the normal course of their sexual development unnaturally advanced by their experiences with Humbert and Vuoso. It is far less acceptable, however, to consider their sexuality outside the discourses of sexualisation and of rape. This is because a notion of sexual agency would risk implying that rape and paedophilia are okay and, worse, that the girls 'asked for it' or in some way consented to their own abuse. It is also less acceptable because a notion of agency grants an autonomy to the girls that cannot be accounted for by conventional assumptions about the 'innocent' exploration of their emerging sexuality and their vulnerability to adult predation. What makes these films unsettling is that it is not so easy to dismiss evidence of the girls' own knowledge and desire. The next section explores this further.

Unthinkable attractions

In the West, paedophilia is regarded as morally wrong and objectionable, yet, when considered according to the logic of an innocence/knowledge binary split within the developmental discourses that define 'coming of age', the issue acquires a new complexity. Derrida's analysis of Lévi-Strauss's work on the prohibition of incest shows how deconstruction destabilises what the opposition of innocence and knowledge – which operates within a broader nature/culture binary – seeks to define and hold in place. Derrida argues that the presumed difference between nature and culture 'finds itself erased or questioned' when it encounters 'a *scandal*, that is to say, something which no longer tolerates the nature/culture opposition' (1978, p. 283)[4]. Incest is something that is scandalous because it '*simultaneously* seems to require the predicates of nature and of culture' (Derrida, 1978, p. 283). To elaborate, Derrida claims that because the prohibition is universal it does not therefore depend on any particular order or cultural norm and so can be considered natural. But as incest is also something that is prohibited, it *is* governed by a system of rules and norms which are culturally and socially variable, making it also cultural. With regard to paedophilia, it is thought that the physical immaturity of children makes them unable to 'have sex', and as this is common to all children, their asexuality can therefore be seen as natural. But what is being suggested following Derrida's work is that 'sex' is actually a cultural construct because it is in this domain that sexual practices are organised, regulated and made meaningful, and this includes the notion of asexuality which paedophilic activity is thought to violate. So to attribute a state of asexuality to children is not the same as their being in a state of 'natural innocence' that exists independently of any particular norm or value system. On the basis of Derrida's interrogation of the incest prohibition, to take the natural innocence of children as culturally attributed to them would thus make paedophilia something scandalous because what makes it wrong could not be contained by the 'inside–outside' relationship of nature to culture or innocence to knowledge. Indeed, Derrida contends that 'from the moment when the incest prohibition can no longer be conceived within the nature/culture opposition, it can no longer be said to be a scandalous fact' (1978, p. 283), and, similarly, neither can paedophilia.

Instead, as something that escapes the concepts of nature and culture, Derrida argues that the incest prohibition (and here I extend his argument to include the problem of paedophilia) is more accurately understood as *preceding* those concepts (1978, p. 283). Derrida argues that the work of 'philosophical conceptualisation' is 'systematic with the nature/culture opposition', but that in order for its oppositional logic to function, the binary leaves 'in the domain of the unthinkable the very thing that makes this conceptualisation possible: the origin of the prohibition of incest' (1978, p. 284). That the incest prohibition cannot be accommodated by the oppositional logic of nature/culture means that the latter does not come *before* the notion of incest by operating as founding concepts grounded in absolute, transcendental truth; rather, they are conditioned or made possible by the space that marks the difference between them. This space of difference, of deconstruction – space that is 'undecidable' – is where 'the origin of the prohibition of incest' (and of paedophilia) resides.

If Derrida's argument holds, this means that the metaphysical distinction made between youth and adult on the basis of innocence/knowledge as it applies to sexuality cannot remain intact. This opposition cannot account for a stage that is 'becoming'; a stage that is based neither in innocence nor in knowledge, or that is both these things at the same time, and is therefore 'undecidable'. Despite the fact that a gradual becoming is exactly what the 'coming of age' discourse implies (and what is implied in the sexualisation literature), in order to be able to maintain the general difference between youth and adult, an *absolute* break is required. We are faced with an all or nothing alternative where there must be a shift from complete asexuality to total sexuality (from absence to presence, nature to culture, innocence to experience, dependence to independence) and not a gradual process from one into the other. Because of this we reach the limits of 'coming of age' in that it prescribes something that is prevented from happening given the oppositional structure it is also supposed to maintain. Recalling Bhabha's discussion of the intentions and effects of mimicry in colonial discourse, when a moment of change, of becoming, *does* happen, and an obvious example of this is the loss of virginity (which I am referring to in general and not in the context of rape), it is therefore seen as wrong, premature, dangerous, transgressive, an 'uncontrollable force' (Lesko, 2001, p. 3). A steadfast belief in the absolute innocence of children – because of their asexuality – makes this loss something to fear and prevent, rather than as necessary for arrival into adulthood. As a result, paedophilia (and underage sex in general) is seen to disrupt and ruin a 'natural' progression towards sexual maturity.

Concomitantly, sexual maturity is imagined as always at risk of arriving 'too soon' and thereby leading to all manner of social pathology in teenagers. According to Lesko, 'teenagers cannot go...forward to adulthood "before their time" without incurring derogatory labels, for example, "immature", "loose", or "precocious"' (2001, p. 123), and, of course, 'slut'. But what remains unseen here is that what is at risk of being lost is only what *functions* as natural, not nature in itself. Derrida would suggest that the attribution of 'natural innocence', by being thinkable as such, makes it always already 'cultural' (that is, governed by a variable system of norms and sanctions). 'Natural innocence' is therefore definable only in terms of its self-difference rather than by virtue of its presumed self-presence, and the implication of this fact is that such a 'state of being' can always be defined differently[5].

What is now of specific concern, however, is that there is a point in current constructions of adolescence where it is physically possible, but not culturally acceptable, for young people (including both tweens and the post-pubescent) to be sexually active and to therefore have a sexual identity. The marker of cultural acceptability is age-based (turning 16 or 18 or 21), but the fact that this marker does not match the physical timing of sexual maturity does little to change both general opinion and the law that sex with a minor is utterly unacceptable. As noted above, and despite physical evidence to the contrary, sexual activity with a minor is thought to violate their 'natural' innocence, and so it is entirely unthinkable that it be seen as anything other than a gross violation of the young person due to an extreme perversion in the adult. Belinda Morrissey writes that 'the legal dictum that one cannot consent to anything which is deemed criminal' means that 'all those classed as...minors cannot consent to any sexual act whatsoever because having sex with someone under the age of consent is criminal' (2005, p. 60). More particularly, Morrissey notes that the implicit innocence and naïveté that is associated with virginity, especially with regard to young girls, means that not only can minors not offer their consent in a legal sense, but to be a virgin actually means to lack *any* ability to consent (2005, p. 59). This conceptualisation of youth offers no space in which a sexual relationship between a minor and an adult could ever not be considered inherently abusive and criminal, and there is no other way to understand youth in this context except as victims.

Lolita and *Towelhead* therefore tread quite dangerous, if not impossible, territory in their respective depictions of a sexual relationship between an adult and a minor that is not wholly abusive for the minor, even though the more acceptable themes of 'innocence lost' (*Lolita*) and the promise of a loving and safe family (*Towelhead*) bring each film to an end. The night before their first sexual encounter, Lolita asks Humbert: 'if I tell you how naughty I was at camp, promise you won't be mad?'. Lolita wakes the next morning and, having slept next to Humbert, whispers her transgression in his ear. Surprised by her confession, he responds: 'you played that with Charlie? *At camp*?'. She replies: 'don't tell me you never tried it when you were a kid?'. 'Never', he says. She then moves and sits on top of him, removes her retainer and begins to untie his pyjama pants, saying: 'I guess I'm gonna have to show you everything'. As Humbert smiles up at her, his voiceover says: 'Gentlewomen of the jury, I was not even her first lover'. In a later scene, Lolita demonstrates her (seductive) power over Humbert by getting him to raise her allowance and to let her be in the school play. Sitting at his feet, she moves her hand up and down his inner thigh as he tries to read his mail: 'I really *do* think it [her allowance] should be two dollars. Am I right?' she asks. Her hand moves higher, '*am I right?*' she repeats. Humbert, aware of what she is doing, relents: 'God, yes. Two dollars'.

Jasira also demonstrates some power of her own, despite Vuoso's abuse and his attempts to absolve himself. Vuoso invites Jasira out to dinner with him and a waiter refers to Jasira as Vuoso's daughter. She giggles and says: 'I'm not your daughter, I'm your girlfriend'. Vuoso is amused by this and replies good-naturedly: 'You're too young to be my girlfriend'. 'No I'm not', Jasira replies. 'You did that thing to me. I'm your girlfriend'. Visibly disturbed by this statement, Vuoso is lost for words. 'Why do you like me?' she asks. He shakes his head. 'I know', she volunteers, 'my boobs'. They both laugh. 'Maybe', says Vuoso, 'but it's more than that'. Jasira tells Vuoso: 'When I grow up, I wanna be in your magazines', to which he immediately says: 'No you don't! Are you a slut? Huh?'. 'I don't think so', Jasira says. 'No, you're not a slut!', Vuoso confirms. 'You're not going to be in those magazines'. He then tells Jasira that if she keeps seeing Thomas she'll be a slut, to which Jasira retorts: 'He's better than you. He only touches me when I say he can'. Dropping Jasira back home,

Vuoso tries to explain, 'I'm not a bad man; I'm really not. I never would have done that thing to you if I'd've known you were still a virgin'. By this time Melina is very suspicious of what's going on between Vuoso and Jasira and tries to get Jasira to talk, but she refuses to engage with Melina. Instead, Jasira organises to interview Vuoso for her school paper, giving them more time to be alone together. When Melina turns up on Vuoso's doorstep during their interview demanding to know what's going on, he becomes angry that she's interfering with them, and Jasira smiles to herself, happy that Vuoso is upset about having their time interrupted.

These and other instances in the films point to the limits of what innocence/knowledge marks as intelligible possibility by having a relationship that, when based on this distinction, is both consensual and abusive at the same time[6]. But what Derrida's argument suggests is that it is only when the difference between nature and culture is taken as self-evident that the problem of teen sexuality exists. This is to say that the binary can only treat behaviour which exceeds its limits (burgeoning sexuality and/or sexual power/agency) as problematic because the behaviour, while conditioned by the binary, threatens the coherence of the distinction and of ideas about the sexual status of young people as naturally occurring.

Here, the second element of the paradox of 'coming of age' can be introduced. The first and overall tension is that 'coming of age' describes a process that is *supposed* to happen given the values and structures of modern society, but is at the same time *prevented* from happening by those very same structures. This is because the oppositional logic of nature/culture or innocence/knowledge on which 'coming of age' is based cannot account for that which belongs to neither side of the binary. This is the second element. We have seen how paedophilia and the problem of youth sexuality upset the binary distinctions that define youth. This makes the space that marks the difference between the binary positions of great significance. It is this space of difference that makes oppositional logic thinkable in the first place, but this means that thinking the absolute difference between innocence and knowledge – on which judgements about paedophilia and youth sexuality are based – actually requires engaging with the space of undecidability. The effect of this engagement is to understand that what appears to be self-evident about each binary position is only ever contradictorily so because each position is grounded in a fundamental relationship with its 'other' and not in an absolute presence with itself. I now turn to an examination of responses to the screening of *Lolita* in Australia to show how both liberal and conservative perspectives on the film do not recognise this originary difference of oppositional logic and so preserve the contradictory logic of 'coming of age'.

'See it and make up your own mind'?[7]

The release of *Lolita* in Australia in April 1999 was met with attempts to ban it (this did not happen with *Towelhead*). Adelaide MP Trish Draper, who led the protest to ban the film, called it 'an encouragement to engage in predatory behaviour against young children' (cited in Harris, 1999, np). Draper succeeded in getting the Office of Film and Literature Classification to review the film's R rating one day after its national release (Schembri, 1999, p. 5). This perspective sees any depiction of paedophilia as dangerous because it would 'make the behaviour acceptable' ('The Case for *Lolita*', 1999, p. 14). Mark Davidson quotes Maryam Kubasek of the National Coalition for the Protection of Children and Families as saying 'however artistically [the new *Lolita* film] is done, it really panders to the paedophile community in the sense that what they want to believe is that children truly are sexual beings and that to initiate them in the sexual experience is doing them a favour' (1997, np). The more liberal response, on the other hand, emphasises the value of exploring the darker sides of society so that they might be better understood, but this side is clear in stating that 'exposition' of such matters does not mean that they are then validated ('The Case for *Lolita*', 1999, p. 14). 'Films that deal intelligently and sensitively with unpleasant subjects deserve to be seen, not banned', argues Jim Schembri. For him, the point of 'worthwhile art' is that it provides an opportunity 'to look into the darker corners of human behaviour and emerge with a better understanding of ourselves' (1999, p. 5). The point of considering these arguments, however, is not to determine which side is more convincing – in this instance, the Classification Review Board upheld the film's R rating ('The Case for *Lolita*', 1999, p. 14) – the point is to note that both sides ultimately condemn paedophilia, and so evidence a failure to engage with 'undecidability' as it operates in moral decisions around sex abuse. For there to be such a thing as right and wrong here, and for us to be able to make decisions based on this, we have to engage with the space that conditions the possibility of both, and, as already noted, that space is 'undecidable'.

In other words, deconstructive logic suggests that if a decision is thought to have a single 'correct' effect or outcome, then there will have been no decision, because there will have been no space in which to recognise what a decision is: a choice between two competing options. As Derrida argues, 'a decision can only come into being in a space that exceeds the calculable program' that would make it an 'effect of determinate causes' (1988, p. 116). For there to be any possibility of coming to a decision about whether sex with a child is wrong, the question must pass through the undecidable; indeed, the very notion of decision 'is structured by this *experience ... of the undecidable*' (Derrida, 1988, p. 116). On this account, decisions are always marked by an indecision in that what seems to be the correct option is thinkable only by virtue of the irreducible possibility that that option could actually be wrong, and this can never be broken from, even in the moment a decision is made. So engaging with the space of the undecidable is therefore engaging with the possibility of an outcome that is 'otherwise'. In this instance, that means risking what seems an irresponsible choice: that paedophilia is not wrong.

To be clear, though, in saying this I am not suggesting that deconstruction supports paedophilia. Deconstructing a moral absolute in this way means dealing with what it seeks to repress and this involves, as previously noted, 'putting a strain on the boundaries' of a dominant way of thinking. It is perfectly okay to prohibit paedophilia, but the point is that how we come to this decision, according to Derrida, involves the ghost of the undecidable. It silently pervades every decision, deconstructing 'from within any assurance of presence' (Derrida, 1992, pp. 24–5). This means that the only way this situation will *not* change is if it always *can* change, and this possibility has to be met with at every moment. This is a difficult and sometimes a dangerous thing to do, but necessary nonetheless for what it enables us to understand about what is normally taken for granted regarding youth sexual identity.

Both sides of the argument over *Lolita*, however, base their positions in the absolute 'wrongness' of paedophilia. Even though they argue differently about how the depiction of Lolita's relationship with Humbert should be treated, having to acknowledge the possibility of the relationship being 'otherwise' (that is, not paedophilic, but consensual or otherwise not in breach of what is considered normal) is intolerable. Once again, though, within deconstruction such a belief is only ever possible based on a foundation that is contradictorily coherent. Whether or not this foundation is unseen, a belief in the absolute wrongness of the relationship is conditioned by, is always already breached by, the opposite possibility. Without an attempt to consider what else is possible – that if constituted differently, the sexual relationship between a minor and an adult might not be inherently wrong – each position can do no more than state and re-state what is thought to be unconditionally wrong about the relationship against another position that, while arguing for a different solution, is doing so for the same reason. With minds already made up, each position prevents the other from making any progress towards getting what they want and so perpetuates debate over something that both sides would wish to have resolved.

The same deconstructive intervention is also required for making sense of the film's external context of production, as it is through this context that the content of *Lolita* is ultimately framed. Barbara Biggs, as a survivor of, and a public speaker on, sexual abuse, argues that if a film like *Lolita* is going to truly deal with something like paedophilia, then it should cast someone in the lead who is actually 12 years old, as the character is portrayed in the original novel (2005, np). In her opinion, the 1962 film cast an actress (Sue Lyon) who looks closer to 18 years old, and while the 1997 version cast a 14-year-old (Dominique Swain) in the role, it made at least some attempt to make her behaviour and body mannerisms those of a young girl (2005, np). The point of her argument, however, is that audiences would have been horrified if an actual 12-year-old, or at least someone who looked 12, was cast, and so would have been less willing to enter into the film's world and the story being told because it would simply be too real. 'Heaven forbid', Biggs writes, that 'viewers would not be able to avoid the thought of something similar happening to their own daughters' (2005, np). Interestingly, commentaries on *Towelhead* make a particular point of noting the age of the lead actress, Summer Bishil, which functions to dispel any such concern. 'Glad to hear Summer Bishil is 19!' says one viewer (Lairymary, 2008, np).

This is an interesting position because it highlights the fact that there comes a point in this debate over the content of these films where 'real life' intervenes and acts as something of a safety net for viewers, a way of not having to risk the 'otherwise' being felt. According to this logic, working once again to the reassuring, yet impossible, certitude of the innocence/knowledge distinction, it would be exploitative and abusive to cast an actual 12-year-old in the role of Lolita, as it would be to cast a 13-year-old in the role of Jasira, especially given the nature and type of the film's sexual scenes. So even though public attention regarding *Lolita's* subject matter has been given on account of its closeness to a real life issue, and even though the film's potential effects on real life have been the cause for so much controversy, any question of the film's relationship to real life is undermined by the legalities and moral ambiguities of having a minor portray the role in such a manner as would be necessary to achieve verisimilitude.

What is more interesting, however, is the claim that the role of Lolita could *only* have been played by a girl at or near that age. On finding Swain to play Lolita, Jeremy Irons, the Humbert Humbert of the 1997 film, said that 'we were lucky to catch her at that age' (cited in Harris, 1999, np). Another girl, he says, 'was the right age but had been in a lot of Hollywood soaps' and so had 'screen reactions' that were 'like a mini-adult'. However the unknown Swain was a 'fawn-like creature who was not pretty and yet because of her youth and lack of self-consciousness she was terribly attractive and also infuriating, all the things Lolita should be' (cited in Harris, 1999, np). Irons' comments point to a brief period where age (14 years) permitted use in such a role, but where body and personality were still that of a young girl which, by the end of filming, Irons says, had passed: 'in just that six months, she had grown about 15cm for a start' (cited in Harris, 1999, np). Irons also notes that Swain had grown 'too old to play the young Lolita' by the time she was filming the scenes where Lolita is 17 (cited in Harris, 1999, np). This suggests that while the casting of a 14-year-old required many precautionary measures – all scenes were videoed, Swain's mother was always present on set and a body double was used in all sexual scenes (Harris, 1999, np) – no one else could have captured the essence of the character: Swain's unselfconsciousness made her ideal to play Lolita, Irons suggesting that it could not be replicated by a more experienced actress, and once that sense was lost, there was no getting it back. The same cannot be said for Bishil's portrayal of Jasira, however, given her age. Instead of a focus on any perceived 'naturalness' in her demeanour, her performance has been described as 'brave' considering how well she handles her character's complex scenes in what is her first film role ('Towelhead is sure to shock', 2008, np).

A contradictory set of ideas is operating here. In one sense, only youth can depict youth, so it is Swain's 'natural innocence' that makes her ideal for the role. But it also makes her vulnerable to the dangers of premature exposure to sex. In another sense, then, to have youth depict youth is to violate what is intrinsic about youth. Perhaps, then, youth should not be depicted by youth. This is to say that if only youth in their perceived natural state of being can offer a depiction of that state, then a deliberate enactment of it contradicts the assumption that it is a state of innocent unknowing, the effect of which is to remove those very youth from that state. The intrinsic, natural qualities of youth innocence cannot therefore be depicted in a direct way, because allowing young people of the correct or exact age to portray roles of the type described here would strip those actors of their 'real life' innocence. This means that youthful innocence can only be represented from outside of itself, which is also to say that these representations of it are not how it actually 'is' for those existing in its 'interior'. So the representation of innocence in these two films is not 'true' or 'actual' innocence if we maintain that it is a pure state of being that cannot be represented or enacted without, in effect, 'spoiling' it.

On this basis, we could afford to worry less about the meaning, effect and implications of films like *Lolita* and *Towelhead* not only for audiences but for the young actors involved in them. They are not being their natural selves on screen; rather, they are offering a rendering of it from an outside position. Except, however, it would also seem that, following Irons' comments, the natural qualities of innocence are *necessary* for such performances. Furthermore, why bother depicting girls' lives if they don't reflect actual experience? Timothy Shary suggests that 'the imaging of contemporary youth [in film] has become indicative of our deepest social and personal concerns' (2002, p. 1). Youth in film is not viewed as fantasy or make-believe; films like this are used as a platform for making sense of real life issues, as demonstrated by the serious debate over the release of *Lolita* in Australia. It may be, therefore, that the actual experience of innocence is rather more like its depiction in these two films. That is, no matter the degree of self-awareness an actor may bring to the role, especially in terms of awareness of their own sexuality, innocence always already exists as 'other' than itself, as outside of those who are deemed to 'possess' it. I consider this issue further in the next section when discussion turns to *Thirteen*, and again in the final part of the chapter. It is also addressed in the next chapter when I look at how the media is actually used to determine the 'real life' characteristics of 'actual' young people.

Now, though, the third element to the 'coming of age' paradox is added. The first element is that 'coming of age' prescribes a process that is supposed to happen, but because the discourse is grounded in the oppositional distinction of innocence and knowledge, in order to be maintained, it cannot account for how youths *gradually* become adult and so 'coming of age' is not able to occur in the way that it is thought it should. The second aspect is that the 'undecidable' element that conditions this conceptual opposition is what makes it possible to know the difference between such oppositions and to therefore be able to operate within them in the first place. However, this 'contradictory coherence' of binary oppositions remains unacknowledged. The third element is that for the distinctions that the space of undecidability marks to exist, they have to remain open to the possibility of being 'otherwise'. This is to say that moral positions regarding the sexual conduct of young people are not the 'effect of determinate causes' (Derrida, 1988, p. 116) but are the outcome of a decision-making process which by definition requires the consideration of alternative positions. Such alternative positions in this instance would be that youth are not necessarily victims if they have a sexual relationship with an adult, it is not necessarily absolutely wrong, and it is not necessarily a violation of what is intrinsic about youth. While moral decisions *do* have real effects, by removing the fixity of notions of youth and abuse, we can engage differently with the 'field... of decidability' (Derrida, 1988, p. 116) and therefore with possibilities that take us beyond current conceptual limits where moral absolutes exist in conflict with the effects they produce.

Thirteen

Thirteen (2003) provides another opportunity to think differently about female youth and the discourse of 'coming of age'. Directed by Catherine Hardwicke, the film depicts life at the extreme end of what might be called teenage rebellion, even though it ultimately offers viewers a return to safer conceptual territory, as do *Lolita* and *Towelhead*. The film nonetheless challenges the limits of possibility regarding youth behaviour and in doing so encounters the paradox of 'coming of age', pointing to its fourth key constitutive element.

Thirteen tells the story of Tracy who, at the beginning of the film, is a typical 'good girl': sweet-natured, happy, polite and friendly. She wears neat clothes, walks the family dog and baby-sits for her mother's friends. But when Tracy enters middle school and the seventh grade, she encounters a pack of girls led by the beautiful and popular Evie. Evie is manipulative of those around her; she lies, steals money and shoplifts, deals and takes drugs, and has casual sex. She wears low-cut jeans with her g-string deliberately visible, and tight, midriff-bearing tops that frame her belly piercing. Tracy is initially unimpressed by Evie, but when Evie's friends make fun of Tracy's clothes ('who let *her* out of the cabbage patch'), she desires a change in herself and pursues a friendship with Evie. Leaving her other friends behind, Tracy embarks on a wild and intense relationship with Evie that sees her steal money and shoplift, have her tongue and belly button pierced, take drugs, have casual sex, and lie to her mother. At home, Tracy's mother, Mel, more 'the hot big sister' than parent, according to Evie, is herself struggling to overcome addiction and is seeing a man she met in rehab who Tracy does not like. Tracy's father is absent, and when he does show up later in the film in the midst of Tracy's chaos, he does no more than throw up his hands when neither Tracy or her brother Mason are able to tell him 'in a nutshell' what the problem is with Tracy. We are given some insight into the reasons behind Evie's behaviour. In Mel's words: 'she's been molested and abused by practically everyone who was supposed to take care of her', and there is a clear textual (or narrative) link between Tracy's somewhat unstable home situation and her desire to follow Evie as well as routinely lock herself in the bathroom and cut her arm with a razor blade as remedy for some of her emotional pain. It would be easy to say that because of this specific framing the film represents what is in fact uncommon for most seventh graders, and so does not need to be seen as any sort of grave threat to, or troubling indication of, the realities of the young of the 'real world' (although the research findings cited in Chapter 2 on the health and well-being of young people perhaps indicates otherwise). What this film demonstrates, however, is precisely the hold that the dominant 'coming of age' logic has over our thinking, such that the logic is affirmed even as it is challenged.

Thirteen was billed as an emotionally raw yet compelling depiction of the real, and frightening, life of young tweens. Alissa Quart claims that the film 'fleshes out ... a new kind of American childhood' where the 'materialism and overly advanced sexual attitudes of tweens far surpasses those of previous eras' (2003, p. 71). In her view, the film constitutes 'a new cinematic gaze that corresponds to this breed of child', a 'teen gaze that projects the desire of young girls rather than those of an adult' (2003, p. 71). But despite its graphic depiction of 'teen limit experience', by the end of the film, 'this uncomfortable truth-telling has been replaced by an after-school-special logic' of restored order (Quart, 2003, p. 71), which feels, according to film reviewer Phillipa Hawker, 'a little too much like a cautionary tale' (2004, p. 7).

However, if, as noted above, the film marks a developmental stage that is 'in between' or 'in transition' to becoming adult, then this stage and the rebellious behaviour that accompanies it, or that is seen to characterise this stage, is part of the normative 'coming of age' process. When developmental logic conceives of a gradual process of preparation for adulthood, then it must also prescribe that teens go through various obstacles, whether or not these are carefully administered and closely monitored, in the service of their eventual arrival at adulthood. In other words, the development of an adult identity calls for a period that is inherently tumultuous and disruptive because it involves passing through a social space that is neither child nor adult. Being a tween is going to upset the boundaries of social acceptability but that is what is supposed to happen given this logic. In Griffin's words, 'dominant representations of youth have simultaneously treated youth as a period of inevitable turmoil and a time for "having a fling", *and* as a time when the path to "normal" life must be found and followed' (2004, p. 16). So however confronting its depiction, and however destructive it might be, teen rebellion has a place in the 'coming of age' discourse, to the extent that it is thought 'wrong' *not* to go through a 'rebellious phase'. Why, then, is it the cause for so much fear? Why should its depiction in *Thirteen* be 'cautionary' and not 'proper', when this is exactly how 'coming of age' has been structured?

'They're not little girls anymore'[8]

If rebellion is accepted because it ultimately leads to an acceptance of the dominant social order then this would by definition make it not rebellious. 'True' rebellion takes us towards the 'otherwise' of thought; it is about engaging with the undecidability of 'coming of age' and of opening up to an unforeseeable outcome. As already noted elsewhere, a space that is 'in between' is actually an unthinkable space given binary logic. If youth is about being in preparation for an adult state of being, then in order to maintain this ideal, young people can never actually arrive at adulthood. If young people are assumed to be intrinsically not present, then they are, in fact, obliged *not* to arrive because this would upset the defining limits of both 'youth' and 'adult'. Teens therefore rebel in the service of nothing. Here, at this conceptual limit, there is an additional aspect of the third part of the paradox of 'coming of age'. For something to count as an event or marker of 'coming of age' it cannot be seen as the consequence of any predetermined knowledge or planned outcome, otherwise there is no 'otherwise' and it would be a foregone conclusion. No moment of transition could therefore be marked: there could only be 'the unfolding of a calculable process' (Derrida, 1992, p. 24). By contrast, Derrida argues that 'to whom it is said "come," should not be determined in advance' (2002, p. 12) for to do so would be to negate the context in which to experience such a thing as, in this instance, 'coming of age'. So for teen rebellion to count towards the event of 'coming of age', there must be an 'interruption of the deliberation that precedes it' (Derrida, 1992, p. 26).

This involves working *with* and not against undecidability in making 'all or nothing' distinctions between youth and adult. This means that teens are either yet to have 'come of age' – yet to have 'done' the things that supposedly mark 'coming of age' – or 'coming of age' will have 'already followed a rule' (Derrida, 1992, p. 24) and occurred. The moments of 'arrival' in the film, such as when Tracy has her first sexual encounter or gets high for the first time, are finite moments, except that once they happen, 'once the ordeal of the undecidable is past (if that is possible)' (Derrida, 1992, p. 24), they cannot be traced back to an origin grounded in what came before, grounded in Tracy's 'youth'. Tracy has instead entered a new conceptual order, but one which, importantly, is no more present to itself than the one before. What is occurring here is not 'the absence of rules and knowledge but . . . a reinstitution of rules which by definition is not preceded by any knowledge or by any guarantee as such' (Derrida, 1992, p. 26).

In other words, the moment of a transition necessitates a break with what Derrida calls a 'horizon of expectation' (1992, p. 26). 'If there were anticipation or programming', he argues, 'there would be neither event nor history' (Derrida, 2002, p. 12). This is because 'it is on condition of the "come" that there is an experience of coming, of the event . . . and consequently, of that which, because it comes from the other, cannot be anticipated' (Derrida, 2002, p. 12). In applying Derrida's line of argument, this condition would make teen rebellion (and becoming sexual), rather than a prescribed developmental stage, a point at which the 'otherwise' is engaged. It would be a point where the 'event' or 'events' of 'coming of age' occur and so rebellion is what institutes a new conceptual order that breaks with what preceded it. To say that adulthood has been successfully prepared for is therefore not the same as having it 'arrive' from youth. The preparation done 'in' youth anticipates an outcome, but the only way that an outcome can come to pass is if its arrival is *not* the expected outcome. This is because youth is adulthood's 'other' and, following Derrida's remarks, we cannot do without this conceptual distinction, even as it is challenged. So, on this basis, the outcome is *not* the outcome, it is something entirely 'new' in the sense that Tracy, for example, will have become something else: adult. This is the fourth element of the paradox of 'coming of age'. Once 'coming of age' has 'arrived' or 'occurred', having passed through the space of undecidability, it will immediately become something else and it will no longer be governed by the horizon of expectation of 'coming of age'. This is to say that youth does not, cannot, 'come'. But while seemingly saying the same thing as above – that youth are 'obliged not to arrive' at adulthood – the difference is that this obligation can now be recognised as the condition by virtue of which adulthood *can* come.

'It's happening so fast'[9]

If Derrida's argument holds, no amount of preparation could prevent us from having to take the risk of the outcome of 'coming of age' being 'otherwise' and of youth slipping away as soon as it does what it is supposed to do, but this is so we can keep making decisions in order to distinguish youth in the kinds of ways discussed here. Derrida likens this process to birth in that a baby 'is prepared, conditioned, named in advance, drawn into a symbolic space' and yet 'despite the anticipations and pre-nominations...the child who comes remains unforeseeable' (2002, p. 12). As with youth, being called to 'come' into adulthood is no guarantee of what will eventually arrive, but this is so 'coming of age', and then adulthood, can continue to exist at all. This carries a further implication: the moment of the transition (decision, event) is always urgent (Derrida, 1992, p. 26). Added to the fourth element of the paradox of 'coming of age', this means that development and change is gradual *and* immediate, accumulative *and* absolute. Earlier, the immediate shift from innocence to experience created great anxiety due to a belief in the premature loss of innocence. Here, interestingly, that same point is re-made. 'Coming of age' *will* always happen 'so fast', but this is the only way it *can* happen, because within the metaphysics of presence, the notion of 'becoming' is undecidable.

In *Thirteen*, there is a mental scrambling by everyone around Tracy that reflects this difficult and contradictory logic. In a clothing store with Tracy and Evie, Mel is initially admiring of Tracy when she parades a new pair of jeans for her, taking a long look of realisation at how her daughter looks suddenly so grown up. In a later scene, however, Tracy and Evie take turns inhaling from an aerosol can and scream at each other to 'hit me!'. They exchange slaps and punches, each getting bruised, Tracy splitting her lip. When at last Tracy hits the floor and passes out, Evie dives to revive her just as they are called outside to eat. Evie forces a languid Tracy to cover her injuries with make up, Evie herself putting a butterfly sticker over a graze on her forehead. Outside, Mel, Tracy's brother, Mason, and a family friend look on in bewilderment as the girls emerge from the bedroom not just hastily covered up but in bizarre dress-up, wigs and feather boas. Evie turns to reveal two fabric eyes stuck on the back pockets of her jeans. 'Say hello to the butt!' she says. The grave look on Mel's face, trying to comprehend this latest spectacle, is palpable. The escalation from playing Barbie dolls to playing drug-induced dress-ups has been swift, just four months. Tracy, it is easy to forget (that is until she is threatened with being held back in school), is still only in the seventh grade.

The social context of the production of *Thirteen* also reflects the difficulties of this encounter with the last element, and therefore *all* the elements, of the paradox of 'coming of age'. As with *Lolita*, the young actors in the film had to abide by strict guidelines during the filming process. For example, the film's DVD audio commentary explains that in a three-way make-out scene with Tracy, Evie and neighbour Luke the guidelines of the manner and kind of touching allowed had to be strictly observed by parents and other officials while being filmed. The girls could tug at the bottom of the boy's shorts, but were not allowed to touch the waistband. The director, Hardwicke, also notes that in the scene Evie had to be stopped from using a bong taken from Luke's mantelpiece because Nikki Reed, the actress playing Evie, was underage. Instead, they had her put it down and rejoin the threesome by having Luke say 'get back here, girl'. She sits back down and pulls off his shirt – the less controversial option, it would seem. While the film was admired for its highly realistic portrayal of 'real' teen life, which includes sex, violence, profanity, drug use and nudity, Catherine Driscoll writes that these are exactly the issues that get 'assessed in considering whether a film is suitable for youth', these are what count towards a restrictive rating (2002, p. 206). It seems ridiculous that minors would ever be allowed to portray these things, however closely regulated and supervised, if by doing so they would involve themselves in things deemed unsuitable for youth to see let alone do, even if they are supposedly depicting what teen reality is really about. What does it mean for the discourse of 'coming of age' that the young actresses be allowed in the film when it is illegal for actual 13-year-olds to see it? (The film was classified MA+ in Australia and R in America). We run into the same conceptual contradiction raised by *Lolita*: that only youth can depict youth, but to have youth depict youth is to violate what is intrinsic about youth.

The result is that *Thirteen* is a film 'about youth but not for youth' (Driscoll, 2002, p. 206). Adults can watch the on-screen transgressions of young teens, yet they can still protect the innocence of young viewers through, in this instance, film classification guidelines. This, however, does not open the way for dealing with the issue that youth are simultaneously regarded as innocent at the same time as their non-innocence is displayed, even if it is only 'performed' as opposed to actually 'experienced'. But, significantly, this is assuming that there is a difference between the two.

The performativity of innocence

The films actually provide a key clue for how to address the conflicts that the paradox of 'coming of age' produces. As things are, the kind of behaviour depicted in all three films becomes a reason to reaffirm the distinction of innocence/knowledge, because every time something happens to mark 'coming of age' it must necessarily happen 'so fast' and it must break with the notion of innocence that previously defined youth. Because this contradicts the notion of 'coming of age' as progressive and gradual, it seems dangerous and premature, even though a young person is doing what they are *supposed* to do in the only way that the binary logic of innocence/knowledge will allow if that logic is to be maintained.

However, for innocence to be represented at all it must already be other than so-called pure innocence, the pure presence of innocence. One of the issues raised earlier (and in Chapter 2's discussion of the Bill Henson case) is that to have young people 'perform' their age is to violate their own innocence. This assumes that innocence cannot be performed, that it can only 'be', which is why only youth can depict youth, even though, technically, it cannot be depicted. As illustrated here and in certain responses to Henson's photography, absolute innocence is not open to being represented, which is also to say, open to being repeated and to therefore being other than what it is. It would seem, therefore, that given the desire to protect the innocence of youth, just the mere thought of making these kinds of films would be enough to do harm. A Giroux-style reading could be applied here in terms of how commercial discourses impinge on or constrain certain forms of youth expression and experience. When there is an underlying assumption of an ideal form of youth, corporate culture, or here, the film industry, can be seen to allow youth to be treated as a product for consumption over and above concern for their well-being. Similarly, Joanne Faulkner describes how contemporary culture works to fetishise innocence. 'Innocence is not supposed to be useful; it is a value that most feel should transcend profit or personal gain' (2011, p. 19). Yet, innocence is seen and used and exploited by the child beauty pageant industry, by the fashion and advertising industries, and most assuredly by the porn industry. But if youth is understood to 'begin' in representation, a notion introduced at the end of Chapter 4, then the relationship between the text and the material, physical world can be seen differently. The films (and Henson's photographs) are not strictly a reflection or representation of a 'natural' state of youth if that so-called natural state is already constituted within a system of differential relations, or is already 'breached' or 'split' from within. So the experience of innocence is made possible precisely because it is not pure, but produced. This will be taken up further in the following chapter.

This way of thinking opens a different way of conceptualising youth within an innocence/knowledge distinction. This traditional binary logic would suggest that for young people to have an opinion about their own experience – or to perform their experience – is not to be 'in' the youth that they are experiencing, because it is assumed that they have a limited self-consciousness about it. On this basis, youth are effectively excluded from discussion over what concerns them and we cannot ask them to articulate their experience as this demands a self-reflexivity that is not attributed to them. The question of whether or not young people are being harmed by exposure to or involvement in this kind of material cannot therefore be asked (or answered) without betraying the truth of youth a developmental discourse posits and is attempting to maintain, preserve and protect. In other words, the discourse depends on that which is unintelligible to it. So to have the issue, problem, debate over teen sexuality actually progress and move on (because as it is now, as already stated, the same old arguments can only be repeated and re-hashed), we *need* to rethink the grounding assumptions of 'coming of age' in order to 'see' its limits as a means of addressing the issues discussed here on paedophilia, sexuality and teen rebellion.

An alternative provided by this deconstructive reading of the three films is that in terms of 'coming of age' we should seek to protect and guide those who 'lack' knowledge rather than those who 'have' innocence – a small but significant difference. This supports Faulkner's claim that 'rather than "letting children be children", we need to let them become adults, by encouraging their social growth and supporting them to participate in the concerns of everyday life' (2010, p. 116). In this way, to gain knowledge is not to violate or 'end' one's innocence as a state that is removed from the concerns of adulthood, but to advance along a course of socio-political development one is already within, because the point is that one was never not within it (to echo the point made in the last chapter that youth are never not within a general reason). So it is possible to discuss such things as youth ethics, self-knowledge, agency, consent and desire and what it means to represent these things in a way not possible within strict binary opposition.

A 'slowly developing sexuality' (Rush and La Nauze, 2006a, p. 1) based in an innocence/knowledge distinction will always be prematurely ruptured because innocence can provide no appropriate moment for its own end if it is taken to exist outside of the adult world of culture and history. But a developing sexuality that is understood as always already within culture grants a different status to youth. If, as Catherine Lumby suggests, 'children and teenagers are not entirely without agency or insight into the adult world' then the 'power relations between children, teenagers, and their adult counterparts are not so asymmetrical or fixed' (2010, np). Even though adults certainly have 'more' knowledge than youth and thus operate on a different intellectual level with different abilities and responsibilities, it is possible to recognise that young people's 'relationship to their bodies, their sexuality, and more broadly to culture and media do not have to be figured as either childlike or adult' (Lumby, 2010, np).

The young teens depicted in the films covered in this chapter support this possibility. Their conduct, sexual and otherwise, is hardly innocent, but it is not altogether 'knowing' either. That they occupy a space or a moment that is neither child nor adult is prescribed as normal by a 'coming of age' discourse, even if the discourse casts these same youth as existing beyond the limits of that norm. To think about youth in the absence of their presumed innocence, however, allows us to view 'coming of age' as a point in their development that includes both an awareness of one's own choices *and* the capacity to fall victim to others' desires. There is no need here to deny all differences between youth and adult forms of subjectivity and to treat them as the same. This approach need not render teen identity any less distinct or important or worthy of protection. Youth can still be other than adult, and make a transition from one to the other, but it can be done without compromising the structure that orders such relations. In other words, a 'situated' innocence is of no less importance than an absolute innocence, but it opens up certain conceptual possibilities that the other does not, which is of vital importance given that what is at stake are issues of safety and abuse, consent, desire and exploitation that are at the heart of debate about the sexualisation of youth.

As noted at the beginning of the chapter, research on tween girls and older youth provides evidence of the critical capacities of young people to make sense of their own lives, cultural contexts and sexualities. These voices complicate popular (and academic) assumptions about youth as vulnerable and at risk, signalling that discussions about teen sexuality need to move on from arguments that are grounded in assumptions of innocence, threat, risk and danger. Such arguments can only be continuously re-hashed on these same terms as they fail to grasp the contradictions that define their use. The critical capacities of youth are not, however, developed independently of these terms in the sense that, as noted in Chapter 3, youth subjects must necessarily use concepts supplied to them by the adult culture to tell their own stories, or to resist or reject the stories offered about them. Jackson and Vares recognise this when explaining the theoretical approach chosen for their research with tween girls: a 'poststructuralist framework enables us to treat our participants' material as simultaneously productive of notions about sexuality and produced by discourses in circulation in their lived lives' (2011, p. 137). This is to say that youth voices are as authentic as they are situated within culture; they do not speak a natural youth discourse and their voices are not strictly their own. But this means that young people may be included in discussions concerning their own health, well-being and development without violating the terms of their status as youth.

The deconstructive reading performed here has revealed that the oppositional logic of nature/culture or innocence/knowledge cannot contain that which it marks as the proper development of female youth and their ideal entry into adulthood. It showed that when the undecidability of oppositional logic goes unrecognised dominant logic becomes problematic because attempts are made to maintain a logic based on absolute distinctions when in fact they are thinkable only because they are *not* absolute. The effect of this is that the discourse of 'coming of age' can only perpetuate a conflict between the desire to protect the innocence of youth while subjecting young people to the demand to 'grow up'. In other words, part of what constitutes teen sex as problematic is to do with the concepts in use.

Alternatively, this chapter has argued that the innocence of youth is always already cultural, and that there is nothing intrinsic or immutable about youth to work from or to seek to protect. By acknowledging the ambivalence of the grounding assumptions of 'coming of age', the issues of safety, abuse, consent, desire and exploitation that are raised by the issues of paedophilia, underage sex and teen rebellion can be considered beyond assumptions of the inherent nature of youth. This does not mean that youth has no firm meaning or will slip from any attempt to make it meaningful, nor is this analysis about replacing a flawed logic with something less problematic. This work involves, as Derrida states, both 'conserving and annulling inherited conceptual oppositions' (1997, p. 105). So rather than getting stuck in a perpetual cycle of fear and panic with regard to the representation and experience of young female sexuality, the deconstructive reading of the three films performed here seeks to move beyond this cycle by revealing the conceptual conditions that lead to such effects. The next chapter pursues a similar aim with regard to the issue of violence perpetrated by young men in the hope of opening up youth identity politics to more productive constitutive and interpretive possibilities.

6
Normal Abnormality: Coming to Terms with Teen Violence and the Undecidability of Youth

Following on from the last chapter's concern with developing a way to more productively respond to issues of sexualisation and the representation of young female sexuality, this chapter explores why it is important that attempts to explain teen violence move beyond normative assumptions about youth. The particular focus of this chapter is the phenomenon of school shootings, specifically, the 1999 Columbine massacre. Columbine is not the most recent or the most deadly school massacre, but in the history of school shootings it represents a defining event in terms of the scale of the tragedy and the depth of its cultural impact. Few other cases have received the same degree of public, media and academic attention in efforts to understand the motivations of the shooters and comprehend the meaning and implications of the event. Searching questions have been asked about the perpetrators' psychology, their upbringing and social environment, their media influences, and their school and peer culture to try and understand their intentions[1].

Unfortunately, such questions continue to be asked of other young men who have carried out subsequent mass shootings. The 2007 Virginia Tech massacre and the 2012 Sandy Hook Elementary School tragedy are two of the most prominent examples of what has become a frighteningly familiar scenario: young men entering schools and university campuses and opening fire into corridors and classrooms using high-powered semi-automatic weapons, killing and injuring dozens of people and ultimately taking their own lives. Of course, the phenomenon of mass shooting extends beyond the classroom. The 2011 Norway massacre and the 2012 Aurora Cinema tragedy have helped render a genre of violence that has become disturbingly familiar yet perpetually shocking. What has also become familiar are the debates that arise in the aftermath of such incidents concerning gun control, violent video games, male alienation, bullying and mental illness as crucial contributing factors in leading young men to commit mass shootings.

Significantly, it is the age of the Columbine gunmen and other teenage shooters that mark school-based massacres as especially aberrant. That people so young should perpetrate such acts against their own peers and in a 'safe' institutional environment that is for learning, growth and preparing for future adult life is particularly shocking and troublesome. That young people are both perpetrators and victims offends against the very notion of youth and what it represents: a future that is yet to come and a time of protected and controlled development. Events like this also therefore offend against the values and order of the wider culture, and as such they demand explanation.

My interest in the Columbine case, however, is that in many respects it has defied adequate explanation. Many explanations for the tragedy are grounded in the context of the two shooters' youth and as such operate from a developmental discourse as conditioned by a presence/absence binary split. I argue that attempts to make sense of the event based on this conceptual opposition are unable to satisfactorily demarcate 'normal' from 'abnormal' youth and this is unacceptable given both the need to account for what happened at Columbine and the ongoing need to protect young people from these kinds of shootings.

In response to this explanatory deficit, I take what may appear to be a risky approach in that, in the face of such an overwhelming and shocking 'real world' event, I am concerned with opening up other interpretive possibilities at a conceptual level. This is done, however, with the same aim in mind as the many other attempts to make sense of Columbine: a desire to preserve and protect young people and to work to prevent this kind of tragedy from continuing to happen. I apply Derrida's notion of iterability and performativity to approach the question of youth intention and this offers a way to make sense of the actions of the two perpetrators that resists totalising claims but brings a greater responsiveness to the work of making sense of what happened. There is no deferral to an underlying logic or a reductive reasoning process, but an affirmation of the need to account for the effects of different explanatory possibilities. Paradoxically, resisting explanatory closure actually allows for an experience of closure or at least for a means of getting closer to a satisfactory explanation, and this work begins by considering the status of Columbine as an event.

The question of 'the event'

In relation to the metaphysics of presence, Niall Lucy writes that events appear as naturally self-evident. They are not made or produced; they simply 'are' (2004, p. 33). Whenever something happens, therefore, we would know exactly what it is and what it means. This approach assumes that there is a sharp distinction between what is actual and what is artificial, and it is on the basis of this knowledge that we are able to construct a 'horizon of expectation' for the event, which is 'a way of knowing the future in advance' (Lucy, 2004, pp. 3–4).

However, to know what actuality is in advance would mean that the future would be closed off to us, for there would be nothing that was not already known. What is required in order for things to happen, therefore, is the possibility that an event will not conform to any existing definition of what is actual and what is artificial (Lucy, 2004, pp. 3–4). As something that actually happens, then, Simon Wortham suggests that an event must exceed its own context and any form of representation of it (2010, p. 48). So even though we need to maintain a distinction between the real and the unreal in order to have a context for experience, we must always experience the event as an unexpected arrival, as unanticipated and beyond our apprehension (Wortham, 2010, p. 48). This is close to what Joanna Zylinska means when she argues, using Kant's notion of the sublime, that there is 'the "event" itself' and then there are 'its different mediations'; how the event is interpreted through language, through particular discourses or frameworks of intelligibility, through different interpretive strategies (2004, pp. 229&234). What makes an event horrific or tragic or shocking is not therefore 'in' the event itself because its direct experience necessarily occurs beyond our ability to know what 'it' is; its meaning is not immediately apparent. Rather, the trauma of an unexpected event is associated with (unwillingly) being put in a position of not knowing what it means, and the struggle of having 'to articulate what defies articulation' based on an existing actual/artificial distinction (Zylinska, 2004, p. 234). The self is deprived of conceptual mastery by the nature of this encounter, and so Zylinska suggests that the discourse of the sublime is often called on to describe such situations where 'the impossibility of representing the event and [the] need to give it a name' puts the authority of the self in question, suspending its sense of 'self-sufficiency and safety' (2004, pp. 242&232). A response is required, demanded, and yet, by definition, 'our cognitive faculties are at a loss to grasp what defies them' (Zylinska, 2004, p. 234). How, then, to respond?

Because what is actual has been exceeded, the actuality of an event has to be 'newly' constructed. This work involves a passage through the undecidable in that every decision about what an event means must necessarily 'engage afresh...with the singularity of the occasion that calls for a decision to be made' and so 'exceed or overrun the conditions of any programme' that posits a particular outcome (Lucy, 2004, p. 150). It is as a result of this decision-making process that an event is put into a context or representable order (which can still 'look' the same as that which was first exceeded by the event). From here it is possible to re-situate the self and define what makes a particular event a tragedy (or something else), because it is possible to work from a 'new' actual/artificial distinction and so determine the what, how and why of something.

However, this is not to articulate what the initial experience of not knowing was, as though that experience had its own reality that could somehow be accessed, even though an understanding of that initial experience that is now possible is all that can count *as* that experience. As Cathy Caruth explains, the direct experience of an event occurs 'as an absolute inability to know it', so its immediacy actually takes the 'form of belatedness' (cited in Zylinska, 2004, p. 234). This means that to have an event happen is to 'make' it and so the significance of an event is an *'effect* of interpretive activities', and not just 'there' to be described (Lucy, 2004, p. 36, my emphasis). A key implication of this approach to the meaning of events is that interpretive activities are not exhausted once a particular decision is made. Making decisions delimits a range of possible explanations for an event by producing particular knowledge about what it is. But if actuality is made rather than given, then it is possible for it to be made differently (Lucy, 2004, p. 6).

However, what is it to make sense of events that seem to require no arguments for their significance since they are manifestly 'important'. It is not necessary, for instance, to make arguments for seeing massively, publicly 'tragic' events as significant. But how is sense made of their manifest significance, and why ask the question other than to 'prove' what is already apparent, to state what that significance 'is'? This is the problem to be addressed here with regard to the event known as the Columbine massacre.

The Columbine massacre

At approximately 11.17am on 20 April 1999, 17-year-old Eric Harris and 18-year-old Dylan Klebold entered Columbine High School in

Littleton, Colorado. Armed with shotguns, assorted automatic weapons and home-made pipe bombs, they shot and killed 12 students and one teacher and wounded 23 others in the hallways, cafeteria and library of the school, and then, after exchanging fire with police officers outside, killed themselves in the library. Their rampage lasted 46 minutes.

This event left the community, the nation and the world in a state of deep shock and disbelief. How could this have happened? Why did it happen? What does it mean? And what do we do about it? How do we begin to make sense of this tragedy? And what constitutes a satisfactory explanation? The notion of the undeconstructible presence of the event as an effect of the movement of supplementarity can be applied here[2]. This is to see that what is manifestly significant about the event is already other than itself as such. A prior opening is required in order for the event to be thinkable in terms of pure presence. In other words, what constitutes the significance of the event is not to be found 'in' the event itself, in a bare description of what actually happened, such as that written above, but through certain mediating factors. To be absolutely clear, though, this is not to say that of itself the event is not important; it is to say that claims of what that manifest importance 'is' are, nonetheless, subject to the effects of supplementarity, to the movement of signification. As such, the various explanations for the Columbine event can be analysed for their particular assumptions about youth, which have taken investigations into the massacre in certain directions rather than others.

The following discussion examines a range of explanations for the massacre that are all reducible to the fundamental assumption of the undeconstructibility of presence and of youth in relation to this, grounded in this. Such work operates on the assumption that it is possible to provide a total explanation for what happened, such as the boys did it because they were under the influence of violent media; they did it because they suffered from mental illness; they did it because they were not 'normal' youth but dangerous criminals. However, I point to where these attempts to explain the significance of the event create effects that an interpretive structure based on presence cannot account for without risking its own intelligibility (the double movement of structure is covered over). The effect of this is that these explanations fall short of the demand for a total explanation and the (implicit) reason for applying such an interpretive strategy in the first place: the preservation and protection of youth and of a mainstream notion of youth. These approaches therefore *fail* to explain the manifest importance of the event and, because of this failure, there is nothing else to do but mark the event as being beyond explanation, because to be less than enough of an explanation is *not enough* given the enormity of the event.

In this case, though, it is clear that there is little option other than to attempt to explain the event; it is *not* okay to affirm the event as being beyond explanation. An alternative, then, is to embrace an excessive inexplicability, or rather, to acknowledge that we will never have explanation enough because the condition of supplementarity is that there is 'always more' (Derrida, 1978, p. 289). The imperative here, therefore, and difficult as it may seem, is to see the event 'otherwise', as other than manifestly significant. From this position, questions can be asked about the function of the concept of youth as deployed in the various explanations for the massacre without compromising the structure on which the work of explanation and investigation is based. In doing this here, and to repeat my introductory remarks, I employ the Derridean concepts of the event, performativity and iterability. I examine why it is counter-productive to seek to reduce this event to a structure of presence, why it is necessary to keep explanatory possibilities open, and what this means for the function of normative notions of youth. Whether or not the event's manifest significance is assumed to be 'just there', such deconstructive work is necessary. It offers, in a word, a more responsive way of working towards the prevention of future shootings and the protection of youth. To this end, I turn now to examine how the event was framed around notions of youth.

How could it happen here? Youth violence in the mainstream

> HATE! I'm full of hate and I Love it. I HATE PEOPLE and they better fucking fear me if they know whats good for em [*sic*]. Yes I hate and I guess I want others to know it, yes I'm racist and I don't mind. Niggs and spics bring it on themselves.
>
> Eric Harris, handwritten journal
> (17 November 1998a)

> It would be great if god removed all vaccines and warning labels from everything in the world and let natural selection take its course. All the fat ugly retarded crippled dumbass stupid fuckheads in the world would die, and oh fucking well if a few of the good guys die to [*sic*]. Maybe then the human race can actually be proud of itself.
>
> Eric Harris, web journal
> (26 September 1998b, 'Vaccines')

The massacre at Columbine sparked panic about something being rotten in the heart of suburbia, something dangerous 'bubbling beneath the surface' in otherwise safe neighbourhoods and communities (Newman, 2004, p. 14). Nancy Gibbs wonders 'what turned two boys' souls into poison', and why do 'smart, privileged kids rot inside'? (1999, np), because what else, other than some kind of contagion, could account for this? In other words, how could it be that white, middle-class suburban boys could perpetrate such an act? What possible reason could they have? How is it that they were even capable of it? And what can be done to prevent it happening again?

According to a US National Academy of Sciences study into lethal school violence, Columbine and other instances of school violence are particular to affluent, suburban communities (2003, p. 1). Previous instances of deadly youth violence, the study notes, involved black and Hispanic youth from socially disadvantaged urban schools and neighbourhoods and were caused by well-understood problems such as 'poverty, racial segregation, and the dynamics of the illicit drug trade' (National Academy of Sciences, 2003, pp. 1&4). However, violence and murder on such a large and horrific scale was completely unexpected in the suburban high school. Because such social conditions were largely absent in suburban communities, they thought themselves insulated from such violence (National Academy of Sciences, 2003, p. 1). Indeed, the study notes that far from demonstrating the structural conditions of the urban environment, most of the communities that had experienced a mass shooting were the demographic opposite: 'thriving economically, having a high degree of social capital, and mostly free of crime and violence' (National Academy of Sciences, 2003, p. 6). As such, the shooters responsible for these crimes 'were not considered to be at high risk for this kind of behaviour by the adults around them' (National Academy of Sciences, 2003, p. 5). In fact, as Christine Griffin suggests (and as Giroux argues, as discussed in Chapter 2), these kids constitute 'the implicit norm against which other groups of young people are judged' (2004, p. 16). As white, middle-class and able-bodied young men they occupy and represent the mainstream, and as such enjoy better educational opportunities and have access to better employment, training services, career options and leisure activities than other racial and socio-economic groups. Compared to their disadvantaged peers, white youth are rarely seen as a 'social problem' or cause for concern (Griffin, 2004, p. 16).

Furthermore, it is these conditions that supposedly produce the kinds of kids who go on to become responsible and productive adult members

of society. Reflecting a dominant developmental discourse, these particular young people are understood to be going through a process of
development towards adulthood for which it is necessary to be protected
and kept at a distance from the adult world in order that they might be
adequately prepared for it. It is not until their eventual transition from
youth into 'adulthood' (which, of course, is not a neat distinction, but it
remains in place nonetheless) that they are considered emotionally and
intellectually mature enough to form and act with intention, to behave
responsibly, and to therefore be held accountable for their actions.

Explanations for the massacre (a range of which are analysed below)
can be seen to work according to these assumptions about youth and
what a developmental discourse marks as actual, calculable possibility
concerning youth behaviour and abilities, and also its particular inabil-
ities. As youth are in a process of development, so they are thought
to lack the necessary stability of identity to cultivate violent intentions. Instead, violent behaviour can be seen to come as a result of
certain negative influences on them because of this inherent instability or vulnerability. Giroux's articulation of a 'youth at risk' discourse
could also be applied here, especially given that the two perpetrators of
the massacre were white, middle-class males – exactly the kind of young
people, Giroux argues, who are afforded the protection that comes with
a belief in their innocence.

A logical response to Columbine, then, would be to assume that something must have adversely affected or influenced the boys' behaviour;
something must have happened to cause them to 'rot inside'. Working
to understand why the shooting happened therefore requires identifying what these causes or influences might be and where they have come
from. As discussed in Chapter 2, Giroux identifies the adverse influence
of corporate culture and the rise of punitive attitudes towards young
people created by adult disinvestment in social services that attend to
young people above and beyond their needs as consumers. By elimi-
nating such negative influences – by investing in a public sphere, for
example – it would be possible to prevent future shootings because
youth could be adequately protected from the negative influences of
corporate culture and so too protected from themselves in their vulnerability to such influences. To make sense of the event by applying
a mainstream notion of youth is, by implication, to work to preserve
this notion of youth. The result – and also the aim – of such work is a
return to or the restoration of an existing order of social relations. In this
case, such order is one in which adults exercise a protective and guiding
authority over (vulnerable, impressionable) youth and work to cultivate

in them certain intellectual, emotional, social and physical capacities, values and desires. Such capacities, values and desires are then applied and managed once adulthood is reached in areas such as work and family, and in response to the demands and expectations of lawful and responsible citizenship.

Why did they do it? Attributions of intention

Much attention in early investigations into the shooting focused on the boys' engagement with violent media and its effect on behaviour. As media scholar Henry Jenkins writes, a 'media effects' tradition is concerned with finding out 'what the media are doing to our children' and not 'what our children are doing with the media' (2006, p. 194). Accordingly, Columbine and other tragedies have been blamed on popular culture. Harris and Klebold were known to have loved and studied the 1994 film *Natural Born Killers* (see Larkin, 2007; Fast, 2008), and Richard Corliss remarks that films like *The Basketball Diaries* (1995) or *Heathers* (1989) make for interesting viewing if one is interested in tracing 'a hindsight game plan for Littleton' (1999, np). In *Diaries* a 'druggy high schooler ... daydreams of strutting into his homeroom in a long black coat and gunning down his hated teacher and half the kids', and in *Heathers* 'a charming sociopath engineers the death of jocks and princesses' (Corliss, 1999, np). Corliss points out that 'revenge dramas' are not new (for example, *Hamlet* and *The Godfather*), and that 'a steady diet of megaviolence may coarsen the young psyche', but the key point here is simple: millions of people see violent movies and do not become violent themselves (1999, np). While there may be *a* connection between violent teen behaviour and violent films, how could it ever be proven to be *the causal* connection?

Something else for which there is more evidence is the boys' involvement with violent video games. Harris was a keen computer gamer and had developed new levels for the game *Doom II*, which he shared online (Fast, 2008, p. 186). Could it be possible that Harris and Klebold were, as one internet investigator believes, 'playing out their game in God mode' when they entered their school? (cited in Pooley, 1999, np). School friend Brooks Brown argues a similar point: 'it was about them living in the moment, like they were inside a video game' (cited in Pooley, 1999, np). However, reporter Eric Pooley questions whether it is 'really possible that the flesh and blood of the maimed and dying was no more real to them than pixels on a video monitor', and if that is indeed the case, then such an explanation 'absolves the killers too easily' (1999, np).

A less reductive alternative offered by Jenkins is to consider why the boys were attracted to dark and violent imagery and why they made use of media in these ways, because, he argues, while different media 'provided them both with the raw materials necessary to construct their fantasies', the 'mass media didn't *make* Harris and Klebold violent and destructive' any more than it can make some other teen creative or sociable (2006, p. 195, my emphasis). While Harris and Klebold's destructive tendencies found exhibition through video games, it is not necessarily *because* of these games that they developed destructive tendencies; Jenkins suggests that such games are a means of expression rather than a cause. This issue will be picked up again later.

With regard to the issue of cause, then, a widely discussed argument for why the boys did it was that they were exacting revenge for having been bullied and marginalised within their school's strict social hierarchy. During the shooting, the boys were reported to have said things like 'all the jocks stand up. We're going to kill every one of you' (cited in Gibbs, 1999, np), and there is much evidence to suggest that the boys did it because they were picked on, bullied and victimised by the school's celebrated athletes or 'jocks'. These are students who stand atop the social ladder and are in a position to deploy both physical and verbal abuse to other students, especially towards the male students who do not meet the strict ideals of manhood (Tonso, 2009, p. 1276). In video messages the boys recorded in the lead up to the shooting (known as the 'basement tapes'), Harris says in one, 'I'm going to kill you all. You've been giving us s--- for years' (cited in Gibbs and Roche, 1999, np). Brooks Brown thinks that 'every time someone slammed them against a locker or threw a bottle at them', they would 'go back to Eric or Dylan's house and plot a little more – at first as a goof, but more and more seriously over time' (cited in Pooley, 1999, np).

Some of the scholarly literature on the shooting links the idea of revenge to notions of masculinity, a connection that has particular pertinence in the context of youth where peer acceptance and social standing, not to mention identity formation, is of paramount concern. Douglas Kellner (2008) considers the actions of the pair as an instance of a crisis of masculinity within a white male identity politics, and Jonathan Fast presents the event as a form of 'ceremonial violence' in which socially disenfranchised individuals become suicidal but, due to narcissistic tendencies, decide to turn their suicide into a public ceremony as a way to achieve adulation (2008, pp. 17–19). Similarly to Kellner, Karen Tonso writes of the production of violent masculinities within ideologies of masculine supremacy. Certain kinds of violence are legitimated, like that attributed to jocks, but not everyone gets to participate in it and those who don't are thus relegated to a lower social status. Harris and Klebold identified with neo-Nazis and with Timothy McVeigh who perpetrated the 1995 Oklahoma City bombing. These figures represent a particular form of masculine rage against a system in which they feel subjugated and thus obliged to rectify. A position of supremacy is owed to them by their culture, and Tonso suggests that Harris and Klebold murdered as a way to 'reclaim their "rightful" place', aligning with a neo-Nazi mindset that assumes a violent right to power in a culture of (white) male privilege (2009, pp. 1277–8). 'Isn't it fun to get the respect that we're going to deserve?' Harris asks on one of the tapes, shotgun in hand (cited in Gibbs and Roche, 1999, np). Equally, however, Tonso suggests that not all men who suffer social humiliations in school appropriate violent masculinities, nor do they 'accept the patriarchal dividend and interpret the world around them using it as a lens for sense-making' (2009, p. 1277).

In contrast, there is also evidence that points to the boys *not* being loner outcasts. A range of accounts of the massacre (see, for example, Larkin, 2007; Fast, 2008; Cullen, 2009a) note that both teens did have a social circle. They achieved good grades in school and held jobs in a local pizza parlour. Klebold engaged in some extracurricular activities and attended his high school prom; Harris was into computers and gaming. However, whether or not the boys were or felt socially marginalised and thus set out to target specific people or subcultural groups within their school (jocks, Christians, academic achievers), the killings were, ultimately, indiscriminate. 'They shot at the math whiz and the actress, the wrestler, the debater, jocks, brains, band members, freshmen, seniors' (Gibbs, 1999, np).

This fact supports the view that the boys actually wanted to annihilate the entire school. Media commentaries marking the ten-year anniversary of the massacre argue that early explanations as to the boys' motives that focused on personal grudges and bullying were entirely wrong and a product of hysteria and mere guesswork (Gumbel, 2009, np). The picture that has emerged from longer-term examination of the evidence suggests that the boys actually wanted to destroy everything. 'I hope we kill 250 of you', says Klebold in one of the tapes (cited in Gibbs and Roche, 1999, np). To this end, the pair placed two propane bombs in the school cafeteria timed to explode when it was full of students taking early lunch. They were designed to kill hundreds of students, leaving the boys to shoot down survivors as they fled the buildings. These bombs failed to explode, forcing the boys to take alternative action (Cullen, 2009b, np; Gumbel, 2009, np).

In light of the view that Harris and Klebold in fact sought mass destruction, a further, and preferred, explanatory approach developed in more recent literature is a psychological one: the boys did it because they suffered from psychological pathology. I will discuss this further in a later section, but for the moment it is an explanation that helps to account for conflicting evidence as to the boys' intentions. On this account, while Harris and Klebold may or may not have had specific targets in mind, and while they may or may not have been the victims of bullying within a jock culture of masculine violence, the rage they expressed towards particular people, groups of people and the world in general can be understood as symptomatic and indicative of their respective pathologies.

However, the ready availability of guns cannot be discounted as a major cause of school shootings and one of the most obvious and straightforward bases for a causal relationship, because, put simply, school *shootings* would not occur in the absence of guns[3] (Newman, 2004, p. 260; Fuentes, 2011, p. 39). School shootings have been shown to not be about attacking individuals, but institutions (National Academy of Sciences, 2003, p. 4), and the use of guns would seem to serve this purpose. As mentioned above, Tonso suggests that Klebold and Harris were attacking the '*systemic* subordination' they felt they suffered within their school (2009, p. 1276). So if their perceived mistreatment was systemic rather than personal, and if, as Kellner suggests, 'the expression of violence through guns ... is perceived as an expression of manhood' (2008, p. 97), then guns serve a useful purpose. They allowed the boys to assert a position of masculine power within the school institution and its social stratifications that denied the pair a sense of that power. On this basis, stricter gun ownership laws could therefore limit, if not prevent, this particular form of violence. Supporting this possibility also is the fact that the Columbine boys did not have to steal their guns, but obtained (most of) them legally through a gun show (Fuentes, 2011, p. 39).

There are, however, reasons to doubt the effectiveness of arguments for greater gun regulation. Aside from America's powerful pro-gun lobby and the country's entrenched gun culture, Nancy Gibbs and Timothy Roche report that the boys defend the friends who helped them buy their guns. In the basement tapes, the boys say that their friends didn't know anything about their intentions and are therefore not to be blamed (1999, np). Harris also states that 'we would have found something else' if they had not obtained their guns this way (cited in Gibbs and Roche, 1999, np). This suggests that even strict gun regulations will not wholly prevent events like this. Furthermore, it would seem that intention is present here before and beyond the issue of gun availability and regulation, not to mention the fact that most young people who grow up with and around guns do not use them for any such violent purpose.

A further possibility, then, is to blame the parents. The glaring question many have asked is how the boys' parents could have missed what was going on with their kids, especially as both of them had been in trouble with the law in the months leading up to the shooting. Was it negligence on their part that allowed this to happen? After Columbine, parents of slain students filed lawsuits against the parents of both boys. Amongst the charges were counts of parental neglect and allowing their sons to amass a stockpile of weapons. These lawsuits were either dismissed or settled out of court (see Kellner, 2008; Cullen, 2009a; Fuentes, 2011). Ultimately, investigators deemed that the parents were not culpable for their sons' actions. But what would be envisaged as a workable response if it were decided that the parents *were* responsible for their sons' actions, especially when all the evidence pointed to the boys coming from stable, 'good' homes? Kate Battan, a lead investigator into the massacre, said that 'they were not absentee parents. They're normal people who seem to care for their children and were involved in their life' (cited in Gibbs and Roche, 1999, np). At the very least, a similar kind of questioning to that being done here concerning youth over what has gone 'bad' in 'good' homes, and by extension in the homes of all of us, would be required because, on this issue, investigators concluded that Harris' and Klebold's parents 'were fooled like everyone else' (Gibbs and Roche, 1999, np). In 2009, ten years after the massacre, Dylan's mother, Susan Klebold, published an essay in *O Magazine* confirming this. She describes her grief over the death of her son and his responsibility for the deaths of others, and her feelings of guilt, humiliation and shame in the face of overwhelming public anger towards her (Klebold, 2009, np). The article presents a devoted, loving mother who failed to notice the degree of her own child's suffering.

What is clear from this discussion is that none of these explanations are quite explanation enough. No one person or one thing is fully accountable or fully without blame. The event cannot be reduced to any completely determinate cause which fully explains what happened and why. It is also easy to pass accountability along. Just as Corliss remarks that 'movies don't kill people, guns kill people' (1999, np), so sceptics of tighter gun control measures argue that 'guns don't kill people', 'people kill people' (Newman, 2004, p. 297). Katherine Newman states that we are left in a truly frustrating situation where there are endless arguments about who is right, and we never reach a point of closure as a result (2004, p. 201). Indeed, exhaustive investigations into targeted school violence conducted by the Secret Service concluded that there is no single, accurate profile of a school shooter (Cullen, 2009b, 34; Fuentes, 2011, p. 37). Similarly, Warnick et al., suggest that the more complex a theory of school violence becomes, the less helpful it is in being able to predict school shootings (2010, p. 376). So even though it is possible to make changes with regard to the circumstances surrounding these events, whether it be more censorship, programmes to improve peer relations, better mental health services, armed security in every school, child-sized bulletproof vests, less guns, or, indeed, *more* guns as a means of self-defence against a shooter, they can never be effective to the point of total prevention because they are not the total cause. When interpretive work is based on a notion that the boys acted under the influence of some negative force and that their intention was not their own, the various attempts by writers (such as those cited here) to determine what or who is responsible, accountable, and therefore who or what is to blame, fail to restore the existing, 'proper' order. But if not as evidence of the effect that something has had on these two boys – social marginalisation affecting identity construction, playing violent video games, and so on – how else can their actions be understood?

Intention of their own

A response, and alternative, to the limits of the types of analysis cited above is to operate under a different (opposing) assumption and consider the shooters as having a fully developed capacity to act with intention. This would be to think of them as being fully accountable for their actions and not as the victims of negative influences or forces because of any particular vulnerability on their part. A further examination of Harris' writing does not require much of a stretch in this direction. Here is an excerpt from his web journal:

> God damn it do not blame anyone else besides me and V [Klebold] for this. Don't blame my family, they had no clue and there is nothing they could have done, they brought me up just fucking fine, don't blame toy stores or any other stores for selling us ammo, bomb materials or anything like that because its not their fault, I don't want no

fucking laws on buying fucking PVC pipes. We are kind of a select case here so don't think this will happen again. Don't blame the school, don't fucking put cops all over the place just because we went on a killing spree doesn't mean everyone else will and hardly ever do people bring bombs or guns to school anyway, the admin. is doing a fine job as it is, I don't know who will be left after we kill but damn it don't change any policies just because of us.

(26 September 1998c, 'Vaccines [cont]')

Additionally, in one of their video messages Klebold predicts that people will say 'if only we could have reached them sooner or found this tape', to which Harris adds: 'if only we could have searched their room...if only we would have asked the right questions'. They also display remorse concerning their parents. 'It f—ing sucks to do this to them', says Harris, 'they're going to be put through hell once we do this'. But he also says that 'there's nothing you guys could've done to prevent this'. Elsewhere he states: 'I can make you believe anything' (cited in Gibbs and Roche, 1999, np).

These comments certainly seem irrefutable; what is there to question here when the pair are so clear on what they are doing and who is going to be affected, and especially as they not only correctly predict people's reactions but negate many of the reasons given by them for their behaviour? This could be taken or treated as a version (indeed, a frightening example) of mimicry, or possibly as evidence of the two boys exhibiting agency and self-awareness in making their own meanings against dominant discourses, to apply the terms of a subculture discourse. Following Hebdige's reading of punk subculture, the boys clearly made a 'spectacle' of themselves via subversion of the signs of middle-class suburban life, school culture and expectations of how young people in these domains should behave (that is, they were the 'least likely' to commit mass murder; they left dead bodies in the halls, cafeteria and library of their school). But in this case, this expression of intention could be treated as something entirely their own rather than treated as an instance of subversion of the dominant culture through mimicry, or even as the effect of corporate models of citizenship that leave individuals to bear personal responsibility for adverse life conditions that may have facilitated such behaviour, as Giroux would suggest.

By assuming that the boys had formed their own intentions, that is, work can be done to protect other young people from them (and others like them) by seeking to identify signs of malicious intent such as those expressed by Harris and Klebold prior to their murderous acts. This is to take their intention as evidence of *difference* from the distinctions of 'normal' youth. Young people who exhibit such intention can therefore be separated from normal youth and dealt with as such (that is, as not normal), and it would be possible for those seeking to explain the actions of 'abnormal' youth to bypass the sense of ambivalence that would come from using justifications for their behaviour that, in the case of Harris and Klebold, have already been subverted or dismissed by the boys themselves (more on this later).

The problem, though, is that the material used to determine that Harris and Klebold acted with pre-formed intention is not wholly different from the kinds of things 'normal' teenagers do and say. Playing violent video games, recording one's angry thoughts or fantasies in a diary or on a website, and keeping to a close friend or group of friends are all 'normal' behaviours for young people. To that extent, they are not ordinarily taken as evidence of serious and fully formed intention to commit mass murder. Seeking to weed out other potential shooters would thus require treating so-called normal – and mainstream – teen behaviour differently. It would mean 'pathologising' such behaviour.

After Columbine, many schools across the US instituted policies of zero tolerance as a way to identify problem students and deal with potential threats. Zero tolerance policies, writes Newman, 'require schools to follow formalised disciplinary procedures after any threat of violence', leaving 'administrators with little discretion to separate serious offenders from casual jokers'. This means that a phrase such as 'I'm going to get you' warrants a suspension irrespective of the context of its utterance (2004, p. 285). This policy is most effective when it comes to dealing with more concrete violations, such as students carrying weapons on campus or being found in possession of bomb-making instructions, but even here there have been instances of undue excess. Annette Fuentes cites multiple examples of disproportionate reactions to minor student infractions in her study of the 'lockdown' approach to American school safety that developed in response to school violence. Rough play in the schoolyard or a bump in the hallway is no longer 'youthful shenanigans' but 'disorderly conduct and assault', and suspensions may be triggered for speaking out in class, tardiness or dress code violations (Fuentes, 2011, p. 53). Despite problems with zero tolerance policies, however, John Cloud reports that many Americans favoured the approach in the aftermath of Columbine as a 'tough-minded' but 'short-term' solution for school violence. The idea was to implement 'more complex approaches' at a later stage to combat and prevent school violence, 'like better mentoring and earlier intervention for troubled children' (1999, np).

The use of profiling or threat assessment programmes to identify problem students is one example of this more comprehensive way of dealing with the threat of youth violence. As Jodie Morse suggests, the focus is on mental detection over metal detection (2000, np). Morse reports on a computer program called 'Mosaic-2000' which works to calculate rough odds on a child's potential to turn violent by building a profile and printing a threat-level report based on answers from 42 questions as developed from the study of other cases[4] (2000, np). Questions include 'is the student harassed by peers?' and 'has the student recently experienced rejection?' (Morse, 2000, np). The assessment is done without the student's knowledge, however, and it is often based only on suspicion – a violent drawing or essay – as opposed to an actual or direct threat. Morse notes that because of this, civil liberties groups contend 'that there is simply no reliable way to weed out the world's Dylans and Erics from their merely cranky classmates without trampling on privacy and constitutional rights in the process' (2000, np).

The work of protecting students by seeking to identify the presence of violent intentions among them therefore has an undesired effect. When 'normal' youth behaviour is the basis for determining dangerous intent, trying to identify students with such intentions ends up treating all youth in the same way. The ability to distinguish abnormal from normal youth is blurred, and educators must adopt 'a psychologically suspicious perspective' towards all students (Warnick et al., 2010, p. 387). But the risk of unfairly or inaccurately identifying a student as dangerous would seem to be one that we cannot afford not to take given what has happened, given that it is potentially a matter of life and death. But this also means having to give up granting students the benefit of the doubt, giving up thinking of them as still developing intellectually and emotionally, and as being in need of guidance and protection. In short, normal 'youth' becomes a threat.

The criminalisation of youth

How, then, is Harris and Klebold's crime to be understood? They committed mass murder, but what is the meaning of this offence with regard to this blurring of distinction between normal and abnormal youth? Newman writes that in US law 'the capacity to form intent is critical in assessing culpability for murder' and that 'in most states, children, particularly those under age fourteen, are deemed inherently unable to form the requisite intent to murder' (2004, p. 183). (As mentioned in Chapter 4, the case of *Roper* v. *Simmons* exempted minors from capital punishment based on a similar ruling of mental incapacity.) Also, Newman writes that the traditional approach in criminal law is one of protection towards defendants and that this is especially the case with regard to juvenile justice, 'for the theory has long been that children can be rehabilitated and that the mission of the system is less to punish than to rescue them' (2004, p. 180). This was the case when, prior to Columbine, Harris and Klebold were arrested for stealing electronics equipment from a van. As this was a first offence, the charges were dropped and the pair were placed on a 'juvenile diversion program' which involved counselling, community service and anger management classes (See Larkin, 2007; Fast, 2008; Cullen, 2009a). But with the event of their later crime, the assumptions about youth underpinning this approach to youth crime were exceeded.

The evidence that Harris and Klebold clearly planned the massacre leaves little alternative other than to mark them as different from youth as defined in legal discourse[5], and as therefore accountable for their crime according to the legal definition of culpability for murder. Supporting this, Newman notes that the attitude of victims' families from other shootings is that offenders should not be allowed to hide behind their youth or confusion about their intentions and should be made to 'confront the enormity of their crimes and be held accountable for the damage they have done' (2004, p. 180). Furthermore, as the boys were 17 and 18 years old, we can assume that had they lived they would have been tried as adults. But the same questions have been raised over shooters as young as 12–14 years. Nathaniel Brazill from Lake Worth, Florida, was 13 years old when he shot and killed a teacher after being sent home for throwing water balloons. Newman writes that his actions sparked debate 'about letting the nature of the crime, rather than the characteristics of the accused, determine whether a defendant should be tried as a juvenile or an adult' and proposals were 'advanced to drop the age of adulthood for the purposes of criminal prosecution to eleven' (Newman, 2004, p. 184). Put another way, it is possible to *decide* the point at which mental capacity is mature enough for the application of adult charges.

Normative assumptions about youth therefore have difficulty containing or accounting for the crime that was committed at Columbine without also losing their explanatory power. It is in the transgression of these assumptions that Harris and Klebold's crime is able to be situated within a legal discourse that provides a context for making a judgement and choosing a definite course of punitive action. But in this context they are defined as adults rather than youth. Only, as demonstrated in the previous section, the manner of defining the transgression is not able to clearly distinguish between normal and dangerous youth, the effect of which is to criminalise not just those who transgress, but mainstream (white, middle-class) youth generally.

Furthermore, in order to appear as though they cover the range of explanatory possibilities that exist, the various oppositions at work here (youth/adult, normal/dangerous youth) rely on the *exclusion* of the fact that 'normal' youth are already set up to be transgressors. As discussed in the Introduction and previous case studies, by being defined as becoming adult, by being in a process of development, youth occupies an undecidable space between child and adult. Anything youth 'do' (that cannot be explained as a result of their lack of adult-level ability) is therefore going to transgress the boundary that marks them as being 'in between'. Defined according to what they are not (child or adult), what young people 'are' is an absence, a lack. In other words, youth 'is' only at its limit. Youth is a lack (of presence, of intention), which can only be contextualised at the moment it is lost, or via its becoming something else. So while young people are doing what they are supposed to do by becoming adult, to actually do so is to exceed the limits of this conceptual framework. Also, following the structure of the event, this transgression is always going to be unexpected and leave that framework at a loss to explain what it has produced even though this unexpectedness is necessary in order for a moment of transition from youth to adulthood to be marked. But as noted in Chapter 5, for this notion of youth as becoming or youth as development to remain intact, and for the structure of social relations it serves to continue to have meaning (adult knowledge and authority over vulnerable youth), that transgression can only be taken as a threat to that order because the kinds of adults this notion of youth is working to produce (responsible, productive citizens) is risked in order to have such adults 'arrive'. What youth 'do' therefore pushes the limits of propriety, and youth are considered to be at risk from premature and uncontrollable development as a result. They are at risk from themselves, in other words.

This approach to youth is self-defeating; it leaves no option but to frame as dangerous and problematic (in order to keep the dominant order of social relations intact) what it desires for and requires youth to do, in order to re-produce and maintain the dominant order of social relations. And when youth (inevitably) deviate from the norm, but in a manner that is considered 'bad', they are defined in their difference from that norm (and issues over the meaning of youth intention are raised again). Work is then done to try and get them back 'on track' (or to 'fix' them because of the external threat they pose), which is to work to a particular definition of 'proper' development that is still, nonetheless, subject to the undecidability of the transition process. Thus attempts to reduce the undesirable effects of this process by seeking to contain development along certain prescribed lines, and so constrain youth behaviour, re-produces the conditions for transgression (that is, a transition from youth to adult still has to be marked). This also risks the youth/adult distinction altogether by both punishing those who transgress and by trying to predict the outcome of a developmental process when it, by necessity, must be broken with in order for the transition to occur.

In trying to define youth crime, then, the interpretive framework provided by a mainstream notion of youth and the work of protection it calls for against such crime actually creates the conditions for the collapse of that framework and the loss of the notion of youth that is thought to be in need of protection. To keep a normative order intact therefore means having to exclude that which cannot be explained by or contained within that existing order, even though such conceptual excess is in fact a result of this interpretive order. We thus have a context for moral panic where a 'group of persons emerges to become defined as a threat to societal values and interests' (Cohen cited in Zylinska, 2004, p. 229). The seemingly natural and logical response to this is to work to reinforce those values and interests that have been threatened, the effect of which is to render aberrant and unknowable something that has come from within. What happens, then, to notions of adulthood that are based on this notion of youth as preparation for the future; what happens when the affluent, white mainstream becomes unsafe from its own children?

Psychopathy and mental illness

According to Dave Cullen, it is because of this interpretive approach that we have been asking all the wrong questions about Columbine. He argues that we should not think in terms of youth at all, and offers a different interpretive framework. 'Quit asking what drove them', Cullen declares, because 'Eric Harris and Dylan Klebold were radically different individuals, with vastly different motives and opposite mental conditions'. In short, Harris was a psychopath and Klebold was a suicidal depressive (2004, np).

As noted earlier, psychological profiling is a prominent feature in contemporary analyses of rampage shootings and diagnoses of a perpetrator's mental illness are common[6]. A team of FBI psychiatrists and psychologists made the diagnosis of Harris and Klebold by examining the written and visual material left by the killers. Cullen notes that the study of Harris in the media focused on his hatred, 'hatred that supposedly led him to revenge'. But clinical psychologist and lead Columbine investigator with the FBI Dwayne Fuselier recognises not hatred, but contempt – 'a far more revealing emotion' (Cullen, 2004, np). Accordingly, Harris' writings are not those 'of an angry young man' picked on by jocks until breaking point, but are those 'of someone with a messianic-grade *superiority* complex, out to punish the entire human race for its appalling inferiority' (Cullen, 2004, np). On this basis, Harris has been interpreted as 'cold, calculating, and homicidal', and the dominant, driving force of the pair and their plan. Klebold, on the other hand, is seen to fit the more familiar mould of someone depressed and suicidal, he 'was hurting inside while Harris wanted to hurt people' (Fuselier cited in Cullen, 2004, np). They were a partnership, but Cullen states that it was Harris' 'pattern of grandiosity, glibness, contempt and lack of empathy' that convinced the psychiatric team that he was a psychopath and therefore the greater force defining what they did and why.

The implication of this diagnosis is that Harris' malevolence existed outside the context of his youth, which means that efforts to explain the event can be taken out of this context as well, bypassing many of the reasons given as to why this event happened, and also their problems. 'Forget the popular narrative about the jocks, Goths, and Trenchcoat Mafia' asserts Cullen, and 'abandon the core idea that Columbine was simply a *school shooting*' (2004, np). According to the FBI team, the school was a 'means to a grander end', which was 'to terrorise the entire nation by attacking a symbol of American life' (Cullen, 2004, np). The school setting therefore steered investigations in the wrong direction. Cullen believes that Harris and Klebold's 'vision was to create a nightmare so devastating and apocalyptic that the entire world would shudder at their power', and they expected this to bring them more than fame, 'they were gunning for devastating infamy' (2004, np).

A major sticking point can be released with this argument: the problem of youth intention. 'Psychopaths lie for sport; they obtain pleasure from deceiving others' (Larkin, 2007, p. 149), and Harris had no trouble deceiving well-meaning authorities, not to mention teachers, parents and friends. This is evidenced in Harris' divergent writings after his electronics theft. Harris wrote a letter to his victim offering his sympathy, but he also wrote an entry in his private (handwritten) journal which expressed opposite feelings:

> Isn't America supposed to be the land of the free? How come, if I'm free, I cant [sic] deprive a stupid fucking dumb shit from his possessions if he leaves them sitting in the front seat of his fucking van out in plain sight and in the middle of fucking nowhere on a Fri fucking day [sic] night NATURAL SELECTION. Fucker should be shot.
>
> (12 April 1998a)

That Harris could be so consciously deceptive is easily accounted for here. As Robert Hare explains, 'psychopaths are not disoriented or out of touch with reality, nor do they experience delusions, hallucinations, or intense subjective distress that characterise most other mental disorders' (cited in Cullen, 2004, np). Instead, 'psychopaths are rational and aware of what they are doing and why', says Hare. 'Their behaviour is the result of choice, freely exercised' (cited in Cullen, 2004, np). So, on this account, the fact that the boys escaped detection is because they engineered it that way, which means we can disregard debate over and problems with policies of zero tolerance and other measures designed to identify signs of trouble in the hope of weeding out potentially dangerous students.

As 'the depressive and the psychopath' there is a way beyond the limits of previous explanations. In Harris's shadow, Klebold's mental illness meant that he possessed a disturbed view of reality and acted on it, but Cullen contends that Klebold 'would never have pulled off Columbine without Harris' (2004, np). And if Columbine had not happened, Cullen thinks that Klebold may have got into trouble perhaps for a petty crime but that this may have led to him getting help and ultimately finding his way to a normal life. But as Klebold's actions are seen to be driven by Harris in this approach, it is the latter's mentality that is the key focus. Defined by the distinctive psychopathic qualities of deceitfulness and 'a total lack of remorse or empathy', Cullen considers Harris to be an entirely different breed of person. 'Not only does he feel no guilt' for his victims, claims Cullen, 'he doesn't grasp what they feel' because 'the truly hard-core psychopath doesn't quite comprehend emotions like love or hate or fear, because he has never experienced them directly' (2004, np). This diagnosis for Harris means that there is nothing anyone could have done. 'Harris was not a wayward boy who could have been rescued', he was 'irretrievable', and, for Cullen, 'his death at

Columbine may have stopped him from doing something even worse' (2004, np).

On the basis of this explanation this event can be separated from other school shootings (and shooters) and the many explanatory inconsistencies that focusing on their youth creates. By the same token, treating this as not 'simply a *school shooting*' preserves the idea that there *are* 'simple' school shootings that *can* be adequately explained by working from assumptions about youth, while here enjoying the satisfaction of answers that the psychopath diagnosis provides. Furthermore, not only is the event able to be explained, it allows for the restoration of an otherwise threatened order of social relations, thus satisfying the desire to protect and preserve youth.

However, even though this reading claims to offer a total explanation for the massacre, such justification can be seen to come as a result of a selective use of the evidence. While Harris is not the first teen to be deceitful, to be so to the degree exhibited by him is seen here to constitute evidence of a level of reason and self-awareness which the average teen is thought not to possess based on existing, normative assumptions (not to mention MRI evidence). Also, within a psychological framework, an inability to comprehend emotions like fear or love, guilt or remorse, is thought to be part of the psychopath's 'make up' and is therefore not a choice a psychopath makes; rather, it is just who they are. Interestingly, however, Harris acknowledges the pain he is about to cause his parents. In final messages recorded with Klebold just prior to the massacre, he states: 'I know my mom and dad will be just fucking shocked beyond belief'. In earlier recordings made on 15 March 1999 Harris says: 'I wish I was a fucking sociopath so I didn't have any remorse, but I do. This is going to tear them apart', and, 'I really am sorry about all this' ('The Basement Tapes', undated). These comments could well be taken as evidence of a psychopath's characteristic deceitfulness, but not necessarily. It is not immediately apparent that this material indicates the presence of a psychopathic personality, rather than being the outcome of yet another explanatory framework (psychology/psychiatry) with certain vested interests.

The problem here though is that this work claims to offer the definitive word on the matter. This is something it could not do, however, if it were to acknowledge that the event only makes sense based on the use of certain information interpreted in a particular way. The point I wish to emphasise (and which the next section will develop more fully) is that the evidence available here carries no intrinsic or self-evident meaning; the charge of psychopathy is an *effect* of an interpretive strategy rather than an inevitable or pre-determined outcome, and one that could be different given a different interpretive context. The claim to comprehensively account for what happened is contingent upon certain factors that, when recognised, actually compromise the integrity of this claim. As such, the diagnosis of psychopathy cannot ensure the restoration and the preservation of a normative order.

The various interpretive approaches outlined here have been shown to fall short of providing enough explanation for what happened and why to ensure the restoration of order. Trying to make sense of Columbine by reducing the singularity of the event to an effect of a structure grounded in absolute presence, which posits youth as fundamentally 'absent', appears to provide a means of restoring order because it is possible to recognise what has gone wrong and how to make it right. It provides a position from which deviations from a norm can be marked, such as the boys did it because they were bullied, because they were not normal youth but dangerous criminals, or because Harris was a psychopath. There is a proper outcome already in place directing interpretive work; it is just a matter of getting there. But it has been shown that the work of reaching this goal has produced effects that the interpretive system cannot account for or allow. The results of these different investigations are both less than and in excess of what they mark as calculable possibility and satisfactory outcome: not providing explanation enough; having to make selective use of available evidence in order to make totalising claims; blurring the distinction between normal and potentially dangerous youth. The problem, however, is that when these explanatory approaches claim to offer a total explanation, anything more or less than this constitutes not just a partial but a total failure of these systems.

In order, therefore, to keep intact dominant structures – in order to (supposedly) be able to make use of these explanatory structures in other cases – there is nothing else to do here but mark the singularity of this event as being beyond explanation. There is too much at stake for an attempt to explain to fail – future shootings and future deaths – so, referring back to Zylinska's work on the discourse of the sublime, it is better to treat the event itself as beyond our ability to interpret it, to know what it means. In other words, as a form of response, or rather a form of non-response, it is better to affirm a Romantic inexplicability. Such a (non)response serves to maintain order by negating, in advance, any attempt to explain. However, even when at a loss to explain what has happened, and even when faced with a situation that defies attempts to articulate it, there is too much at stake *not* to attempt to explain.

That so many deaths have occurred from this kind of violence is enough to demand that an attempt be made, even if it means failing to (fully) explain the event. As the next section will demonstrate, it is actually in failing to fully explain the event that there is a way forward.

Explaining the inexplicable: Intention and iterability

As noted at the beginning of the chapter, to discuss the meaning of the event as an effect of interpretive activities changes what it means to discuss things in terms of presence. By looking at what conditions the status of something as singular, coherent, present, it is possible to offer a different response to a situation where the self is deprived of 'conceptual mastery' (Zylinska, 2004, p. 242). The attempts to explain the Columbine event that have been detailed so far have sought to regain that sense of mastery in a manner that resulted in losing sight of what it was attempting to protect and preserve: a normative notion of youth and the social structure it serves. But, as Judith Butler writes, because events happen without our express intent or deliberate action, because they come at the limit of an actual/artificial distinction, we are returned 'not to our acts and choices, but to the region of existence that is radically unwilled' (2001, p. 38). We are returned to 'the primary impingement' that is prior to any 'us' and 'them', 'you' and 'me': the originary trace. As discussed in Chapter 4 on the teen brain, the trace marks 'the lack at the origin that is the condition of thought and experience' (Spivak, 1997, p. xvii). Ungraspable in itself but never non-existent, the trace is that which opens up and always keeps open the future because it prevents anything from coming into presence. Instead, things always 'keep on be-coming' (Lucy, 2004, p. 61). In effect, this is to acknowledge the limits of self-knowledge (that is, self-knowledge is not wholly present to oneself), and this understanding opens up a less reductive way of considering the notions of identity and intention as they apply to Harris and Klebold.

According to Derrida, the metaphysics of presence assumes that a speech act involves the communication of consciousness, of one's full self-presence, and therefore that one means what one says (1988, p. 8). However, the condition of having intention in a singular and direct sense is only possible because it does not originate 'in' one's consciousness, but rather as an effect of the trace-structure of language. Jonathan Culler writes that when there is a 'lack at the origin', a statement of intention can only be understood as such – it can only be what it 'is' – in relation to that which is it is not: a non-serious utterance, a parody or repetition (2007, p. 120). An original utterance or intention does not mark a pure presence; rather, it emerges as such through an encounter with what is other to it, with what is inauthentic or derivative. The communication of intention is therefore defined via the possibility of its repetition. Imitation thus makes possible what is 'original' and 'authentic' and a direct intention signifies as such 'only if it is iterable' (Culler, 2007, p. 120). This condition of repeatability, what Derrida calls iterability, or the structure of iteration, means that an intention that animates an 'utterance will never be through and through present to itself and to its content' (1988, p. 18). The experience of having intention comes because it is not a singular and unrepeatable thing, but it is on condition of its repeatability that it can appear to be a singular and unrepeatable thing. In other words, the ideality of the notion of intention as presence is an effect of iterability (Lucy, 2004, pp. 60–1).

If there is no immediate apprehension of the meaning of intention in oneself or in others, we cannot say that intention is strictly one's own. Derrida argues that 'this essential absence of intending the actuality of utterance, this structural unconsciousness, if you like, prohibits any saturation of the context' (1988, p. 18). On this basis, there can only be an experience of having one's intentions met, understood or carried out, based on the possibility of them being misunderstood, or of being interpreted otherwise. Intention must be based on this possibility if it is to have any meaning or any effect (Lucy, 2004, pp. 56–7). This does not mean, however, that 'the category of intention' disappears; it still has a place, 'but from that place it will no longer be able to govern the entire scene and system of utterance' (Derrida, 1988, p. 18). Instead, as an effect of iterability, intention can be understood performatively (as dependent on context for its meaning), and there are two noteworthy effects of this with regard to the discussion of Columbine.

The first effect is that there is no guarantee in advance that one will be understood to mean what one says. For example, Gibbs and Roche write that 'it's easy now to see the signs' of threat in 'how a video-game joystick turned Harris into a better marksman, ... [h]ow Klebold's violent essays for English class were like skywriting his intent', but the problem, they say, 'is that until April 20, nobody was looking. And Harris and Klebold knew it' (1999, np). But to approach their intention as an effect of iterability is to understand that the context for making sense of their intention did not 'exist' until *after* the event, as the result of the application of a particular interpretive framework and its assumptions about youth and intention. This means that Harris and Klebold's intentions were not there to be 'seen' prior to the event, even if someone *was* looking for them. As Jenkins writes, 'Harris and Klebold's websites exposed their darkest thoughts, fantasies, and plans to public scrutiny. They were *hidden in plain sight*, there for anyone to see' (1999, np, my emphasis). Their intentions were indeed 'missed' when, prior to the shooting, Harris made threats against schoolmate Brooks Brown. The Brown family reported their concerns about Harris to local police but the report was never investigated[7] (Fast, 2008, p. 194). Similarly, in the basement tapes Harris recalls that his mother saw the butt of a gun poking out of his gym bag but that she thought it was just his BB gun (Gibbs and Roche, 1999, np).

The second key effect is that there is no way for the boys to predict and thus control the effects of their intentions; their intentions exceed them. For example, while the boys predicted infamy for themselves, it was not for them to know that a dramatic stage play of the event would go into development (see www.davecullen.com/columbine). Furthermore, it was not for the boys to know that someone would create *Super Columbine Massacre RPG!*, a role-playing video game in which players experience the massacre from the boys' perspective as pieced together from their writings and other material. The game's creator, Danny Ledonne, explains in his 'Artist's Statement' that he began the project to deepen understanding of the massacre and by doing so push 'the envelope as to what a video game can be' (undated, np). Ledonne is seeking to 'confront real cultural issues' in a form traditionally used for entertainment purposes only. The game 'implores introspection' on the player's part about the society we are living in rather than serving to glorify what happened in any way (Ledonne, undated, np). Ledonne writes: 'SCMRPG dares us into a realm of grey morality with nuanced perspectives of suffering, vengeance, horror, and reflection' (undated, np). Here, too, of course, it was not for Ledonne to know that despite his very clear intentions as to the game's purpose that it would not be used for destructive ends. In September 2006, 25-year-old student Kimveer Gill opened fire at his Montreal college killing one person and wounding 19. Police found website postings that listed *Super Columbine Massacre* as his favourite game. It was reported that Gill wore a trench coat as Harris and Klebold had done, and his online writings speak about his hatred of jocks and preps alongside many pictures of himself posing with guns. 'Life is a video game you've got to die sometime', he writes ('Columbine link to Montreal mass shooting', 2006, np).

Identity and the role of the media

With this last quote and these activities in mind, it is interesting and important to note the place of the media in this case. By this I don't mean the fact that events like these become media spectacles, attracting saturation coverage. Rather, it is important to note how the media has served to disturb conceptual oppositions concerning what counts as actual and artificial regarding the presence of intention and discussion of the boys' identities, and how this disturbance enables an alternative way of making sense of Columbine. Jenkins argues that 'new media technologies' enable 'a more participatory relationship to media culture' (1999, np). In a hyper-mediated, or media-saturated, society, he contends that youth have the chance to actually do what they have always done in terms of seeking out ways of gaining self-mastery and self-control – of cultivating identities – but the difference, he says, is that this is no longer taking place out of doors, and, for the most part, out of sight of parents. Jenkins suggests that teens have access to a world beyond the (protective and regulative) realms of home and family and school, and, one could add, following Giroux, beyond the corrupting commercial sphere that constrains possibilities for self-expression. And yet these activities are increasingly taking place *in* areas such as family rooms and bedrooms (1999, np).

Jenkins argues that the increased visibility of youth culture, thanks to the media, is shocking to parents because they are discovering that there is much they do not know about their children's association with cultural material, some of it violent and dark. The problem, as he sees it, is adults' unfamiliarity with how the media is used by teens. Participatory media forms offer access to a huge range of ideas and information and Jenkins suggests that teens take and make many and varied (and certainly not always dark and violent) meanings of and from them. For kids, 'the computer has become a central point of access to their peer culture' and it is a profoundly social tool, whereas for adults, it is predominantly 'a tool of the workplace or the classroom' (1999, np). Jenkins contends that this lack of adult understanding leads to perceptions of the media as dangerous because 'our children seem to be going places where we [adults] cannot follow them', even though this is happening right in front of 'us' (1999, np). What is missing here, on Jenkins' account, is an appreciation of how media technology and different media content is enmeshed in practices of performativity and how these operate in constituting 'presence'. Or, to call on the terms provided by (sub)culture theory, what is missing is an awareness of how youth construct their own culturally significant meanings separate from adult culture. Jenkins' sees this lack of understanding evidenced in the typical adult response of banning specific media images. Jenkins argues, however, that this 'will have little or no impact on the problem of youth crime, because doing so gets at the symbols' and 'not at the meanings those symbols carry' in informing the social reality and identity of teens (1999, np). This perspective indicates a need to alter perceptions about the agency and self-awareness of youth, or rather, the lack thereof, that is implied by conventional assumptions.

To illustrate, Harris and Klebold maintained personal websites and made a series of video recordings detailing their plans, played online video games, and enjoyed certain violent movies and music. When Harris explains himself and Klebold as 'a select case', when he explains that he is a racist, when he states that he will 'feel no remorse, no sense of shame' (Harris, undated), and when they anticipate and negate the many explanations for their behaviour – 'don't blame my family . . . don't blame the school', 'if only we could have reached them sooner' – they make use of a range of already available images and ideas about youth (and other subjectivities) and ways of speaking about them that precede and exceed their use of them, that are not their own. In the basement tapes, the boys discuss how movies will be made of their story and Harris says he used 'a lot of foreshadowing and dramatic irony' in preparation for that (cited in Gibbs and Roche, 1999, np). He had written a poem in which he imagines that he is a bullet, and in the tapes he quotes from Shakespeare's *The Tempest*: 'Good wombs hath borne bad sons' (Gibbs and Roche, 1999, np). 'Directors will be fighting over this story', says Klebold, and they even discuss who they could trust with the script: 'Steven Spielberg or Quentin Tarantino' (Gibbs and Roche, 1999, np).

The difficulty here is that for Harris and Klebold to frame themselves using these terms and ways of speaking, to self-consciously shape a 'narrative' for what they were doing, is not to 'be' the youth that is described by these ways of speaking. Instead, it is to speak the discourses that adults speak about youth – that is, from an 'adult' speaking position. Traditionally, and as discussed in the previous chapter on the notion of innocence, it is adults who ascribe meaning to youth behaviour, and understood developmentally, it is assumed that what they are describing about youth is self-evident and naturally occurring. It is also assumed that whatever youth is understood to be, young people do not know themselves as being such things. In other words, because, as youth,

Harris and Klebold supposedly lack certain abilities – including the ability to be so self-reflexive – it is logical to blame parents, teachers, violent films and so on for their behaviour. But for them to position themselves in this self-reflexive manner is to be outside this notion of youth. And this is not just because they ask not to be held to it; the same would apply even if they wished to identify with this way of thinking.

However, if, as noted above, everything originates according to a structure of iteration or a fundamental repeatability, then it would not be possible to reduce who the boys really were or 'are' to anything outside of youth discourse. Rather, and to repeat the statements made at the end of Chapter 4 regarding the interpretation of MRI scans, and Chapter 5 on the depiction of innocence, it would be possible to understand that the boys' subjectivity begins in and as representation. On this basis, what youth 'is' cannot be accounted for by pointing to the physical, material existence of young people, and not just because, in this instance, the boys' real lives gave little or no indication of what was really going on with them. Even as they appeared to live the lives of seemingly normal teenagers prior to the shooting, the actuality of this is informed by a particular notion of youth that is not given 'but actively produced' in ways that are 'hierarchising and selective', and in the service of particular 'forces and interests' (Derrida, 2002, p. 3). An assumption that the boys should lack the ability to be self-referential, as well as arguments that they are other than normal youth, criminals or psychopaths, can all be read as textual effects rather than as evidence of an absolute state of being. This is because, on this account, the boys' actuality cannot be wholly separated from or opposed to a concept of the virtual, to something that has been made.

The particular role of the media in this case is an obvious example of this non-opposition at work. Even though ideas about movie narratives and what makes a good tragedy, for example, provided a framework for some of Harris and Klebold's actions, this is not the same as saying that it was violent films that made them do it or that gave them the idea to do it, or that a desire for fame motivated them (as many have suggested). However, neither is it possible to discuss their motives *outside* of this material. There is no other material to use to establish the 'true' nature of the boys outside the media-based material they used and produced. But it is this material that marks them as other than 'normal' youth because in their use of different media they self-reflexively speak the discourse of 'normal' youth. This means that it is not possible to confine or reduce the boys' actions or identities to an actual/virtual or real/manufactured split; to something that is 'natural' over and against something that is 'made'. But even the absence of media would not alter the performative or textual aspect of identity. If the boys did not make use of particular ways of speaking provided by the media, they would utilise some other way of speaking. In this way, we cannot say that the enhanced means by which it is possible to define oneself via the media, as described by Jenkins, makes the young people who do so other than youth. What counts as 'normal' youth is already other than itself (as inherent or natural) if we accept that it cannot be thought except as and through representation as conditioned by the movement of supplementarity.

Also, a particularly powerful reason for arguing why we must rethink traditional approaches to youth is because Harris and Klebold's media-based existence has had – and continues to have – real and tangible effects. In his web journal Harris promises that 'we will haunt the life out of anyone who blames anyone besides me and V' (1998c), and Gibbs and Roche note that while the Littleton community searched for answers and needed to understand the boys after the shooting, the last thing the survivors wanted was 'to see these boys on the cover of another magazine, back in the headlines, on the evening news' (1999, np). What does it mean that they remain so real even though they no longer exist? They have a spectral 'presence', and, in a way perhaps not meant by Harris, have made good on their promise. Their mediated or media-based 'existence' upsets or puts in question what counts as actual and virtual, and thereby what it means to exist. As was mentioned at the beginning of the chapter concerning metaphysical events, to insist on knowing the difference between what is actual and what is artificial requires knowing exactly what everything actually 'is', and Harris and Klebold cannot be accommodated by that certainty because they 'exist' outside or beyond such an opposition. This is because their actuality, their existence, has been determined since their deaths. All we have to work with to make sense of actual events and their very real effects (not just death and injury, but changes to school policy, the treatment of other shootings, and so on) is what has been 'made' by them and about them. This means that calling on an actual/artificial distinction to account for the event cannot adequately do so because the evidentiary material does not conform to that opposition, this material exceeds the limits of the opposition.

Yet, in another way, it is for the dead victims (and for future victims) that people – survivors and investigators – seek meaning and search for answers. It is in establishing the actuality of their deaths that their lives can be properly honoured and those left behind can 'move on'. But this cannot happen by insisting on containing the event within a particular actual/artificial, real/unreal, being/non-being distinction. Because the figure of the spectre 'is neither pure spirit or soul nor simple reincarnation or living body, neither exactly dead or alive, absent or present' (Wortham, 2010, p. 194), a notion of spectrality disturbs an ability to decide what something is based on absolute difference. Therefore, there is an obligation to make decisions about what counts as actual and virtual because it is not possible to defer to some pre-existing determination of them; they are now understood as spectral or textual effects. This demonstrates why it is necessary to open up the interpretive possibilities of 'youth' as a means of being able to discuss Columbine, rather than being forced to exclude 'youth' on the basis that the Columbine 'event' fails to conform to a notion of youth that is under adult authority and control.

In other words, what Harris and Klebold did is not simply explained by saying that it was their own absolute self-present intention at work. But that they did act with intention does not make them other than (normal) youth either. And to punish them for having malicious intention does not necessarily mean that all youth must bear within them the possibility that they are all potential criminals (or worse). If intention is not strictly one's own, if there is differance at the origin, if things 'keep on be-coming', and if iterability and supplementarity are the conditions that shape the being of *all of us*, then the fact or issue of the boys' youth – their age and the specific issues and activities that are linked to their age – is actually *incidental* (as opposed to essential) to this event, and, indeed, to *any* event. While this claim may appear to contradict much of the argument that has preceded it, it is actually the key that opens the way for thinking about youth against an alternative that would lose sight of it altogether. This means: the boys committed horrendous deeds and such behaviour can and should be condemned, but the choice to define them through the distinctions of youth is ultimately an arbitrary one (we could choose not to have a concept of youth at all). However, it still matters a great deal that we *do* have a concept of youth, if for no other reason than to maintain the distinctions of adulthood, which we would lose if we gave up, and gave up on, youth.

To treat youth as incidental rather than essential, therefore, is to open the possibility of 'choosing' to deploy *a* concept of youth (as distinct from 'the' concept of youth) in order to make sense of the event – or, indeed, to choose otherwise – and such a decision would be made in the name of developing a more expansive sense of the possibilities of youth. As Butler argues, we cannot 'forget that we are related to those we condemn, even those we must condemn', otherwise 'we lose the chance to be ethically educated or "addressed" by a consideration of who they are and what their personhood says about the range of human possibility that exists' (2001, p. 30). So to 'choose' youth – which comes thanks to being made aware of the conditions through which the very possibility of 'youth' emerges – rather than 'fall back' on it based on some notion of essence or absolute truth, is to make a larger and more enabling choice regarding how to understand the specific embodied experiences it frames and is called on to explain, which affects everyone, not just the young.

Ethical inexplicability and the undecidability of youth

This larger choice is conditioned by an understanding that, as performatively constructed and interpreted, any account of 'who one is' is always going to be less than and in excess of itself. This means, according to Butler, that 'any effort made "to give an account of oneself" will have to fail in order to approach being true', so we must not expect an answer to the question of who one is that will satisfy us (2001, p. 28). If the limits of self-knowledge are acknowledged as that which actually opens the possibility of having self-knowledge, then we should allow the question to remain open. Our pursuit of and desire for recognition and understanding should therefore remain open as a desire rather than be resolved through satisfaction (Butler, 2001, p. 28). This means that when we make decisions about what happened at Columbine and why, about who is responsible and what to do about it, it will never be explanation *enough*. But rather than this being a problem or an ethical failure, as is imagined within the metaphysics of presence, this is to affirm what can be called an excessive or responsive inexplicability. Where a Romantic inexplicability marks the failure of a demand for resolution, here an affirmation of the fallibility of explanation marks a demand *against* resolution as a means of getting *to* an explanation.

An excessive inexplicability allows us to reflect on the boys in a responsive way rather than in a reductive way as we cannot defer to a pre-existing structure, nor can we ignore existing structures completely. The point is not to try to 'escape' binary thinking – there is nowhere else to 'go' – but it is about being placed at the point of having to decide what the difference is between things. Yet, because of iterability and supplementarity, a capacity to make moral or ethical judgements is not exhausted once a decision is made (Butler, 2001, p. 30). It is on the condition of its repeatability that any particular decision is possible, so coming to a decision as to the meaning of an event like Columbine is possible because it could always in fact be made differently, and this potential remains in place even after a particular decision comes to pass. This means that there is no final resolution, the demand to explain remains open, and so judgement is always deferred. But by being positioned at the point where a decision must always be made as to what something means – when ethical judgement is sustained rather than resolved – so we become responsible for, and can experience self-knowing through, our decisions (Butler, 2001, pp. 30–1).

This allows us to understand that Columbine and the discussion of Columbine is undecidably about youth (as are other cases of shooting tragedies perpetrated by teens). To respond to the demand to explain the inexplicable is, as stated at the beginning of the chapter, to 'engage afresh...with the singularity of the occasion that calls for a decision to be made' (Lucy, 2004, p. 150). To seek to reduce the singularity of the event to the effect of a general structure posited by the metaphysics of presence, which assumes a purity of distinction between youth and adult and normal and dangerous youth, means that in order for that ideal to be met and maintained, it must exclude 'certain essential traits of what it claims to explain or describe – and yet cannot integrate into the "general theory" ' (Derrida, 1988, p. 117) or else risks its collapse. The only recourse in this instance is to affirm the inexplicable singularity of the event. The undecidable, however, having to decide what 'there is' means, is what 'opens the field of decision or decidability' (Derrida, 1988, p. 116). While this serves to affirm the fundamental inexplicability of events in general, it is what *enables* discussion about them specifically. An undecidable relation to youth therefore opens discussion about youth and requires us to take responsibility for youth because we are called to make decisions about it as there is no already-right answer to what youth 'is'.

This undecidable relation to youth does not mean giving up on trying to prevent future shootings by working on, in this case, issues of media violence, gun availability, school environment, mental illness and so on, but we must begin from 'differance' rather than presence in order to 'get' these things. The goal of this analysis is the same as other responses to Columbine – the preservation and protection of youth (that is, actual young people and a notion of youth) – but the reasoning underpinning this analysis is different from existing responses. This chapter has sought to develop a way of responding to the event that is not limited to, for example, thinking in terms of media effects or the inherent vulnerability of youth as these ways of thinking cannot satisfactorily demarcate between 'normal' and 'abnormal' youth behaviour. This is important because it is one thing to be opposed to events that cause death, but our response to such events must not be to prevent events from happening at all – which is to be prevented from making decisions about them. The existing ways of explaining the event covered here, which would result in the affirmation of a Romantic inexplicability, leave us without that capacity. In other words, to give up making decisions and judgements would be to give up the event, which would be to give up youth and close off the future (and youth *as* the future, and the future of adulthood). As Derrida asserts, 'the coming of the event is what we cannot and must never prevent, another name for the future itself' (2002, p. 11). To this he adds: 'we are only ever opposed to those events that we think obstruct the future or bring death, to those events that put an end to the possibility of the event' (2002, p. 11). Columbine was one such event and it is right that we oppose it for these reasons. But it is for these same reasons that our response to this event must embrace an excessive inexplicability if we are to do more in working towards a future that is without school shootings than render unthinkable what we most desire to understand about it.

7
Conclusion

This book has demonstrated that contemporary academic and popular debates over 'youth issues' reproduce a limited range of discourses. The case studies have shown how these discourses rely on essentialist and totalising assumptions about youth the operations of which actually serve to undermine the explanatory possibilities such assumptions articulate in the work of making sense of youth. I have argued that young people exceed the limits of what dominant discourses mark as possible when young people act *in accordance with* these discourses. In this way, 'youth problems' can be tied to the very manner of conceptualisation of youth. Thus, to the extent that youth discourses create effects that limit or close down possible solutions to a range of youth issues, attending to the discursive construction of youth is necessary.

A deconstructive approach to youth works to challenge the flawed logics currently operating in much academic, policy and media discourse by opening up youth discourses to the limits of knowledge, and by embracing the undecidability or inexplicability of youth. A deconstructive reflexivity provides opportunities for productive intervention and critical analysis that existing knowledge frameworks and research methods do not, if only because these frameworks contribute to the problems they also attempt to solve. The text-based analysis performed here has allowed me to trace how the dominant discourses of a range of social domains have a direct impact on the parameters of public discourse and work to determine the contextual frames of everyday life. Whether popular or academic, such texts contribute to the construction and maintenance of shared value systems, beliefs and attitudes that are mobilised in specific situations and contexts. While this kind of close reading of texts may be an exercise that is somewhat removed from direct social interactions, it nevertheless connects with

171

and addresses the very structures and frameworks through which the meaning of social interaction is constructed and interpreted. As such, the deconstructive analysis undertaken throughout this book has the potential to transform the seemingly more 'concrete' conditions or processes that define the forms in which youth behaviour may be rendered intelligible. This potential applies to young people themselves as much as to their self-appointed guardians in the media and in academia.

Approaching youth according to the Derridean notions of supplementarity, iterability and performativity offers a means of 'coming to terms' with violent and other extreme events, with the transition from innocence to experience, and with the development of reason, rather than 'falling back' on notions of youth innocence and a lack of self-awareness as grounding and founding aspects of identity and selfhood. An understanding of truth and being as textual effects requires that the meaning and effects of categorical boundaries such as that between child and youth or youth and adult be the subject of deliberate attention rather than be taken for granted. The difference in coming to decisions about the meaning of youth rather than reducing youth behaviour to assumptions about their absolute nature as determined by biology or neurological function does not mean that key boundaries and distinctions are dissolved; rather, they are open to reaffirmation, but with a vital opening to the possibility of being made 'otherwise'.

This is important to consider since, regarding Columbine, concerns about youth violence have not ceased, and neither, of course, have school shootings. But if it is accepted that youth is a fundamentally undecidable concept, then questions of youth violence may be approached not in terms of a reductive search for causes or motives but by refusing totalising explanations for what happened. As argued in Chapter 6, accepting the excessive inexplicability of youth allows for issues of youth intention, responsibility and accountability to be directly addressed as opposed to evidence of these being taken as signs of abnormality or of the presence of some corrupting force.

Similarly, fears about the premature sexualisation of girls via the media continue to be expressed. Yet if the discourse of 'coming of age' does in fact generate the conflicting demands, identified in Chapter 5, that youth innocence be preserved at the same time as maturity be attained, then a notion of innocence as performative offers a way to imagine how young women may indeed undergo a process of 'coming of age' that is not inherently transgressive of social norms. Thus it would be possible to re-cast debate around innocence and sexual maturation and the many sensitive issues that accompany it beyond notions of youth that could only ever affirm the innocence of youth against its inevitable loss.

Research into youth brain function offers empirical evidence that appears to confirm, rather than reveal the reasons for, familiar and entrenched beliefs about the social and emotional incompetencies of young people. However, as demonstrated in Chapter 4, the fundamental contradiction of desiring and expecting that youth develop a capacity for reason that is neurologically absent (the problematic effects of which are played out in a range of social contexts and institutional settings), may be resolved if the 'Reason' which youth supposedly arrives at is but a specific form of 'reason'. The rethinking of the teen brain research offered in the chapter establishes 'youth' as a potential opening to another form of reason – one which can affirm reason as a (social) project rather than as a cerebral function. This means that when it comes to questions of appropriate policy aimed at regulating but also nurturing desired mental and emotional qualities and thus behavioural outcomes in the young, or when it comes to trying to understand why teens think and behave the way they do, or responding to changing social conditions that impact on youth, the imperative would be to scrutinise the effects of standards of reason on youth with regard to their cognitive capacities, not to 'discover' any 'natural' quality of Reason inherent in such capacity. In this way, none of the importance or value that is attached to reason and to the development of high-order mental function is lost, but a far less deterministic approach (and the limited outcomes it offers) may be taken in the treatment of young people in relation to such value.

Additionally, a deconstructive transformation of discourses on youth potentially enables new forms of *self*-understanding on the part of youth. Evidence of this can be found by considering how young people are increasingly turning to new and digital media for their identity, culture and social connections. Existing and traditional approaches to youth have been shown to be limited in their capacity to account for the youth they themselves articulate, and this is only exacerbated when new media project youth identity and activity into realms such approaches consider problematic, if not inaccessible – sexuality, performative identity, self-conscious activity and so on. Boundaries of appropriate behaviour regarding sex, violence and ethics are rendered more permeable under regimes of new media. Corporeal or biological understandings of youth identity and development come under increasing stress as linear temporality dissolves via new media – a space where prior cultural and social limits to access, to expression, to social relations, come unstuck. As was shown with regard to the Werribee Kings, the Gobs 2012 case and the Columbine case, young people therefore have the opportunity to articulate themselves through new media in ways not previously available to them, and these technologies are the central means through which attempts are made by others to understand them.

Furthermore, new media technologies are already proto-deconstructive in the sense that they have no centre, their hold on meaning is often fleeting, their creation of identity is unstable, they encourage performativity and they transcend normal frames of space and time. As such, these technologies can accommodate the structural tension that is at the heart of youth. As shown in Chapter 2 and in the case studies, youth is impossibly poised between childhood and adulthood, between immature affective responses and intuitive adult logic, and new media negotiate and often collapse similar tensions between binaries of public/private, self/other, community/individual and privacy/display. So as youth collapses and diverges into the flows of new media in ways that until recently were perhaps philosophically possible but never historically realisable on any kind of scale, it seems increasingly clear that youth and discussion about youth – its behaviour, morality, sexuality, corporeality – has, thanks to new technology, become more clearly the discursive construct deconstructionists would argue that it always has been.

It seems, therefore, that the moment for a deconstructive thinking of youth has never been more pertinent. The slippages and instability that deconstruction finds at the heart of discourse, and particularly in discourses concerning youth, seem to become increasingly manifest in the relations of youth to new media. In this way, and somewhat paradoxically perhaps, the context of new or digital media offers to bring the deconstructive critique into a more 'concretely' realised form at the same time as deconstruction offers to transform the seemingly concrete conditions that define youth.

Consequently, rather than working from an assumption that it is possible to offer a total explanation for the meaning of youth, keeping the demand to explain youth *open* brings the possibility of responding to youth problems differently and more productively. To be made aware of the conditions of possibility for youth is to treat youth not as natural, essential or inherent, but as an effect of discourse, as already in representation. By being open to the possibility of choosing 'otherwise', it is possible to respond to so-called youth problems in a way that tries to avoid reproducing conditions for the same problems to occur. In other words, to make a choice to deploy 'a' concept of youth, rather than 'the' concept of youth, in responding to youth issues and problems offers a way *beyond* the limits of youth as they are currently experienced.

Such an approach need not entail dismantling a notion of youth altogether. Neither does it necessarily attempt to replace a flawed logic with a superior one, or to render impossible any attempt to say something meaningful about youth. The deconstruction of the discursive limits of youth performed here is undertaken in the hope that the aims, ideals and expectations that youth discourses shape might actually be carried out – all the while remaining open to the possibility that such ideals might be less than ideal after all. It also seems clear that the time is right for a deconstructive approach to youth to be articulated, and this book has attempted to set the parameters in place for a deconstructive thinking of youth. This is not an approach that would replace other ways of thinking youth, but seeks rather to work alongside them and to ask for greater attention, care and reflexivity in thinking youth. As youth itself becomes more unstable, more deconstructive, as it resists attempts at containment and categorisation at all levels, perhaps a deconstruction orientated towards the question of reflexivity and responsibility points a way forward.

Notes

2 The State of Contemporary Youth: Conceptual Underpinnings of Dominant Youth Discourses

1. This selection of literature offers a representation of particular ways of speaking about youth. The selection is neither exhaustive nor genealogical as the aim of the chapter is not to provide a history of ideas regarding youth, but to offer an account of discursive statements about youth. Authors and texts other than those I have chosen to focus on could of course be examined in performing this work, but this particular selection of theoretical paradigms is broad enough to allow for the examination of diverse claims about youth that connect with a wide range of contemporary youth issues. Furthermore, as I am seeking to identify assumptions about youth that underpin and are common to multiple perspectives, a different choice of literature would not change this purpose, nor would it necessarily alter the findings.

2. See, for example, Ariel Levy *Female Chauvinist Pigs: Women and the Rise of Raunch Culture* (2005); Gail Dines *Pornland: How Porn Has Hijacked Our Sexuality* (2010); Patrice Oppliger *Girls Gone Skank: The Sexualisation of Girls in American Culture* (2008); Natasha Walter *Living Dolls: The Return of Sexism* (2010); M. Gigi Durham *The Lolita Effect: The Media Sexualisation of Young Girls and Five Keys to Fixing It* (2009); Diane E. Levin and Jean Kilbourne *So Sexy So Soon: The New Sexualised Childhood and What Parents Can Do to Protect Their Kids* (2009); Melinda Tankard Reist (ed.) *Getting Real: Challenging the Sexualisation of Girls* (2009); Sharna Olfman (ed.) *The Sexualisation of Childhood* (2008).

   See also *Corporate Paedophilia: The Sexualisation of Children in Australia* (2006) and *Let Children Be Children: Stopping the Sexualisation of Children in Australia* (2006) by Emma Rush and Andrea La Nauze; the Senate Standing Committee on Environment, Communications and the Arts Inquiry into the 'Sexualisation of children in the contemporary media' (2008); *Young People and Sexting in Australia: Ethics, Representation and the Law* (2013) by Kath Albury, Kate Crawford, Paul Byron and Ben Mathews; *Letting Children Be Children: Report of an Independent Review of the Commercialisation and Sexualisation of Childhood* (2011) by Reg Bailey; *A Qualitative Study of Children, Young People and 'Sexting'* (2012) by Jessica Ringrose, Rosalind Gill, Sonia Livingstone and Laura Harvey; 'Sexting, consent and young people's ethics: Beyond Megan's story' (2012) by Kath Albury and Kate Crawford.

3. See http://www.carlyryanfoundation.com/ for information on the murder case.

4. The controversy ignited again in October of the same year when it was revealed that Henson had previously been allowed to scout for models at a St Kilda primary school in bayside Melbourne ('It is important', 2008, np). The

principal who had allowed and accompanied Henson on his walk through the playground subsequently found herself the subject of a government investigation into her conduct, but was later cleared of any wrongdoing (Tomazin et al., 2008, np; Tomazin and Smith, 2008, np).

5. See Andy Bennet and Keith Kahn Harris' 'Introduction' in *After Subculture: Critical Studies in Contemporary Youth Culture* (2004) for an outline of key criticisms of the CCCS model of subcultural resistance. See also Muggleton (2000), Hodkinson (2007).

4 Reasonable Unreason: The Limits of Youth in the Teen Brain

1. The new scientific field of epigenetics is demonstrating that environmental factors may actually influence the genetic code (see Cloud, 2010).

5 Presumed Innocent: The Paradox of 'Coming of Age' and the Problem of Youth Sexuality

1. More generally, the interdisciplinary field of 'girl studies' offers detailed readings of contemporary femininity, girlhood, girl cultures and girls' voices. See, for example, Driscoll (2002; 2008), Harris (2004a, 2004b), McRobbie (2000), Currie, Kelly and Pomerantz (2009), Johnson (1993) and Walkerdine, Lucey and Melody (2001).
2. For an excellent interrogation of the concept of adolescent girls' sexual empowerment in the context of media sexualisation, see Gill (2012) and Lamb and Peterson (2012).
3. For analyses of the historical construction of children, childhood, innocence and sexuality, see Egan and Hawkes (2010), Kehily and Montgomery (2009) and Ariès (1962).
4. My adaptation of Derrida's work on incest to a contemporary discussion of paedophilia is intended to address how the discourse of 'coming of age' comes up against its own limits in attempts to explain youth sexuality. I use Derrida's argument on incest to help identify a struggle to account for the presumed nature of youth using binary terms that do not allow for an ambivalent middle space to exist, yet upon which the terms are dependent. While Derrida argues that the origin of the prohibition of incest cannot be explained by a nature/culture opposition, it may also be said that it cannot be identified *outside* of terms that are culturally constructed. This means that to proceed as though the notion of incest comes *from* a nature/culture distinction is to therefore be limited in attempting to explain where the prohibition originates. This is a problem because incest has a socially constitutive role. Its prohibition forms the basis of social relations and the moral order that shapes them, and this fact cannot be adequately accounted for.

In a similar way, youth functions as an excluded third term on which a child/adult binary depends for its conceptualisation and subsequent social function. To attend to youth as an ambivalent third term that is constitutive of a child/adult binary is to upset the foundations upon which paedophilia is conceptualised as a violation of cultural norms about youth that are produced by the distinctions of child/adult, nature/culture and innocence/knowledge. This, however, does not prevent judgements about the problem from being made at all; it just removes any assumption as to their grounding in the absolute nature of youth. In other words, arguments about and different responses to paedophilia are used in this chapter as examples of where the paradoxical logic of the discourse of 'coming of age' gets played out. The issue is used to demonstrate how the discourse cannot accommodate an ambivalent space that exists in between the binary distinctions that define the discourse. To that extent, the discussion here does not address paedophilia generally or *as such*, but rather as a *context* in which the questions of youth sexuality (and hence the discourse of 'coming of age') emerge. More specifically still, the focus is on two representations of seemingly consensual paedophilic relationship – hence on two representations of a potentially active relationship on the part of (a) youth to (her) emerging sexual being. What is at stake in this discussion, then, is the potential for the discourse of 'coming of age' to coherently account for the emergence of youth sexuality, and not the question of paedophilia's justifiability or otherwise.

5. For example, the natural innocence attributed to virginity is imagined differently in light of the phenomenon of 'born again' virginity. For women, the perceived emotional 'purity' of virginity may be reclaimed by choosing to abstain from premarital sex, and physical virtue may be regained by undertaking hymen reconstructive surgery. Women who wish to reclaim their virginity are able to do so not because they could ever return to a state of natural innocence that is presumed to come with being a virgin – and which implies a *lack* of sexual knowing – but because their knowledge of sex enabled them to make a *choice* about what they wanted it to mean. If virginity supposedly marks a state of absolute innocence, then this phenomenon would not be possible. The fact that it *is* possible both physically and socially would appear to confirm Derrida's theory that what is classified as natural is always already cultural. This is to suggest that 'virginity' never actually existed as something pure and natural in the first place. Rather, it only 'appeared' as such in the moment it was made intelligible in the cultural domain, and therefore, by definition, in its 'disappearance' as pure and natural. So a desire to reclaim one's virginity is only possible because 'virginity' is not something that was ever naturally 'there' to begin with.

6. A primary focus on the notion of innocence in the particular discussion of paedophilia presented here is because the analysis of the discourse of 'coming of age' has called for it, and not because I am arguing that this is the defining problem of paedophilia in general. This chapter is concerned with paedophilia insofar as it is a means of addressing the limits of the discourse of 'coming of age' and its basis in an innocence/knowledge binary split. Extensive and multidisciplinary literature exists on the meaning of and issues surrounding paedophilia, encompassing socio-critical, criminological and psychoanalytical perspectives. See, for example, Goode (2009), Seto (2008), Socarides and Loeb (2004) and Kincaid (1998).

7. The phrase 'see it and make up your own mind', used here as a subheading, is a tagline from the 1997 film version of *Lolita*.

8. This phrase is one of the taglines from *Thirteen*.

9. This is another tagline from *Thirteen*.

6 Normal Abnormality: Coming to Terms with Teen Violence and the Undecidability of Youth

1. For thorough accounts of the massacre and detailed portraits of the lives and psychologies of Dylan Harris and Eric Klebold, see Peter Langman's *Why Kids Kill: Inside the Minds of School Shooters* (2009), Ralph W. Larkin's *Comprehending Columbine* (2007), Jonathan Fast's *Ceremonial Violence: A Psychological Explanation of School Shootings* (2008) and Dave Cullen's *Columbine* (2009).
2. See Chapter 3 on the structurality (or supplementarity) of presence for an explanation of Derrida's work on the notion of supplementarity.
3. Gun reform is an ongoing issue in the US with different legislation enacted under different administrations. Shooting tragedies reignite debate, but often without lasting reform. In the wake of the 2012 Sandy Hook Elementary School tragedy in which 20 children (aged six and seven) and six adults were killed, the Obama administration committed to new gun control laws including bans on the sale of certain types of assault weapons.
4. See also Marcel Lebrun's *Books, Blackboards, and Bullets: School Shootings and Violence in America* (2009) for examples of different checklists educators may use to assess potential student threats.
5. However, this is not necessarily the case within a neuroscience discourse, despite the fact that this discourse informs legal decisions about minors. The boys' activities could be viewed as consistent with a 'fuzzy trace theory' approach to youth and a verbatim style of reasoning as discussed in Chapter 4.
6. Mental illness was a major focus of investigation into the Virginia Tech massacre and gunman Cho Seung-Hui, as well as the Aurora Cinema shooter, James Holmes. Similarly, the case against Norway massacre gunman Anders Breivik hinged on the question of his sanity.
7. The troubling behaviour of Virginia Tech gunman Cho Seung-Hui had also attracted attention from his university teachers prior to his rampage. Yet despite efforts to alert campus authorities, no action was taken (Kellner, 2008, p. 51).

References

Albury, K. and Crawford, K. (2012) 'Sexting, consent and young people's ethics: Beyond Megan's Story', *Continuum: Journal of Media and Cultural Studies*, 26.3, 463–73.

Albury, K., Crawford, C., Byron, P., and Mathews, B. (2013) *Young People and Sexting in Australia: Ethics, Representation and the Law* (Kelvin Grove, Queensland: ARC Centre for Creative Industries and Innovation and the Journalism and Media Research Centre, University of New South Wales).

American Psychological Association (2007) *Report of the APA Task Force on the Sexualisation of Girls: Executive Summary* (Washington, DC: American Psychological Association).

An Education [DVD] (2009) Dir. Lone Scherfig. Perf. Carey Mulligan, Peter Sarsgaard, Alfred Molina. Sony Pictures Classics.

Ariès, P. (1962) *Centuries of Childhood: A Social History of Family Life* (London: Jonathan Cape).

Australian Labor Party (2008) 'Media Statement', *National Binge Drinking Strategy*, http://www.health.gov.au/internet/ministers/publishing.nsf/Content/mr-yr08-nr-nr159.htm (accessed 21 June 2013).

Bachelard, M. and Mangan, J. (2008) 'Photos "in realm of porn" under state laws', *The Age* [Melbourne], 25 May, np, http://www.theage.com.au/news/national/photos-in-realm-of-porn-under-state-laws/2008/05/24/1211183189564.html (accessed 28 May 2008).

Bailey, R. (2011) *Letting Children Be Children: Report of an Independent Review of the Commercialisation and Sexualisation of Childhood* (United Kingdom: Department for Education).

Bennett, A. (1999) 'Subcultures or neo-tribes? Rethinking the relationship between youth, style and musical taste', *Sociology*, 33.3, 599–617.

Bennett, A. and Kahn-Harris, K. (2004) 'Introduction' in Andy Bennett and Keith Kahn-Harris (eds.) *After Subculture: Critical Studies in Contemporary Youth Culture* (Basingstoke: Palgrave Macmillan), 1–18.

Bennett, A. and Hodkinson, P. (eds.) (2012) *Ageing and Youth Cultures: Music, Style and Identity* (Oxford and New York: Berg).

Bessant, J. (2008) 'Hard wired for risk: Neurological science, "the adolescent brain" and developmental theory', *Journal of Youth Studies*, 11.3, 347–60.

Bhabha, H. K. (1994) *The Location of Culture* (London and New York, Routledge).

Bhabha, H. K. (1996) 'The other question' in Padmini Mongia (ed.) *Contemporary Postcolonial Theory: A Reader* (London: Arnold), 37–54.

Biddulph, S. (2008) 'Art or not, it's still exploitation', *The Age* [Melbourne], 28 May, np, http://www.theage.com.au/news/opinion/art-or-not-its-still-exploitation/2008/05/27/1211654026964.html (accessed 28 May 2008).

Biggs, B. (2005) '*Lolita* is still pretty naïve and dangerous', *Daily Telegraph* [Sydney], 29 November, first edn, np, http://infoweb.newsbank.exproxy.lib.monash.edu.au (accessed 17 January 2006).

Bishop, E.C. (2012) 'Examining the raunch culture thesis through young Australian women's interpretations of contradictory discourses', *Journal of Youth Studies*, 15.7, 821–40.

Bita, N. (2009) 'Play in, politics out for new early learning manifesto', *The Australian*, 2 April, np, http://www.theaustralian.news.com.au/story/0,25197, 25277353-601,00.html (accessed 3 April 2009).

Brown, T. (2006) 'Wild child' [television programme], *Sixty Minutes*, Nine Network Australia, 6 August, Transcript, http://sixtyminutes.ninemsn.com.au/stories/ tarabrown/259431/wild-child (accessed 2 February 2013).

Buckingham, D. (2000) *After the Death of Childhood, Growing Up in the Age of Electronic Media* (Cambridge: Polity Press).

Buckingham, D. (2003) *Young People, Sex and the Media, The Facts of Life?* (Basingstoke: Palgrave Macmillan).

Butler, J. (1992) 'Contingent foundations: Feminism and the question of "postmodernism"' in Judith Butler and Joan W. Scott (eds.) *Feminists Theorise the Political* (London: Chapman and Hall, Inc.), 3–21.

Butler, J. (1993) *Bodies That Matter: On the Discursive Limits of 'Sex'* (London and New York: Routledge).

Butler, J. (1999) *Gender Trouble: Feminism and the Subversion of Identity*, 10th anniversary edn. (London and New York: Routledge).

Butler, J. (2001) 'Giving an account of oneself', *Diacritics*, 31.4, 22–40.

Butler, J. and Scott, J. W. (1992) 'Introduction' in Judith Butler and Joan W. Scott (eds.) *Feminists Theorise the Political* (London: Chapman and Hall, Inc.), xiii–xvii.

Carrington, B. and Wilson, B. (2004) 'Dance nations: Rethinking youth subcultural theory' in Andy Bennett and Keith Kahn-Harris (eds.) *After Subculture: Critical Studies in Contemporary Youth Culture* (Basingstoke: Palgrave Macmillan), 65–78.

Casey, B.J., Getz, S., and Galvan, A. (2008) 'The adolescent brain', *Developmental Review*, 28, 62–77.

Chaney, D. (2004) 'Fragmented culture and subcultures' in Andy Bennett and Keith Kahn-Harris (eds.) *After Subculture: Critical Studies in Contemporary Youth Culture* (Basingstoke: Palgrave Macmillan), 36–48.

Choudhury, S. (2009) 'Culturing the adolescent brain: What can neuroscience learn from anthropology?', *Social Cognitive and Affective Neuroscience*, 5.2–3, 159–67.

Choudhury, S., Nagel, S.K., and Slaby, J. (2009) 'Critical neuroscience: Linking neuroscience and society through critical practice', *BioSocieties*, 4.1, 61–77.

Clarke, J., Hall, S., Jefferson, T., and Roberts, B. (1976) 'Subcultures, cultures and class' in Stuart Hall and Tony Jefferson (eds.) *Resistance Through Rituals: Youth Subcultures in Post-War Britain* (London: Hutchison & Co.), 9–74.

Cloud, J. (1999) 'The Columbine effect', *Time*, 6 December, np, http://www.time. com/time/magazine/article/0,9171,992754,00.html (accessed 19 November 2006).

Cloud, J. (2010) 'Why genes aren't destiny', *Time*, 18 January, 27–31.

'Columbine link to Montreal mass shooting' (2006) *The Sydney Morning Herald*, 15 September, np, http://www.smh.com.au/news/World/Columbine- link-to-Montreal-mass-shooting/2006/09/15/1157827121127.html (accessed 15 September 2006).

Cooper, H. (2008) 'Rudd sets aside $53-million to tackle binge drinking', *PM*, ABC Radio National, 10 March, Transcript, http://www.abc.net.au/pm/content/2008/s2185516.htm (accessed 28 March 2008).

Corliss, R. (1999) 'Bang, you're dead', *Time*, 3 May, np, http://www.time.com/time/magazine/article/0,9171,990878,00.html (accessed 19 October 2006).

Cox, R. (1996) *Shaping Childhood: Themes of Uncertainty in the History of Adult–Child Relationships* (London and New York: Routledge).

Crawford, C. (2006) 'A sequel to the Werribee sex crimes DVD is believed to show the thugs involved in a break-and-enter spree', *Herald Sun* [Melbourne], 29 October, np, http://www.heraldsun.com.au/news/victoria/dvd-thugs-made-break-in-sequel/story-e6frf7kx-1111112434066 (accessed 8 February 2007).

Crosby, C. (1992) 'Dealing with differences' in Judith Butler and Joan W. Scott (eds.) *Feminists Theorise the Political* (London: Chapman and Hall, Inc.), 130–43.

Cullen, D. (2004) 'The depressive and the psychopath', *Slate*, 20 April, np, http://www.slate.com/articles/news_and_politics/assessment/2004/04/the_depressive_and_the_psychopath.html (accessed 19 October 2006).

Cullen, D. (2009a) *Columbine* (New York: Twelve).

Cullen, D. (2009b) 'Columbine was not a typical teen killing – there's no such thing', *The Times* [London], 1 May, 34.

Culler, J. (2007) *On Deconstruction: Theory and Criticism After Structuralism*, 25th anniversary edn. (New York: Cornell University Press).

Currie, D., Kelly, D.M., and Pomerantz, S. (2009) *Girl Power: Girls Reinventing Girlhood* (Peter Lang: New York).

Curry, D. (2008) 'From a night out into a nightmare', *Canberra Times*, 30 November, np, http://infoweb.newsbank.com.ezproxy.lib.monash.edu.au (accessed 28 February 2009).

Davidson, M. (1997) 'Is the media to blame for child sex victims?', *USA Today Magazine*, 126.2628, np, http://www.questia.com/library/1G1-19782197/is-the-media-to-blame-for-child-sex-victims (accessed 17 January 2006).

DeLisi, M., Wright, J.P., Vaughn, M.G., and Beaver, K.M. (2010) 'Nature and nurture by definition means both: A response to males', *Journal of Adolescent Research*, 25.1, 24–30.

Department of Education, Employment and Workplace Relations (undated) 'Early years learning framework', Australian Government, http://deewr.gov.au/early-years-learning-framework (accessed 9 January 2013).

Department of Health and Ageing (undated) 'Campaign messages', *Drinking Nightmare*, Australian Government, http://www.drinkingnightmare.gov.au/internet/drinkingnightmare/publishing.nsf/Content/about-the-campaign#Campaign%20messages (accessed 9 January 2013).

Derrida, J. (1978) *Writing and Difference*, Alan Bass (trans.) (London: Routledge & Kegan Paul).

Derrida, J. (1982) *Margins of Philosophy* (Chicago, Ill: University of Chicago Press).

Derrida, J. (1988) *Limited Inc* (Evanston, Ill.: Northwestern University Press).

Derrida, J. (1992) 'Force of law, the "mystical foundation of authority"' in Drucilla Cornell, Michel Rosenfeld and David Grey Carlson (eds.) *Deconstruction and the Possibility of Justice* (London: Routledge), 1–67.

Derrida, J. (1997) *Of Grammatology*, Gayatri Chakravorty Spivak (trans.), Corrected edn. (Baltimore: The Johns Hopkins University Press).

Derrida, J. (2002) 'Artifactualities' in Jacques Derrida and Bernard Stiegler (eds.) *Echographies of Television*, Jennifer Bajorek (trans.) (Cambridge: Polity Press), 3–27.

Derrida, J. and Roudinesco, E. (2004) *For What Tomorrow ... A Dialogue*, Jeff Fort (trans.) (California: Stanford University Press).

Dines, G. (2010) *Pornland: How Porn Has Hijacked Our Sexuality* (Boston, MA: Beacon Press).

Dodds, D. (2011) 'The new science of the teenage brain', *National Geographic*, October, 42–59.

Driscoll, C. (2002) *Girls: Feminine Adolescence in Popular Culture and Cultural Theory* (New York: Columbia University Press).

Driscoll, C. (2008) 'Girls today: Girls, girl culture and girl studies', *Girlhood Studies*, 1.1, 13–32.

Dubecki, L. (2006) 'A ratbag element that crossed the line to criminality', *The Age* [Melbourne], 26 October, 3.

Dubecki, L. (2008) 'Small-minded attitudes cloud responses to art', *The Age* [Melbourne], 26 May, np, http://www.theage.com.au/news/opinion/ smallminded-attitudes-cloud-responses-to-art/2008/05/25/1211653847046. html (accessed 28 May 2008).

Durham, M.G. (2009) *The Lolita Effect: The Media Sexualisation of Young Girls and What We Can Do About It* (Woodstock, NY: Overlook Press).

'DVD mob "like Nazi camp guards"' (2006) *The Age* [Melbourne], 25 October, np, http://www.theage.com.au/news/national/dvd-mob-like-nazi-camp-guards/ 2006/10/25/1161699377397.html (accessed 8 February 2007).

'DVD school in despair' (2006) *The Age* [Melbourne], 27 October, np, http://www.theage.com.au/news/national/dvd-school-in-despair/2006/10/ 27/1161749297302.html (accessed 8 February 2007).

Easy A [DVD] (2010) Dir. Will Gluck. Perf. Emma Stone, Amanda Bynes, Penn Badgley. Sony Pictures.

Egan, R.D. and Hawkes, G. (2010) *Theorising the Sexual Child in Modernity* (New York: Palgrave Macmillan).

Elkind, D. (1998) *All Grown Up and No Place to Go: Teenagers in Crisis* (Massachusetts: Addison-Wesley).

Epstein, R. (2007a) *The Case Against Adolescence: Rediscovering the Adult in Every Teen* (California: Quill Driver Books).

Epstein, R. (2007b) 'The myth of the teen brain', *Scientific American*, 17, 68–75.

Fast, J. (2008) *Ceremonial Violence: A Psychological Explanation of School Shootings* (Woodstock, NY: Overlook Press).

'Father's plea, destroy "disgusting" DVD' (2006) *The Age* [Melbourne], 24 October, np, http://www.theage.come.au/articles/2006/10/24/1161455691124.html (accessed 24 October 2006).

Faulkner, J. (2010) 'The innocence fetish: The commodification and sexualisation of children in the media and popular culture', *Media International Australia*, 135, 106–17.

Faulkner, J. (2011) *The Importance of Being Innocent: Why We Worry About Children* (Port Melbourne: Cambridge University Press).

Fischhoff, B. (2008) 'Assessing adolescent decision-making competence', *Developmental Review*, 28, 12–26.

Frith, S. (2004) 'Afterword' in Andy Bennett and Keith Kahn-Harris (eds.) *After Subculture: Critical Studies in Contemporary Youth Culture* (Basingstoke: Palgrave Macmillan), 173–8.

Fuentes, A. (2011) *Lockdown High: When the Schoolhouse Becomes a Jailhouse* (London and New York: Verso).

Gerrard, M., Gibbons, F.X., Houlihan, A.E., Stock, M.L., and Pomery, E.A. (2008) 'A dual-process approach to health risk decision making: The prototype willingness model', *Developmental Review*, 28, 29–61.

Gibbs, N. (1999) 'In sorrow and disbelief', *Time*, 3 May, np, http://www.time.com/time/magazine/article/0,9171,990870,00.html (accessed 19 October 2006).

Gibbs, N. and Roche, T. (1999) 'The Columbine tapes', *Time*, 20 December, np, http://www.time.com/time/magazine/article/0,9171,992873,00.html (accessed 19 October 2006).

Giedd, J. (2002) 'Interview: Jay Giedd', *Inside the Teenage Brain*, Frontline, PBS online, http://www.pbs.org/wgbh/pages/frontline/shows/teenbrain/interviews/giedd.html (accessed 25 January 2013).

Giedd, J. (2008) 'The teen brain, insights from neuroimaging', *Journal of Adolescent Health*, 42, 335–43.

Gill, R. (2012) 'Media, empowerment and the "sexualisation of culture" debates', *Sex Roles*, 66, 736–45.

Gill, R. and Scharff, C. (2011) 'Introduction' in Rosalind Gill and Christina Scharff (eds.) *New Femininities: Postfeminism, Neoliberalism and Subjectivity* (Basingstoke: Palgrave Macmillan), 1–17.

Giroux, H. A. (1996) *Fugitive Cultures: Race, Violence and Youth* (London and New York: Routledge).

Giroux, H. A. (2000) *Stealing Innocence: Corporate Culture's War on Children* (New York: Palgrave).

Giroux, H. A. (2002) 'The war on the young: Corporate culture, schooling, and the politics of "zero tolerance"' in Ronald Strickland (ed.) *Growing Up Postmodern: Neoliberalism and the War on the Young* (Lanham: Rowman & Littlefield), 35–46.

Giroux, H. A. (2009) *Youth in a Suspect Society: Democracy or Disposability?* (New York: Palgrave Macmillan).

Golding, P. and Murdock. G. (1991) 'Culture, communications, and political economy' in James Curran and Michael Gurevitch (eds.) *Mass Media and Society* (London: Arnold), 15–32.

Goode, S.D. (2009) *Addressing Adult Sexual Attraction to Children: A Study of Paedophiles in Contemporary Society* (Hoboken: Taylor & Francis).

Grice, E. (2006) 'Gone to the dogs, the girl who ran with the pack', *The Age* [Melbourne], 19 July, np, http://www.theage.com.au/articles/2006/07/18/1153166383022.html (accessed 20 July 2006).

Griffin, C. (2004) 'Representations of the young' in Jeremy Roche, Stanley Tucker, Rachel Thomson and Ronny Flynn (eds.) *Youth in Society: Contemporary Theory, Policy and Practice*, 2nd edn. (London: Sage), 10–18.

Gumbel, A. (2009) 'The truth about Columbine', *The Guardian* [United Kingdom], 17 April, np, http://www.guardian.co.uk/world/2009/apr/17/columbine-massacre-gun-crime-us/print (accessed 19 November 2012).

Harris, A. (2004a) *Future Girl: Young Women in the Twenty-first Century* (London and New York: Routledge).

Harris, A. (ed.) (2004b) *All About the Girl: Culture, Power, and Identity* (London and New York: Routledge).

Harris, E. (1998a) *Handwritten Journal* (10 April 1998 to 3 April 1999), transcript, http://acolumbinesite.com/eric/writing/journal/journal.html (accessed 16 November 2012).

Harris, E. (1998b) 'Vaccines', *Web Journal*, 26 September, acolumbinesite.com, http://acolumbinesite.com/eric/writing/plans.gif (accessed 16 November 2012).

Harris, E. (1998c) 'Vaccines (cont)', *Web Journal*, 26 September, acolumbinesite.com, http://acolumbinesite.com/eric/writing/plans2.gif (accessed 16 November 2012).

Harris, E. (undated) 'Pissed', *Web Journal*, acolumbinesite.com, http://acolumbinesite.com/reports/pissed.gif (accessed 16 November 2012).

Harris, S. (1999) 'The will of Irons', *The Advertiser* [Adelaide], 6 March, 2nd edn., np, http://infoweb.newsbank.com.ezproxy.lib.monash.edu.au (accessed 17 January 2006).

Hartley, J. (1992) *Tele-ology: Studies in Television* (London and New York, Routledge).

Hawker, P. (2004) 'Story of a bad girl with a cautionary pig tale', *The Age* [Melbourne], 11 March, A3, 7.

Heaven, P.C.L. (2001) *The Social Psychology of Adolescence*, 2nd edn. (Basingstoke and New York: Palgrave).

Hebdige, D. (1979) *Subculture: The Meaning of Style* (London and New York: Methuen).

Hentges, S. (2006) *Pictures of Girlhood: Modern Female Adolescence on Film* (Jefferson, NC: McFarland).

Hodkinson, P. (2007) 'Youth cultures: A critical outline of key debates' in Paul Hodkinson and Wolfgang Deicke (eds.) *Youth Cultures: Scenes, Subcultures and Tribes* (New York: Routledge), 1–22.

Houlihan, L. and Metlikovec, J. (2006) 'Public outrage met by boasts, laughter', *Herald Sun* [Melbourne], 26 October, np, http://www.news.com.au/breaking-news/public-outrage-met-by-boasts-laughter/story-e6frfkp9-1111112418619 (accessed 8 February 2007).

'Inside the Teenage Brain' [television programme] (2002) *Frontline*, PBS, www.pbs.org/wgbh/pages/frontline/shows/teenbrain/ (accessed 25 January 2013).

'It is important to get a proper perspective on Henson' (2008) *The Age* [Melbourne], 7 October, np, http://www.theage.com.au/opinion/editorial/it-is-important-to-get-a-proper-perspective-on-henson-20081006-4v0e.html (accessed 8 October 2008).

Jackson, S. and Vares, T. (2011) 'Media "sluts": "Tween" girls' negotiations of post-feminist sexual subjectivities in popular culture' in Rosalind Gill and Christina Scharff (eds.) *New Femininities: Postfeminism, Neoliberalism and Subjectivity* (Basingstoke: Palgrave Macmillan), 134–46.

Jenkins, H. (1999) *Congressional Testimony on Media Violence*, 4 May, np, http://web.mit.edu/m-i-t/articles/dc.html (accessed 23 March 2008).

Jenkins, H. (2006) *Fans, Bloggers, and Gamers: Exploring Participatory Culture* (New York and London: New York University Press).

Johnson, L. (1993) *The Modern Girl: Girlhood and Growing Up* (Sydney: Allen & Unwin).

Juno [DVD] (2007) Dir. Jason Reitman. Perf. Ellen Page, Michael Cera, Jennifer Garner. Fox Searchlight Pictures.

Kehily, M.J. and Montgomery, H. (2009) 'Innocence to experience: A historical approach to childhood and sexuality' in Mary Jane Kehily (ed.) *Introduction to Childhood Studies* (Maidenhead: Open University Press).

Kellner, D. (2008) *Guys and Guns Amok: Domestic Terrorism and School Shootings from the Oklahoma City Bombing to the Virginia Tech Massacre* (Boulder, CO: Paradigm Publishers).

Kelly, P. (2012) 'The brain in a jar: A critique of discourses of adolescent brain development', *Journal of Youth Studies*, 15.7, 944–59.

Kincaid, J. R. (1998) *Erotic Innocence: The Culture of Child Molesting* (Durham and London: Duke University Press).

Kinkade, L. (2012) 'Ruining lives' [television programme] *Today Tonight*, Seven Network Australia, April 4.

Klebold, S. (2009) 'I will never know why', *O Magazine*, November, np, http://www.oprah.com/world/Susan-Klebolds-O-Magazine-Essay-I-Will-Never-Know-Why (accessed 16 November 2012).

Lairymary (2008) 'Your rating, Towelhead', *At the Movies*, ABC TV (online) http://www.abc.net.au/atthemovies/txt/s2355353.htm (accessed 1 January 2013).

Lamb, S. and Peterson, Z. (2012) 'Adolescent girls' sexual empowerment: Two feminists explore the concept', *Sex Roles*, 66, 703–12.

Langman, P. (2009) *Why Kids Kill: Inside the Minds of School Shooters* (New York: Palgrave Macmillan).

Larkin, R.W. (2007) *Comprehending Columbine* (Philadelphia, PA: Temple University Press).

Lebrun, M. (2009) *Books, Blackboards, and Bullets: School Shootings and Violence in America* (Lanham, Maryland: Rowman & Littlefield).

Ledonne, D. (undated) 'Artist's statement: A meditation on Super Columbine Massacre RPG!', *Super Columbine Massacre RPG!*, columbinegame.com, http://www.columbinegame.com/statement.htm (accessed 17 November 2012).

Lerner, H. (1987) 'Psychodynamic models' in Vincent B. Van Hasselt and Michel Hersen (eds.) *Handbook of Adolescent Psychology* (New York: Pergamon Press), 53–76.

Lesko, N. (1996) 'Denaturalising adolescence: The politics of contemporary representations', *Youth and Society*, 28.2, 139–61.

Lesko, N. (2001) *Act Your Age! A Cultural Construction of Adolescence* (London and New York: Routledge Falmer).

Levin, D.E. and Kilbourne, J. (2009) *So Sexy So Soon: The New Sexualised Childhood and What Parents Can Do To Protect Their Kids* (New York: Random House).

Levy, A. (2005) *Female Chauvinist Pigs: Women and the Rise of Raunch Culture* (New York: Black Inc.).

Locke, J. (1989) *Some Thoughts Concerning Education*, John W. Yolton and Jean S. Yolton (eds.) (Oxford: Oxford University Press).

Lolita [DVD] (1997) Dir. Adrian Lyne. Perf. Jeremy Irons, Dominique Swain, Melanie Griffith, Frank Langella. Pathe and The Samuel Goldwyn Company.

Lucy, N. (1995) *Debating Derrida* (Carlton South: Melbourne University Press).

Lucy, N. (2004) *A Derrida Dictionary* (Oxford: Blackwell).

Lumby, C. (2010) 'Ambiguity, representation, and sexuality', *CLCWeb: Comparative Literature and Culture*, 12.4, np, http://docs.lib.purdue.edu/clcweb/vol12/iss4/5.

Maffesoli, M. (1996) *The Time of the Tribes: The Decline of Individualism in Mass Society* (London: Sage).

Males, M. (2009) 'Does the adolescent brain make risk taking inevitable? A skeptical appraisal', *Journal of Adolescent Research*, 24.1, 3–20.

Males, M. (2010) 'Is jumping off the roof always a bad idea? A rejoinder on risk taking and the adolescent brain', *Journal of Adolescent Research*, 25.1, 48–63.

Marcus, C. (2008) 'Growing up: Why it can really get you down', *Sydney Morning Herald*, 21 September, np, http://www.smh.com.au/lifestyle/life/growing-up-why-it-can-really-get-you-down-20090407-9yrp.html (accessed 25 September 2008).

Martin, P. J. (2004) 'Culture, subculture and social organisation' in Andy Bennett and Keith Kahn-Harris (eds.) *After Subculture: Critical Studies in Contemporary Youth Culture* (Basingstoke: Palgrave Macmillan), 21–35.

McKinney, J. P. and Vogel, J. (1987) 'Developmental theories' in Vincent B. Van Hasselt and Michel Hersen (eds.) *Handbook of Adolescent Psychology* (New York: Pergamon Press), 13–33.

McRobbie, A. (1994) *Postmodernism and Popular Culture* (London and New York: Routledge).

McRobbie, A. (2000) *Feminism and Youth Culture*, 2nd edn. (London: Macmillan).

McRobbie, A. (2007) 'Postfeminism and popular culture: Bridget Jones and the new gender regime' in Yvonne Tasker and Diane Negra (eds.) *Interrogating Postfeminism: Gender and the Politics of Popular Culture* (Durham: Duke University Press), 27–39.

Medew, J. (2007a) '"Callous" teens escape jail for sex attack film', *The Age* [Melbourne], 6 November, 3.

Medew, J. (2007b) 'Judge opts for rehabilitation and education over punishment', *The Age* [Melbourne], 6 November, 3.

Medew, J. (2007c) 'Film of attack on girl shown to parents', *The Age* [Melbourne], 18 October, 3.

Miletic, D. (2006) 'Outcry over teenage girl's assault recorded on DVD', *The Age* [Melbourne], 25 October, np, http://www.theage.com.au/articles/2006/10/24/1161455722271.html (accessed 8 February 2007).

Miller, N. (2008) 'Generation unwell', *The Age* [Melbourne], 26 September, 15.

Moore-Gilbert, B. (1997) *Postcolonial Theory: Contexts: Practices: Politics* (London and New York: Verso).

Moore-Gilbert, B., Stanton, G., and Maley, W. (1997) 'Introduction' in Bart Moore-Gilbert, Gareth Stanton and Willy Maley (eds.) *Postcolonial Criticism* (New York: Addison Wesley Longman), 1–72.

Morrissey, B. (2005) ' "I'm not that innocent": Teenage girls and the problem of consensual sex', *Southern Review*, 37.3, 58–72.

Morse, J. (2000) 'Looking For trouble', *Time*, 24 April, np, http://www.time.com/time/magazine/article/0,9171,996695-2,00.html (accessed 19 October 2006).

Moshman, D. (1999) *Adolescent Psychological Development: Rationality, Morality, and Identity* (New Jersey: Lawrence Erlbaum Associates Publishers).

Muggleton, D. (1998) 'The post-subculturalist' in Steve Redhead, Derek Wynne, Justin O'Connor (eds.) *The Clubcultures Reader: Readings in Popular Cultural Studies* (Oxford: Blackwell), 167–85.

Muggleton, D. (2000) *Inside Subculture: The Postmodern Meaning of Style* (Oxford and New York: Berg).

The National Academy of Sciences (2003) 'Executive summary' in *Deadly Lessons: Understanding Lethal School Violence* (Washington, DC: The National Academies Press), 1–8.

Nayak, A. and Kehily, M.J. (2008) *Gender, Youth and Culture: Young Masculinities and Femininities* (Basingstoke: Palgrave Macmillan).

Newman, K. S. (2004) *Rampage: The Social Roots of School Shootings* (New York: Basic Books).

Norris, C. (1982) *Deconstruction: Theory and Practice* (London and New York: Methuen).

Olfman, S. (ed.) (2009) *The Sexualisation of Childhood* (Connecticut and London: Praeger).

Oppliger, P. (2008) *Girls Gone Skank: The Sexualisation of Girls in American Culture* (Jefferson, NC: McFarland & Company).

Petrie, A. (2006) 'Parents tell of horror at DVD attack', *The Age* [Melbourne], 27 October, np, http://www.theage.com.au/news/national/parents-tell-of-horror-at-dvd-attack/2006/10/26/1161749253955.html (accessed 27 October 2006).

Phillips, S. F. (2007) *The Teen Brain* (New York: Chelsea House).

Pooley, E. (1999) 'Portrait of a deadly bond', *Time*, 10 May, np, http://www.time.com/time/magazine/printout/0,8816,990917,00.html (accessed 19 October 2006).

Quart, A. (2003) 'Review of *Thirteen*', *Film Comment*, 39.4, 71.

Redhead, S. (1997) *From Subcultures to Clubcultures: An Introduction to Popular Cultural Studies* (Oxford: Blackwell).

Rennie, R. (2006) 'Coonan warns of internet's underbelly', *The Age* [Melbourne], 25 October, np, http://www.theage.com.au/news/national/coonan-warns-of-internets-underbelly/2006/10/25/1161749173525.html (accessed 8 February 2007).

Reyna, V.F. and Farley, F. (2007) 'Is the teen brain too rational?', *Scientific American*, 17, 60–7.

Reyna, V.F. and Rivers, S.E. (2008) 'Current theories of risk and rational decision making', *Developmental Review*, 28, 1–11.

Ringrose, J., Gill, R., Livingstone, S., and Harvey, L. (2012) *A Qualitative Study of Children, Young People and 'Sexting': A Report Prepared for the NSPCC* (United Kingdom: NSPCC).

Rivers, S.E., Reyna, V.F., and Mills, B. (2008) 'Risk taking under the influence: A fuzzy-trace theory of emotion in adolescence', *Developmental Review*, 28, 107–44.

RMIT University (2012) 'Bachelor of social science (youth work)', *RMIT University*, http://www.rmit.edu.au/programs/bp191 (accessed 7 May 2012)

Ross, C. J. (2009) 'A stable paradigm: Revisiting capacity, vulnerability and the rights claims of adolescents after *Roper* v. *Simmons*' in Michael Freeman and Oliver Goodenough (eds.) *Law, Mind and Brain* (Farnham, Surrey: Ashgate), 183–98.

Rousseau, J. J. (1969) *Emile*, Barbara Foxley (trans.) (London: Everyman's Library).

Rush, E. and La Nauze, A. (2006a) *Corporate Paedophilia: Sexualisation of children in Australia* (Discussion Paper no. 90, The Australia Institute), http://www.tai.org.au/documents/dp_fulltext/DP90.pdf (accessed 17 June 2012).

Rush, E. and La Nauze, A. (2006b) *Letting Children Be Children: Stopping the Sexualisation of Children in Australia* (Discussion Paper no. 93, The Australia Institute), http://www.tai.org.au/documents/downloads/DP93.pdf (accessed 17 June 2012).

Sacco, D., Argudin, R., Maguire, J., and Tallong, K. (2010) *Sexting: Youth Practices and Legal Implications* (Youth and Media Policy Working Group Initiative, Berkman Center for Internet and Society at Harvard University, Research publication no. 2010-8, June 22), http://cyber.law.harvard.edu/publications (accessed 12 May 2012).

Said, E. W. (1978) *Orientalism* (London: Routledge & Kegan Paul).

Schembri, J. (1999) 'Humbert, humbug and the pursuit of happiness', *Sunday Age* [Melbourne], 11 April, late edn., 5.

Senate Standing Committee on Environment, Communications and the Arts (2008) *Sexualisation of Children in the Contemporary Media* (Canberra: Commonwealth of Australia).

Sercombe, H. (2010a) 'The "teen brain" research: Critical perspectives', *Youth and Policy*, 105, 71–80.

Sercombe, H. (2010b) 'The gift and the trap: Working the "teen brain" into our concept of youth', *Journal of Adolescent Research*, 25.1, 31–47.

Seto, M.C. (2008) *Pedophilia and Sexual Offending Against Children: Theory, Assessment, and Intervention* (Washington, DC: American Psychological Association).

Shary, T. (2002) *Generation Multiplex: The Image of Youth in Contemporary American Cinema* (Austin, TX: University of Texas Press).

Shtargot, S. (2007) 'Werribee DVD youths plead guilty, avoid jail', *The Age* [Melbourne], 21 July, np, http://www.theage.com.au/news/national/werribee-dvd-youths-plead-guilty-avoid-jail/2007/07/20/1184560043673.html (Accessed 21 July 2007).

Socarides, C.W. and Loeb, L.R. (2004) *The Mind of the Paedophile: Psychoanalytic Perspectives* (London: Karnac Books).

Spinks, S. (2002) 'Adolescent brains are works in progress, here's why', *Inside the Teenage Brain*, Frontline, PBS online, http://www.pbs.org/wgbh/pages/frontline/shows/teenbrain/work/adolescent.html (accessed 25 January 2013).

Spivak, G. C. (1988a) 'Can the subaltern speak?' in Cary Nelson and Lawrence Grossberg (eds.) *Marxism and the Interpretation of Culture* (London: Macmillan), 271–313.

Spivak, G. C. (1988b) *In Other Worlds: Essays in Cultural Politics* (London and New York: Routledge).

Spivak, G. C. (1997) 'Translator's preface' in Jacques Derrida *Of Grammatology*, Gayatri Chakravorty Spivak (trans.), Corrected edn. (Baltimore, MD: Johns Hopkins University Press), ix–lxxxvii.

Steinberg, L. (2008) 'A social neuroscience perspective on adolescent risk-taking', *Developmental Review*, 28, 78–106.

Strauch, B. (2004) *The Primal Teen: What New Discoveries About the Teenage Brain Tells Us About Our Kids* (USA: Anchor Books).

Sunstein, C.R. (2008) 'Adolescent risk-taking and social meaning: A commentary', *Developmental Review*, 28, 145–52.

Tankard Reist, M. (ed.) (2009) *Getting Real: Challenging the Sexualisation of Girls* (North Melbourne: Spinifex).

Tasker, Y. and Negra, D. (2007) 'Introduction: Feminist politics and postfeminist culture' in Yvonne Tasker and Diane Negra (eds.) *Interrogating Postfeminism: Gender and the Politics of Popular Culture* (Durham, NC: Duke University Press), 1–25.

'Teen Brain' [television programme] (2005) *Catalyst*, ABC TV, http://www.abc.net.au/catalyst/stories/s1424747.htm (accessed 25 January, 2013).

'Teens think sexting is normal' [television programme] (2012) *Weekend Sunrise*, Seven Network Australia, April 7, http://au.tv.yahoo.fcom/sunrise/video/-/watch/28870112 (accessed May 7 2012).

Terry, B. (2012) 'School girls offered sex for money' [television programme], *Seven News* (Australia), 4.30pm edn., April 4, http://www.youtube.com/watch?v=fUHwoNsdH0Q (accessed 8 May 2012).

'The Basement Tapes' (undated) *dylanklebold.com*, http://dylanklebold.com/columbine-shooting-facts/the-basement-tapes/ (accessed 25 February 2013).

'The Case for *Lolita*' (1999) *Sydney Morning Herald*, 12 April, late edn, 14.

'The DVD that shocked the nation reveals some nasty truths' (2006) *The Age* [Melbourne], 26 October, 14.

Thirteen [DVD] (2003) Dir. Catherine Hardwicke. Perf. Holly Hunter, Evan Rachel Wood, Nikki Reed. Fox Searchlight Pictures.

Thornton, S. (1996) *Club Cultures: Music, Media and Subcultural Capital* (Hanover: Wesleyan University Press).

Tilley, T. (2012) *Hack* [radio programme], Triple J, ABC radio, April 4, http://mpegmedia.abc.net.au/triplej/hack/daily/hack_wed_2012_04_04.mp3 (accessed April 24 2012).

Tomazin, F., Jackson, A., Rood, D. and Strong, G. (2008) 'Henson principal could face suspension', *The Age* [Melbourne], 7 October, np, http://www.theage.com.au/national/henson-principal-could-face-suspension-20081006-4v1y.html (accessed 8 October 2008).

Tomazin, F. and Smith, B. (2008) 'Principal in clear over Henson', *The Age* [Melbourne], 8 November, np, http://www.theage.com.au/national/principal-in-clear-over-henson-20081107-5k8j.html (accessed 25 February 2009).

Tonso, K.L. (2009) 'Violent masculinities as tropes for school shooters: The Montreal massacre, the Columbine attack, and rethinking schools', *American Behavioural Scientist*, 52.9, 1266–85.

Towelhead [DVD] (2007) Dir. Alan Ball. Perf. Summer Bishil, Aaron Eckhart, Peter Macdissi, Toni Colette, Maria Bello. Warner Independent Pictures.

'Towelhead is sure to shock' (2008) *The Age* [Melbourne], 6 October, np, http://www.theage.com.au/articles/2008/10/05/1223145161855.html (accessed 8 October 2008).

Turner, G. (2003) *British Cultural Studies: An Introduction*, 3rd edn. (London and New York: Routledge).

Walkerdine, V., Lucey, H., and Melody, J. (2001) *Growing Up Girl: Psychosocial Explorations of Gender and Class* (New York: New York University Press).

Wallis, C. (2004) 'What makes teens tick', *Time*, 10 May, 46–53.

Walter, N. (2010) *Living Dolls: The Return of Sexism* (UK: Virago).

Ward, A. (undated) 'Feral children', *FeralChildren.com: Isolated, Confined, Wolf and Wild Children*, http://www.FeralChildren.com/ed/index.php (accessed 27 June 2009).

Warnick, B.R., Johnson, B.A., and Rocha, S. (2010) 'Tragedy and the meaning of school shootings', *Educational Theory*, 60.3, 371–90.

Weinzierl, R. and Muggleton, D. (2003) 'What is "post-subcultural studies" anyway?' in Rupert Weinzierl and David Muggleton (eds.) *The Post-subcultures Reader* (Oxford and New York: Berg), 3–23.

Williamson, B. (2012) 'Suspended school girls need support, child psychologist' 891 ABC Adelaide, April 5, http://www.abc.net.au/local/stories/2012/04/05/3471666.htm#.T545FagPEPM (accessed 12 May 2012).

Wortham, S.M. (2010) *The Derrida Dictionary* (London and New York: Continuum).

Young, R. (1990) *White Mythologies: Writing History and the West* (London and New York: Routledge).

Young, R. (2000) 'Deconstruction and the postcolonial' in Nicholas Royle (ed.) *Deconstructions: A User's Guide* (New York: Palgrave), 187–210.

Ziffer, D. (2006a) 'YouTube yanks assault DVD' *The Age* [Melbourne], 26 October, np, http://www.theage.com.au/news/national/youtube-yanks-assault-dvd/2006/10/26/1161749222232.html (accessed 8 February 2007).

Ziffer, D. (2006b) 'Don't blame me for those evil bastards', *The Age* [Melbourne], 26 October, 3.

Zylinska, J. (2004) 'Mediating murder: Ethics, trauma and the price of death', *Journal For Cultural Research*, 8.3, 227–46.

Index

Note: Letter 'n' followed by the locators within bracket refer to notes.